Purchasing and Providing Health Care

A PRACTICAL GUIDE

Norman Vetter

Stanley Thornes (Publishers) Ltd

First published 1997 by:
Stanley Thornes (Publishers) Ltd
Ellenborough House
Wellington Street
CHELTENHAM
GL50 1YW
United Kingdom

97 98 99 00 01 / 10 9 8 7 6 5 4 3 2 1

A catalogue record for this book is available from the British Library

ISBN 0-7487-3293-4

Typeset by WestKey Limited, Falmouth, Cornwall.
Printed and bound in Great Britain by TJ International, Padstow, Cornwall

Contents

Dedication

I dedicate this book to my wife, Sarah, who is trying to make it work at the sharp end and who did not complain about not being mentioned in the last book.

Preface

Most of the examples I have used have been ones that I have used or seen used in my work. They will therefore tend to have a Welsh flavour. I think most will export reasonably well. I have tried to make it plain where Welsh Office policies differ from the UK generally but will, inevitably, have missed some differences.

Acknowledgements

I would like to acknowledge the help given me in the preparation of this book by Dr Gillian Todd and Ms Melanie Walker who commented on the text. Thanks for data are due to Dr Sharon Hopkins, Dr Su Vui Lo and Dr Michael Burr. Special thanks to Ms Julia Evans who word-processed most of it many times.

The purchaser–provider principle

1

HISTORICAL DEVELOPMENT

Managed competition is 'a beautiful animal in fairyland but unseen on earth' – a unicorn:

> *Representative Pete Stark, Democratic chair of the House of*
> *Representatives sub-committee on health in 1993*

Managed competition in the health service was set up in the UK when Margaret Thatcher was Prime Minister. Managed competition, by its nature, needs managers. This was a U-turn for Mrs Thatcher for, when she first became Prime Minister, she said that she would get rid of bureaucracy in the UK, including many of the managers of the health service. Her government was convinced, and had convinced the nation, that the public sector was wasteful. They said this was because it did not have the pressures of competition in a market to keep it lean and striving for efficiency. There was, and still is, a feeling that the very size of the huge health and social welfare budgets must mean that they are capable of being trimmed.

There was also a growing antiprofessional mood suggesting that closed groups such as teachers, doctors and lawyers were making the rules for their own ends. They seemed to be unaccountable to the public for what they did. The two pressures – to reduce bureaucracy and to control the medical profession – were to be resolved by the development of competition. This allowed some increase in management numbers but relied on managed competition using an internal market to control the costs generated by doctors. Butler [1] suggested that four important developments, under the Thatcher government, led to the internal market:

- The growing importance of management
- Income-generating schemes
- Contracting out services to private companies
- The development of an internal market.

The growing importance of management

Mr, later Sir, Roy Griffiths, looked at the management of the National Health
Service (NHS) in England [2]. Although the Griffiths inquiry did not cover
Scotland, Wales or Northern Ireland, the government applied the main recommendations to the UK. Sir Roy was deputy chairman and managing
director of Sainsburys, the supermarket chain, and wanted to bring a managerial, business-like approach to the NHS.

The existing management of the health service then revolved around the
idea of consensus management. The previous group of management consultants brought in to advise on the management of the NHS, the McKinzey
group, had favoured this approach. Sir Roy swept this aside in favour of strong
management and a feeling that one had to know where, and indeed with whom,
the buck stopped [3]. Thus general managers took over the health service. This
meant that, at each level of command, it would be clear who, among the
managers at any rate, was in charge.

Income-generating schemes

The schemes of income generation set up at that time in the UK health service
have never been terribly important as a means of obtaining cash. My own
hospital developed a series of tatty shops selling cheap merchandise. Other
hospitals were more entrepreneurial, but the income has not made much
difference to hospital budgets. The schemes were important as a way of
suggesting a new ethos in the health service. There was a move from the drab
corridors of a public institution to the trestle tables of the cheap jewellery-
sellers. I remember a colleague in the early days suggesting that there was a need
for someone to sweep through the entrance halls of our hospitals overturning
these 'money changers in the temple'. In our district, at least, no-one felt
suitably qualified for the task. These attitudes give a feeling of the sense of
separateness from markets that was then common. There was, in the hospitals,
at best a sense of service, and at worst a sense of paternalism to patients.
Well-off people found the latter irritating; poor people found it intimidating.

Contracting out services

Contracting out was a more important policy. In 1983 health authorities were
told to use a competitive tendering process to decide who should do their
cleaning, catering and laundry [4]. Private contractors competed with the

people supplying the existing services; generally, the in-house service tendered for the work. Some of the trusts made reasonably large financial gains [5]. Despite this, the change was, again, more important as a symbol. Private companies were allowed to invade the health service. The change was also a sad one. The most poorly paid in the health service, who are also among the most poorly paid in the country, had their salaries and rights squeezed, with virtually no-one fighting for them. At the same time, in the same corridors, some of the most highly paid people in the country, the consultants, continued to provide services with only minimal pressure on them to improve efficiency.

The internal market

The internal market did not appear to me, as an observer at the time, to be an obvious answer to the problems that appeared to be facing the health service. There was, as there has regularly been in the UK, a rise in concern about the future of the health service because of lack of funding. The final straw may well have been a report from the Presidents of the three senior Royal Colleges [6] stating unequivocally that the NHS needed more money.

The government promised considerable changes, but they did not provide more money. The most obvious radical change that they could have made would have been to alter the financing of the health service from the existing tax-based service to an insurance-based one. However, even the right-wing government of the day felt that this would be a more expensive method of providing services. Perhaps, more importantly, the changes would be very obvious to the public as their methods of payment altered. The general public had, and still has, a great sympathy with the existing health service, despite its problems. The government therefore confined its intervention to changes in the administrative structure of providing the service, which would not affect patients directly. Alain Enthoven, an American management guru, first proposed many of the changes, including the idea of an internal market.

Alain Enthoven

In a small monograph in 1985 [7], Alain Enthoven set out his ideas for the future of the NHS in the UK. This appears to have been influential in encouraging some of the changes in 1990. It also helped to reject others that were possible candidates, especially the move to an insurance-based system.

New technology

Enthoven made a special point about the widespread support given to the NHS by the public in the UK. He also said that that it was very efficient. Despite this, he suggested that it would need to produce even more value for money in the future. He did not believe that such a small cash investment could allow the service to use 'effective new medical technology' for all the patients who needed it. It is a common fallacy that health services depend heavily for their effective development on high technology, whether in the development of machinery or of new drugs. The health service as an industry is a low user of technology, and many effective new approaches do not require additional technical contributions [8].

Problems of changing the NHS

Enthoven also mentioned the difficulties of making changes in the NHS. He gave high praise to the staff and their ability to maintain quality. My impression was that he could not understand the NHS culture of muddling through, nor the level of decrepitude that is accepted, especially the quality of the buildings. Virtually the only pressures towards improving the state of buildings in the NHS since its inception have been the building and fire regulations. Those hospital planners 'lucky' enough to find themselves looking after buildings with death watch beetle or which are fire traps have been able to persuade the government to give them the money to rebuild.

Enthoven commended the establishment of general managers at authority and hospital levels but felt that this did not go far enough. He favoured competitive tendering as a wedge for other changes. He pressed hard for NHS managers to know their costs and to buy from the private sector where this appeared to be cheaper. In hindsight, it is interesting to see how little impact this competition with the private sector has had.

Enthoven then had a swipe at the specialty of community medicine. This may have precipitated the specialty to change its name to 'public health' soon after. Enthoven stated, wrongly, that community medicine specialists had no management training and suggested that the doctors' leadership would improve if management training were given to selected consultants. My experience suggests that we have not, so far in the UK, made careers in top-level management attractive to doctors involved in clinical work.

Inequality of access

Enthoven also looked at the unequal access to services in the UK. He suggested that people should obtain their services wherever they wished, not only within their own health authority area. He went on to say, 'This line of thinking could lead to an Internal Market Model for the NHS. Each District (health authority) would receive a *per capita* revenue and capital allowance. It would continue to be responsible for providing and paying for comprehensive care for its resident population, but not for care for other people without current compensation at negotiated prices. Each District would resemble a nationalized company. It would buy and sell services from and to other health authorities and trade with the private sector. In such a scheme District managers would be freed to use all their resources most efficiently'. This was the first mention of an internal market for the NHS. Interestingly, Enthoven suggested it in the context of competition between different health authorities. Each, he thought, would be vying with the others to persuade patients to travel into their area for the best services. In retrospect, this is unlikely to have had any effect. I will provide data later in this book suggesting that UK patients are reluctant to travel any distance for better services.

Enthoven also suggested that, in competition with others, doctors would impose controls on each other that they would never dream of accepting if the government tried to impose them. He suggested that clinical freedom would give way to effective control of quality and cost-effectiveness. There is an implication here, as with many people writing about medical costs, that the key to success is to make doctors take cheaper options when treating their patients. There seems little evidence of this from the USA where doctors already compete more directly with each other for services than they do in any other developed country.

THE NHS AND COMMUNITY CARE ACT 1990 – THE PURCHASER–PROVIDER SPLIT

The health authorities, until 1990, oversaw the planning of the health service and delivered the services. Within each authority were a varying number of units: hospitals, community services, ambulance services. The purchaser – provider split set up an internal market by separating the central planning function of the health authority from its services. The centrally based group comprises the purchasers, the units the providers. Initially, the term 'procurers' was used for the new health authorities. Thankfully for those of us who had to tell people what we did for a living, this term rapidly disappeared. Later, the term commissioning was used for purchasing, but this too has gradually become less common.

The task of the purchasers was to reach the best compromise between cheapness and quality for each of the services they bought. The providers – hospitals, community units and others – split off to form self-governing trusts. These trusts compete with each other, as part of the internal market, for the money held by the health authorities. The health authorities decide which of the competing providers should get the money for providing a service by winning contracts. The home purchaser pays for people who belong to one area but are taken ill in another.

The NHS and Community Care Act also put into place the central Management Executive led by a chief executive. The Management Executive included career civil servants and NHS managers, together with some people brought in for their expertise. At health authority level, the Act made changes to the boards of health authorities. Before the Act, boards of 15–20 members ran the health authorities. Many of these people had a special political or professional interest in the NHS; some were local councillors. They were often slow to reach a consensus because of their conflicting political ideologies. Executive and non-executive board members have replaced these people. The executives are the full-time managers at the top of the organization, headed by a chief executive. They usually include a finance director, a medical director, a nursing director and one other, often someone involved with the development of the trust or marketing. They are balanced by the non-executive directors, who are part-time, in theory giving about half a day a week to the work. In practice, this often amounts to much more.

The Secretary of State chooses the new chairmen of both health authorities and trusts. There are usually five executives and five non-executives on each board, with the chairman holding the balance. The regional offices choose the non-executives for the health authorities and trusts. In turn, the non-executive members appoint the executives. The chief executive, once chosen, takes part in the appointment of his or her executive director colleagues.

An odd market where everything's (almost) free

The buyers and sellers in this market are not as free as those selling their wares in Petticoat Lane. Indeed, one might think that it is a strange market where all the goods are free over the counter and everyone, whether buying or not, helps to pay for the goods on the 'never never', as taxes. The good news for those paying is that the total amount of goods paid for every year is restricted to a certain amount at the beginning of the year. As a result, the sellers will, on occasion, run out of things to sell. In that situation, buyers have to queue until more goods arrive. I will resist the temptation to squeeze this analogy into whether the goods are cheap and shoddy or of good quality, nor indeed into whether they would be legal under the Sale of Goods Act as 'fit for their purpose'.

Provider competition

The essence of the managed market in the UK is that there is competition for the health authority's finance. The competitors are the NHS trusts, the public providers, private health providers, voluntary bodies and any others who wish to provide health services [9]. The arrangements for NHS trusts [10] are such, especially in their system of capital funding, that they do not have a natural advantage over other providers who are not within the health service. However, the NHS trusts are several orders of magnitude bigger than the private and voluntary providers and in most cases can provide a cheaper and more comprehensive service than can the independent groups.

Enthoven, in his suggestions for reform of the health service, did not envisage two main areas of change that the government introduced. The first of these was self-government for hospitals, developing into trusts; the second was general practice fundholding. These two planks of the reform appear to have evolved as a result of following a logical line of argument within the government. Some people thought, at the time, that they had reached an illogical conclusion.

The rise of primary care

The American management gurus did not seem willing to suggest changes to primary care, especially the general practitioner service. When the government set up the NHS in 1948, general practitioners were given little status, possibly because of their opposition to it. Despite, or possibly because of this, the 1948 Act insisted that all patients should see a general practitioner before being seen by a hospital consultant. This is an unusual requirement for a health service but appears to have served the UK well. The general practitioners have acted as filters for patients who need specialist care. The system appears to have been responsible for keeping down the demand for secondary care in this country.

General practitioner fundholding

An important part of the NHS and Community care Act 1990 was the development of general practitioner purchasing. This allows general practitioners to apply for fundholding status. General practitioners who opt to become fundholding practices have to have a list size of at least 5000 patients. General practitioners with 3000 or more patients can opt to hold the budget for outpatient and community care only. There are slight differences in the rules in Wales, Scotland and Northern Ireland. Fundholding practices are purchasers of secondary services. They are given a budget taken from the health authority allocation to cover the cost of certain non-emergency inpatient and outpatient care. This also covers the cost of their prescribed drugs and the staffing costs of the practice. They draw up contracts with the hospital or community trusts specifying the cost of the service and its quality.

At present, general practitioner fundholders purchase about 8% of the trusts' budgets. About half of the population were registered with fundholding practices in 1996. Practices are increasingly being encouraged to opt for total fundholding. In this case, practices are given most of the costs incurred by their patients, including their emergency care, out of the health authority budget.

THE GROWTH OF THE INTERNAL MARKET

People often say that the NHS is slow to change. The NHS is an organization that costs £40 billion a year, with management costs of about 6% of the total.

I believe that the people in the organization have shown the most amazing adaptability over the past 25 years. The management costs compare with British Rail, which, before privatization, had management costs of about 12%. There were some teething troubles in the health service. There were instances in the early days of trusts in which the purchasers and providers were dealing in different measures in the contract. I have seen examples where one group believed the contract to be measured in the number of patients seen (discharges and deaths), whereas the other based the contract on the number of days patients were in hospital (bed-days). Considerable confusion followed when the bills came in. Nevertheless, managers in the health service have adapted very rapidly to a new way of working.

Models abroad

The good, or maybe bad, news about all the UK changes is that no other country is satisfied with its health system. There appear to be three types of problem:

- *Finance*. Every country thinks it pays too much for its health service. The USA has managed to develop a system of high administrative costs with low control over the service. The UK, has in contrast, low administrative costs and a high degree of control. Most other countries fall between these two extremes, but none are happy about the amount they spend.
- *Delivery of services*. All developed countries seem to have doubts about the quality or the access of patients to their services. Poor people do not, even when the service is free at the point of delivery, have equal access to services.
- *Efficiency*. There is a common belief that all health services can be made more efficient. This leads to more central control of the way in which services are provided. This has recently led to the use of guidelines and detailed descriptions of how we should provide health care intended to allow managers more control over the clinicians. The government ostensibly brought about these changes to improve the effectiveness of care. There may be an antipathy between efficiency and effectiveness which most governments feign not to appreciate.
- *Limits to health care*. Some believe that redefining what the health service provides will clarify what they are trying to do. This ranges from a belief in more prevention and health promotion and taking personal responsibility for one's health, to restricting health care to the acute treatment of diseases that have effective treatment.

Several recent examples of the problem in defining health care have arisen recently in the NHS. One was a row about whether the health service should provide some or no continuing care for elderly people. Others have included arguments about whether the treatment of scars, other forms of cosmetic surgery and assisted fertilization services should be provided on the NHS. Some people believed that these things are not what health care is about.

Other problems

Most countries agree about the nature of the problems. They also seem to judge their inability to reach the health care Nirvana as being due to similar obstacles:

- There are not enough data. If health and what health care should do are not defined, it is difficult to know what the data should be about.
- There is not enough money spent on prevention, and conversely there are too many hospital beds and too many doctors. A primary care-led service is said to have merit.
- Poor coordination and communication abounds within the health service, in particular poor collaboration between hospital and general practitioners. There is also poor communication between health and other services. This is most often used as another way of saying that the other organization is not doing its fair share.

Markets and health

Health services left to unmanaged market forces have a number of problems. Ill people are generally poorer, less able to judge the most effective treatment and less able to choose between different treatments than people who are not ill. People find it difficult to understand the complexities of health care and cannot make decisions about what services they prefer when they are well. Private providers of health services are therefore as keen as public providers that patients should not have to pay up at the 'point of sale' as they, believing that their service is best, want patients to make a rational decision.

Competition in health services probably does constrain costs [11]. It is curious therefore that the government monitors the organization so heavily. It seems that the main reason for this is that the government and the purchasers do not trust the provider trusts. Some trusts, as I write, are having to make detailed submissions to government departments monthly. The central control on the trusts, despite much rhetoric about giving trusts the freedom of the market approach, is greater than ever.

Strengths and weaknesses of the internal market

Strengths

The strength of the internal market for purchasers is that they can specify what they buy in as much or as little detail as they wish. The purchaser has a reasonably free rein, although there are some limits, including giving the provider 12 months warning about proposed major changes in the service. The Department of Health has also issued general strictures not to undermine the viability of trusts. In practice, purchasers have been responsible about their demands on providers. After all, only a few years back they were colleagues in the same organization. Many people, especially in management, move from one side of the service to the other. General practitioner fundholders have not been as gentle on their providers, but they have the benefit of knowing that they represent only a small part of a trust's budget.

All areas and providers have their black spots, which may be a specialty, a service or an individual. The internal market does not solve all problems, but it does allow purchasers to have the ultimate sanction if things are not improving, that sanction being to remove the contract from one provider and give it to another. For providers, the new system has given them more freedom to develop and try to sell new ideas. The boards of the trusts have a greater stake in their work for, if a trust fails, the non-executives will be out of an (albeit part-time) job. There is greater pressure for hospitals and community units to keep within their budgets than there was before the development of the market. Trusts have to be aware of what they do well and to concentrate on that, rather than trying to do a wide range of tasks, some badly.

This aspect of the market has been disappointing. Some trusts have been fast to develop new, exciting approaches to the delivery of services, but these are a minority. Generally, the trusts have been on the defensive, worrying about their budgets and trying to keep their heads down.

Weaknesses

There is now built-in competition between providers so that collaboration between them is difficult. There are also problems, especially for general practitioner fundholders, of buying in rare services. The need to make overt choices when purchasing one of two alternatives, a central point of the internal market, can also be seen as a weakness. This is the case if the choice is not explained to the public promptly and clearly. Trusts that lose services that they have provided for some years tend to cry foul to the press. Sometimes the decision not to give a service, even at the individual patient level, can hit the headlines. This is only a weakness of the service if the purchaser or provider in question is unable to give coherent reasons for the decisions. Unfortunately, there is no tradition within the health service for doing this, so patients often get a distorted view of the service.

There is a new overt emphasis on costing. Health authorities, trusts and general practitioner fundholders produce annual reports, which have to include detailed costs. This emphasis upon money appears to make the service appear less altruistic than it has in the past. There has been a long tradition in medicine, from the days of the voluntary hospitals [12], of giving free treatment, and the NHS inherited some of this ethos, so that until recently there has been only sporadic talk about the cost of effective care.

Mrs Thatcher's favourite image of the market was of a group of coster-mongers vying with each other about the price and quality of their goods to sell their wares. In this model, price is not something one mentions as an afterthought: it is shouted as part of the marketing. The new internal market in the health service was different from such a free approach. It had to keep within budget and to provide a full range of medical care free at the point of use. It is hard to envisage a group of costermongers developing a managed market under such constraints. It might just do so under heavy threat from the local spivs. It is interesting to surmise about who has that role in the health service.

COST PRESSURES ON HEALTH SERVICES

An ageing population

The problems faced by hospital services, be these increasing costs or the changes needed to make them more efficient, always seems to come back to the cost of caring for and treating elderly people. People say that increasing demands from elderly people and the increasing severity of their disabilities use up more and more hospital services. Eminent people often lead this debate about the increasing numbers of elderly people and their potential effect upon

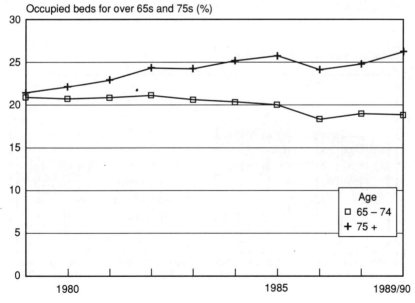

Figure 1.1 The proportion of 65–74 year olds (□) and those over 75 years (+) in England.

the health and social services [13,14]. Despite an intuitive feeling that more old people means more disabled people, the three components – an ageing society, dependency and the use of health services – are not linked.

A high proportion of hospital beds is occupied by people aged 65 and over. Figure 1.1 shows the percentage over the past 20 years. The proportion, especially of those over 75, has been increasing gradually but not dramatically. There was a change in the way the numbers were collected in 1986/87, accounting for the fall between 1985 and that year. These changes are small when one reflects that the proportion of people aged 75 and over has increased in the UK during that time by 50%.

Will more elderly people mean more ill people?

Studies have looked at the idea of healthy life expectancy or life expectancy without disability for elderly people [15]. Researchers have studied populations of elderly people over time to clarify this. Eighty-five year old people in 1989 were found to require considerably less assistance to go about their normal lives than were people of that age in 1982 [16]. Figure 1.2 shows that from 1976 to 1986 there was an increase in life expectancy for both men and women aged 65 and 75 years of age. When the researchers divided life expectancy into periods with and without disability, the period without disability increased. In contrast, the period with disability remained relatively constant or, in the case of women aged 75, rose at first up until 1981 and then fell again [17].

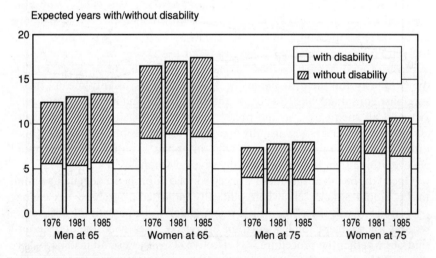

Figure 1.2 Expected years of life without disability remains constant, whereas that with disability rises over time.

Technological pressures

The development of most modern technologies requires money and, in the majority of cases, a lot of it. The social and political stimuli for the development of new ideas appear to be increasing in their effect. An important spur appears to be the increase in communications, especially television, which itself promotes change. The media tend to support an exaggerated view of science and scientific discovery that suggests that each new study is a breakthrough and every new product will be a success. They appear to have fostered a belief that we understand virtually all medical problems and a notion that there is a technical answer to all health problems.

Does the internal market make rationing more or less likely?

If purchasers are knowledgeable about, for instance, which services are most effective and which are not, spending by the health service may be contained. It will not, at least, have to rise as much as if ineffective services were being developed or maintained. With this proviso, the internal market should make the health service more effective and rationing less necessary. Comments in some newspapers have engendered some confusion by stating that health authorities that refused to buy ineffective care were rationing.

Tentative rationing that failed – sex change operations

A number of health authorities have made decisions that some forms of therapy traditionally given by the health service should no longer be provided. Examples usually seem to involve a puritan approach. Breast augmentation, liposuction and forms of plastic surgery for improving the looks of patients, in contrast to improving their health, are usually targets. 'Sex change' operations are also unpopular with health authorities toying with rationing. The authorities modify most of these strictures by a statement to the effect that they will pay for them 'if clinically indicated'. This usually means that a specialist consultant has to endorse the therapy. Specialist consultants refer virtually all such cases, so the policy tends to be meaningless. The health authority's grand gesture usually manages to get it into hot water about rationing with the local politicians who, in public, say that everyone should get everything free. It does not usually save any money.

One of the health authorities I worked for had published a document stating that it would not, 'except where clinically indicated', purchase 'sex change operations'. I was therefore a little taken aback to be passed, for decision, a request for payment for just such an operation. I searched the literature to find out whether the procedure was effective. This was not an instance where one could look up a number of studies with randomized controlled trials. The problem and the treatment were too rare for there to be enough cases for any real comparison of people who had and had not had the procedure. There were some studies of those who had had the procedure against those still waiting for it. The first part of my learning curve was to call the procedure 'gender reassignment' as sex change is, of course, impossible. The second was to discover that physicians in the USA had already drawn up guidelines on how to select suitable candidates [18]. The Dutch had studied a reasonably large group of them and found that the procedure had, subjectively, been beneficial to the patients involved [19]. The evidence, in other words, seemed as good, if not better, for the procedure than for many other rare or indeed some common procedures. I agreed to the payment, but the patient changed his mind.

WHAT TO BUY AND SELL

More recently, purchasers have been improving their ability to specify what they do and do not want to buy. Many health authorities now emphasize that they wish to buy only effective services. In the USA, the same pressure – to reduce spending on health – by federal health schemes led to the rapid development of guidelines of best practice for virtually every medical problem one could mention [20]. These guidelines are used to monitor the work being carried out in the health maintenance organizations and the federally funded budgets.

In the UK, another set of projects grew up around this question of effective treatment. Instead of the traditional agreement by the great and the good about the details of how to care for patients with different diseases, or to develop guidelines as in the USA, groups of people began to collect and criticize the scientific evidence. Researchers brought together this evidence, as published trials, and judged each trial against preset measures to decide whether each was of a reasonable quality. They combined, as so-called meta-analyses, the results of those trials that passed the tests. Thus there may be six good trials, using standardized criteria for what constitutes good, about whether, for example, special units for treating people with a stroke are effective. The results of the trials on helping stroke patients to recover from their disabilities are combined. This increases the number of patients and allows one to reach an average effect.

There are, however, detractors from this approach [21]. Some people say that glueing together a series of trials that were, individually, unable to answer a question simply multiplies the defects of each of the separate trials in one big one. If there is not a trial with sufficient power to answer the question about whether a treatment works or not, such an approach is surely the best use of the existing data. Without such trials, meta-analyses are compromises, but they do appear to be better than their individual component trials. On occasions when a single trial with sufficient power has been set up later, the meta-analyses have usually been found to be justified. Others say that this approach stultifies new ideas coming from individual clinicians. Overall, the people promoting evidence-based medicine seem to be aware of these problems and make the point that clinicians need to use the combined data from trials in conjunction with their personal expertise. There have been many years of individual practitioners doing unusual and unproven things to patients, so a little stultifying may be no bad thing. In my experience, those who are good at caring for patients individually also tend be well clued-up on the research evidence.

<table>
<tr><td>

2

</td><td>

Purchasing: responsibilities and principles

</td></tr>
</table>

VALUES IN PURCHASING AND PROVIDING

'Where there is no vision the people perish . . .' [22]

The *Oxford Shorter English Dictionary* defines a value as 'worthy of esteem for its own sake; that which has intrinsic worth'. In the NHS, we are dealing with values all the time. Programmes relating to effectiveness of treatment, quality improvement, equal opportunities, the Patient's Charter and rationing health care rely on sets of values. Despite this, there is no statement of the primary values underlying the structure, policy and work for the NHS or for parts of it. A single code for all the professions within the health service is asking too much. However, the board of directors of health authorities consulting the populations they serve and the professionals they use should develop a set of values. This would provide an important backbone for the development of strategic and operational changes.

The need for values

Organizations work according to certain sets of values, whether stated or unstated, agreed or not. The advantage in identifying and agreeing them is that, when crises come, the organization has a better chance of reacting consistently and agreeing to a plan of action. If purchasers wish to pass on the utilitarian principle of 'the greatest good for the greatest number', they must, for example, have a view of what this means for screening patients. These people have no disease, yet the money for screening is taken from the budget for treating acutely ill patients.

Purchasers setting up contracts with providers will need to make decisions between different services and to decide which should have priority. The

Department of Health, in its *Health of the Nation* document, has suggested certain principles for the development of services. These usually relate to the effectiveness and efficiency of services or make a general comment about 'improving health'. However, a shoe factory that did not make shoes or made terrible shoes would not describe making usable shoes as a value. It would see making shoes as the *sine qua non* of its existence. It might, however, need to decide whether to make the best shoes or the cheapest ones, or come to a better compromise between these two options than did other people. The company would choose to value high quality or cheapness. The difficulty for the health service is that it is not clear what it is in the business of selling as there is a spectrum of possibilities. The way it sets its values will help to decide which choice it makes.

The spectrum is not exhaustive, nor does any health service come from only one area: most are a mixture. However, each approach inevitably has its own set of values:

- Health for all, with health as the 'sense of complete mental, physical and social well-being'. This covers the whole population, with interventions in many fields beyond the traditional health areas. It tends to be a politicized approach and can clash with government policies in budgeting.
- Health promotion, with health seen as being taught. The approach follows closely the research evidence for the avoidance of disease. The approach relies on population data and is geared to the whole population. There is some politics involved. Health educationists have clashed heavily with the government in the UK on the promotion of information about sex, drugs and tobacco.
- Health services for providing reassurance for patients. There is an emphasis on screening for many diseases, including some that are quite rare. This gives reassurance to large numbers of people that they are 'normal'.
- Health services for 'cradle to grave' care. Advocates of this approach suggest that 'all effective services should be free'. This diverts attention towards deciding what is effective.
- Health services for 'health gain'. Those in need of health care are defined as those who will gain appreciably in terms of mortality and morbidity by receiving health services. The approach tends to be a bit indecisive concerning what to do for people who are not going to get better.
- Acute health interventions only. There is a need to define what services provide acute medical care. Others are seen as 'social care' and taken out of the remit of the health service. The argument about whether the NHS should provide long-term care for elderly people got into trouble with this approach.

It seems to me very difficult to set up a set of values until one decides what the health service is aiming to provide.

What values?

Andrew Wall [23] has suggested four values for the development of management in the health service:

- Justice
- Value for the community
- Value for the individual
- Sense of duty.

David Seedhouse, in his book on ethics [24], has suggested a similar four:

- Respect persons equally
- Create autonomy
- Respect autonomy
- Serve needs before wants.

One reason for the need for values is when priorities have to be made for scarce resources. The Oregon State government [25] had a particular problem, as many of its citizens were uninsured for health care costs. They decided that they would like to provide a basic package of care for all of their uninsured population but could not afford all available services for everyone. They decided to set priorities for different types of medical care, based on a set of values. The following shows the list of ethical values drawn up:

- Prevention
- Quality of life
- Cost-effectiveness
- Ability to function
- Equity
- Effectiveness of treatment
- Benefits large numbers
- Mental health and chemical dependency
- Personal choice
- Community compassion
- Impact on society (e.g. infectious diseases)
- Length of life
- Personal responsibility (lifestyle).

The public supplied these values at community meetings and individual phoned interviews. They were grouped into three: essential to basic health care, of value to society and of value to the individual. Prevention and quality of life appeared in all three. Benefits to many, an impact on society and cost-effectiveness were the three others described as being essential. Many of these are not, strictly speaking, values but characteristics of a functioning service. There will be trade-offs between one type of service and another, and values help one to decide which of these should have priority when trade-offs occur.

Values in practice

One researcher [26] highlighted the values that exist in hospitals by studying 24 hospitals into which a large number of innovations were introduced during a 6 month period. The importance given to these innovations suggested the values held by managers. The researchers classified them into four groups along two axes. The first axis had at one end an emphasis on flexibility, versus at the other end control. The second related to internal versus external changes (Figure 2.1).

The most notable finding of this study was that the 'flexible, internally orientated' group was good at the development of training for their staff, but this group contained by far the smallest number of innovations. Half of the hospitals questioned did not have any innovations of this type. Only three hospitals failed to introduce innovations in the 'external orientation, control' group. This suggests that hospital managers are, at present, concerned with controlling the external environment rather than developing their staff. Managers are keeping close control over the way in which their people work and, while aiming to care for their patients, this care does not seem to extend towards the staff working for the organization. It has often been suggested that caring organization are likely to fail to care for those who work in them.

Problems with values

Many health authorities, including my own, follow a strategy, although this may not be stated in such terms, of giving highest priority to the most severely and acutely ill. This makes some areas of work, especially in health promotion

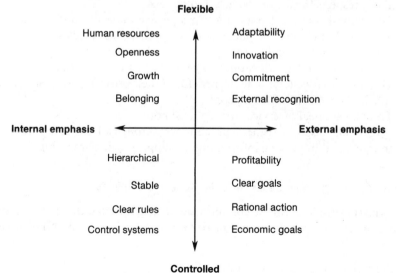

Figure 2.1 Types of organization and their values.

and primary care, of low priority. A number of other possible approaches are possible, but all have their difficulties.

There are a number of general approaches to choosing what we should do first:

- Equity is given pre-eminence. Expensive treatments are limited in favour of cheaper ones.
- The greatest potential for improving health. Purchasing is based on the greatest number of lives saved and disabilities avoided. Smoking prevention by the general practitioner tends to be most effective here.
- Accessibility. This tends to favour primary care. Acutely ill people have less priority.
- The best possible service for everyone. This is likely to run out of money on services of marginal value.

PURCHASING AND PROVIDING: WORKING IN PRINCIPLE

The implementation of the NHS and Community Care Act 1990 began in 1991 with the creation of the first round of trusts and a few general practitioner fundholders. Since then, hospitals, community services and ambulance services have become trusts separating off from the health authorities.

Functions of health authorities since the providers left

- To develop strategies to meet national and local priorities.
- To be responsible for public health functions.
- To establish the local population perspective of health and health care needs, and to involve the public in developing local strategies.
- To help to increase public understanding of health and health care issues.
- To advise on budget allocations to general practitioner fundholders.
- To ensure that general practitioners fulfill their providing and purchasing role in the interests of local people.
- To purchase health services for the local population.
- To provide support to general practitioners through advice, investment and training, and to provide information to support their purchasing.

Other changes brought about since the Act came into being

A review in 1994 confirmed a commitment to competition rather than collaboration within the purchaser and provider split. It said that the NHS should have:

- A market structure that is competitive
- Good information on prices and quality

- Providers motivated to be efficient and purchasers motivated to act on behalf of patients
- A price structures that gives the opportunities for providers and purchasers to choose patients on the basis of costs of services
- Capital control by the Department of Health, although trusts are to be encouraged to borrow money from the private sector under a Private Finance Initiative.

These changes appeared to expect the purchasers to be more aggressive in pressing providers for the best cost and quality deal. Government advice since the full implementation of the 1990 Act has tended to swing. At times it has advocated an aggressive approach, with emphasis on making providers compete with one another for cost and quality. At other times, it has emphasized the need for purchasers to maintain the viability of trusts and work collaboratively [27].

Competitive tendering

Compulsory competitive tendering for clinical services is one aggressive approach that has not, been promoted nationally by the Department of Health, although some health authorities have experimented with it. In the early 1980s, rules were set out by the government for competitive tendering for non-clinical services. The reason for the lack of interest in competitive tendering for clinical work has been partially because of the uproar among clinicians that this causes. In addition, most clinical professionals have contracts that are difficult and costly to alter or terminate, so that changes are difficult to bring about if the tender goes to a new provider.

PRESSURES OF CHANGE UPON SERVICES

Problems of re-tooling

One of the greatest problems faced by both purchasers and providers has been to work in a new way with what have often seemed to be very old tools. New training and retraining with very small budgets has made changing things difficult, but this has been small beer compared with two main difficulties. This first of these has been to alter the perceptions of the staff, whether clinical or non-clinical, to the idea that the service given should be of the highest quality. This is what I call the 'if you want me to call you by your surname you'd better go to BUPA' syndrome. The second has been the extreme lengths to which government departments have gone to keep tight control of the whole process in, sometimes, hilarious contrast to the rhetoric about market forces and free competition that they release to the press.

Problems with bringing about rapid change in the NHS

The health service is a very large organization, employing about a million people in the UK. In theory, the trusts and purchasers act as independent units within the whole. However, the government, aware of the large amount of money spent on the health services, keeps strict control on the amount of freedom that health authorities and trusts have. A recent example was about salaries for doctors and nurses. Trusts were initially told that they had local discretion to pay whatever they wished. However, after some negotiation, the Pay Review Body for doctors made a national settlement. The nursing unions, after some negotiation, forced a compromise that resulted in the great majority of nurses in the country receiving a 3% pay rise. The workforce of the health service is so vast in number and the amount of money so great, that the government of the day finds it impossible not to interfere.

The health backlash: the example of the learning disabilities service

A number of important lessons to anyone involved in fundamentally changing health services can be learned by studying the learning disabilities service. This service has aimed to reduce to a minimum the number of clients the health service holds in large institutions. The first lesson has been that change is very slow. The Mental Handicap Strategy was set up in 1984 in Wales, with a belief that the resettlement of the great majority of people out of the hospitals and into smaller, more friendly units would have been completed within 5 years, certainly within 10. In fact, this process has been much slower than was foreseen. Between one-third and one-quarter of the patients then in hospital still have to be moved out. The first large inappropriate learning disability hospitals may close in late 1997 in Wales, this despite, for once in the health service, no lack of resources.

The first stages suggested that the process would not be very difficult. Some clients moved to their families, others to small groups with social services personnel looking after them. Social services set up day facilities for these people to have interesting and fulfilling activities during the day. Others took care to ensure that the new homes were not institutional in nature. Some attempts were made to find employment for learning disabled people, and some sheltered employment facilities were set up.

In the mean time the institutions found that, with the less disabled clients leaving first, there was increasing pressure on the staff. The community teams were recruiting staff, especially nurses, from the hospitals, with the result that people regarded the nurses left behind as the less able ones.

The high concentration of very disabled people in the remains of the institutions made people look at what was holding back the remaining clients. It appears that it is difficult to resettle three main groups of people: some clients have mental illnesses as well as learning disabilities, others have severe physical problems; another group is difficult to manage socially. This 'challenging behaviour' group sometimes falls foul of the law and may need to be legally detained, for some time at least, in secure accommodation.

The time taken to resettle the clients and the nature of the problems experienced by them has led the health service to take a new, more detailed look at learning disabled people. It was originally thought that almost all clients in institutions would be transferred to the care of social services. If they had health problems, they would be able to use the general health services, general practitioners and hospital services when necessary. This approach is gradually being revised so that units for people with challenging behaviour are developing under the care of health services.

These overall changes have resulted in more attention being paid to the specialty, so that it grew in status as a medical academic and research-based specialty. These people are much more willing and interested in caring for the patients than has been the case in the past. There has therefore, owing to increased interest in and funding of the clients, been a backlash from the health service to keep a higher proportion of these people in the services than was initially envisaged.

INVOLVING GENERAL PRACTITIONERS IN PURCHASING

Health authorities have an obligation, during contracting, to involve general practitioners and the community. One study [28] into this showed that the group of health authorities the researchers visited was making efforts to consult local general practitioners and community health councils to ensure that contracts met their wishes. The researchers asked community health council respondents about conferring with health authorities about their plans. The council members were generally satisfied with the consultation from the health authority: over half of them were always consulted, and all of them believed that the health authorities had altered their plans in response to suggestions. They also kept the community health councils up to date on their plans.

The researchers then asked the local general practitioners whether the health authority consulted them. There was a great difference between the six authority areas studied. Four out of 10 of the general practitioners said that their health authority never consulted them. In contrast, a similar proportion felt that all or some of their comments had been taken into account. One-quarter said they had commented but the authority had ignored the comments. The health authorities with the best record were those which had established local purchasing teams. The teams visited the practices in their area every 6 months to discuss contracts and purchasing intentions. Some health authorities included general practitioner fundholders on their commissioning teams to make sure that contract terms and conditions were similar in the fundholding and non-fundholding practices.

Another approach was for health authority staff to visit all the general practices for informal meetings. On these visits, the staff went through the annual health plan and discussed services that the health authority did and did not want to purchase in future. When asked whether the contracts that health authorities had made with acute hospitals were appropriate for their patients' needs, one-quarter of the general practitioners said that they were always appropriate. Two-thirds said that the contracts were only sometimes appropriate.

Monitoring contracts

General practitioners were more likely to be involved in contracting than in monitoring the hospital's performance against their contracts. General practitioners' views are particularly valuable for monitoring hospital care as detailed patient information is often difficult to get from hospitals. General practitioners who are in direct contact with the patients who have been in hospital are in a unique position to help with monitoring.

The survey also asked for views on whether general practitioners felt that their patients had benefited from the internal market. Nearly half of the general practitioners thought that some of their patients had benefited, but many others were not convinced of the benefits, despite the efforts of the health authorities.

PURCHASING WHAT?

In any market, one is usually clear about what is on sale, but this is not the case for health services, which naturally makes them difficult to purchase and provide. There are so many factors that affect health that Lalonde (the Canadian Minister of Health in 1974) said that 'everything which has an effect on life has an effect on health'. He described the 'health field concept', which identifies four categories of influence on health:

- *Human biology* includes those aspects of health that are a consequence of basic biology, the genetic inheritance of each person and the natural consequences of maturing and ageing.
- *Environment* describes those matters related to health that are outside the human body and over which people have little or no direct control. Things included in this category are the quality of air, water supplies and sewage, noise pollution, passive smoking, fear of crime and unemployment, and the social environment in which we live.
- *Lifestyle* reflects those aspects of life over which individuals have control, such as smoking, alcohol consumption and diet, sexual habits, exercise and other personal choices about life. There is some overlap between

environment and lifestyle features. Political pressure on governments could change some aspects of the environment. Some aspects of lifestyle are constrained by what is available and what is considered to be normal and acceptable. One could debate the control that people have over, for example, smoking in a profession or family where it is the social norm.

- *Health care organization* describes the medical services provided to treat and prevent illness and care for patients.

Lalonde proposed that factors from one or more of the four categories of the health field concept could account for the causes of any health problem. He suggested that it was possible to analyse the relative significance of each category for each health problem. The model can be useful even if the reasons for a disease or other problem are not understood.

What affects health?

McKeown [29] considered those factors that improved the health of the UK population in the past 200 years. His conclusion was that the decline in mortality and increased expectation of life that have occurred are due to environmental, behavioural (equivalent to Lalonde's lifestyle category) and therapeutic changes, in that order of importance. He considered that the most important environmental change was better nutrition for the population, which had been brought about by improved farming techniques to produce more good-quality food. The improved distribution of goods due to the development of the canal, railway and road networks also played a very important part. A wide range of cheap, good-quality food has been promoted by the development of the huge supermarket chains in the Western world. These have some disadvantages for poor and elderly people without transport, although most provide a cheap bus service to the outlet.

Other important environmental changes are hygiene improvements caused by the development of clean water supplies, sewage systems and food-handling techniques. The improved hygiene has helped to reduce the impact of infectious diseases on the population. However, McKeown argues that this was secondary to the effect of the nutritional benefits that produces a healthier population more able to withstand infectious diseases. The most important behavioural change was in reproductive practices, leading to the decline of the birth-rate, spacing of families and a fall in family size.

Therapeutic advances such as immunization and antibiotics became available a long time after the measures described above had already caused a dramatic fall in mortality. Nevertheless, there has been a substantial decline in the mortality and morbidity from some diseases such as diphtheria and poliomyelitis and the eradication of smallpox following the introduction of effective medical interventions, mainly forms of immunization.

The effect of health services on health

Popular belief equates the level of health with the quality and quantity of health services available rather than with other determinants of health. Health services are responsible for the health care organization category of the health field concept, with only limited involvement in the other areas. However, the health services attempt to influence other determinants of health, with the intention of improving the overall health of the population.

Interactions of the health fields

Health education directed towards individuals and society as a whole can influence lifestyle. Legislation can have an effect: a ban on tobacco advertising can reduce smoking habits, and seat belt legislation has dramatically increased the proportion of individuals wearing them. Legislation making it illegal to drive with high concentrations of blood alcohol has cut down on deaths due to drink-driving. Prevention of disease is better than treatment if that prevention involves simple lifestyle changes. If these changes were adopted by the whole population, it would be more effective than dramatic changes adopted by a small number of people.

A good example of this is the use of seat belts, which has saved many lives and avoided a great deal of suffering. It is noteworthy that when seat belts were provided in all cars by law, a relatively small proportion of people wore them. The main improvements in health occurred when legislation was brought in to make the wearing of belts compulsory. The main effect was as a result of legislation, rather than due to exhortations from the health or education professions. In a similar way, the most effective means of reducing smoking in the population as a whole is known to be for the Chancellor of the Exchequer to increase the tax on, and therefore the price of, cigarettes.

Government legislation is also important, as laws to reduce pollution and to promote safety of food, water supplies and workplaces influence the environment. This raises the question of whether the health services should have a political role in pressing the government to take legislative action in these areas.

Human biology is more difficult to influence, but research in this area has produced useful knowledge. The abnormal genes responsible for many genetic disorders are being identified. The possibility of achieving genetic manipulation is increasingly close, although there are difficult ethical, moral and financial considerations, of which the financial problem may be the greatest. Severe genetic defects are rare, and therapy is likely to need to be customized to each person receiving it. Drugs companies may find it impossible to develop a therapy needed by enough people world-wide to pay for its development. Some related therapies, such as using genetic material to deliver drugs to particular organs or abnormal tissues in, for example, cancer therapy, may have more general application and therefore be able to pay for its development.

Such discoveries are bringing this area into the health services field. Present techniques to prevent the birth of seriously handicapped individuals are designed to identify genetic disorders antenatally to allow the abortion of an affected baby. More usefully, for people at high risk, genetic abnormalities can be identified before test-tube embryos are implanted into the mother.

Society spends large sums of money on health services. At the same time, it tolerates and even encourages harmful behaviour and environmental hazards. The examples of smoking and road transport are so obvious that the arguments do not require repetition. Changes to the lifestyle and environment categories could have a much greater impact on health than could increased spending on health care. This ambiguity often results in a feeling that the health service is trying to run up the down escalator.

Working with non-health groups – joint planning

It can be seen from the complexity of the health field concept that services providing health care, social care, education and housing, voluntary bodies and private organizations often need to work together. This relationship can be very complex and often fraught with problems. In the 1980s, research was carried out on the role of health authority members. It also examined the relationship between the different organizational levels of authorities and internal, professional and organization-based pressures on their policies [30–32]. This showed that the structure and development of committees, the personalities and interests of members and whether they met informally outside the meeting were important for helping or disrupting the work involved in making decisions.

Groups have studied the problems faced by people from large organizations trying to cooperate. This degree of working together can be described in five increasingly intimate ways [33]:

- Communication and consultation
- Cooperation
- Coordination
- Federation and teamwork
- Merger.

Webb researched joint planning and financing [34] between the health and social services. He said that the main barrier to collaboration was the need to protect the interests of the organizations. Different groups had to follow different priorities and maintain a satisfactory professional image. An old-fashioned need to build empires was less important. Webb also suggested that collaboration that is inappropriate or forced in some way can often disable the outcome that both groups want to achieve.

Challis showed that, at a time when money was scarce, the main spur to collaboration was the possibility of obtaining funds as part of the collaboration. Another aspect that helped was the possibility of large organizations using their money to help smaller organizations. The *quid pro quo* was that the smaller ones would often help to carry out the larger ones' strategies. The health and social services often use small amounts of money to set up groups of people with similar problems – self-help groups. As an example, stroke clubs give information and help to provide some simple forms of therapy to people who would otherwise be difficult to contact. Voluntary groups commonly do a great deal of health service-funded work with mentally ill people. Their success is due to the informality and non-establishment image of the voluntary group. On occasion, two organizations with the same problem may pool resources to solve it, but this is less common.

Spurs to collaboration

Research has shown that when two large organizations try to work together, they need to decide from the start the degree of collaboration necessary to achieve what they want. This is the case whether the organizations are purchasers and providers within the health service or health authorities and trusts with social services. Friendships between key members of the different organizations are extremely important to allow close cooperation and collaboration. At lower levels of the hierarchy, a merger of the different professionals in a separate management structure is sometimes needed for the process to work best. Problems of this kind often arise when services that are separate need to work together on a project. Community mental health teams often come into this category. They require health and social services staff to work closely. This is sometimes done by setting up a separate administrative structure for the teams, which is contributed to by the health and social services.

A particular problem now occurs in the health service when two or more trusts need to work in collaboration, as all the pressures in the internal market encourage competition between them. A common problem has been the development of community-based child health services, as mentioned in Chapter 11. The paediatric community-based nurses and sometimes community paediatricians are often under one trust, the hospital-based paediatricians under another. Trusts, by the way that they have been set up, find it difficult to cooperate with each other except under the closest external scrutiny to ensure fair play. Again, a separate management team for children's services is sometimes the answer to the rivalry between the trusts.

To date, little work has been carried out to examine the difficulties resulting from the need to coordinate the plans of these groups. There is a particular problem for services, such as those for the learning disabled, mentally ill and disabled people. The people providing the service work under the NHS and Community Care Act 1990, which means that they have to include the interests and wishes of the patients who use their services and the people that care for them into their plans.

The people doing the planning can include the views of users and carers in a number of ways. Planning groups can attend users' forums or they can co-opt people who use the service and their carers. This approach has caused considerable difficulty in some places, despite the advice of many of the voluntary agencies. There is no obvious way of choosing a representative of these groups, and those that are chosen may become overwhelmed by the high-pressure tactics of the people representing the large organizations. Those chosen may also find themselves increasingly separated from the people whom they were meant to represent. They often find themselves defending the actions of the large organizations to their erstwhile friends, as they become more aware of the restrictions placed on these organizations.

My view is that we should acknowledge these problems and reduce the formal joint planning mechanism. Where cooperation is needed, the service acting as prime mover should be responsible for ensuring that there is no clash of interest with the others. The interests of health service users and carers is then the responsibility of the prime mover. The elected councillors would perform this function for social services departments and others run by the local authorities. Effective collaboration and avoidance of conflict will continue to be key issues in the effective delivery of much of health care.

CONCLUSION: THE MAIN TASKS

Purchasers

Purchasing health care within the health services divides naturally into a number of processes.

Planning

- Monitoring existing contracts and learning lessons
- Assessing government policy changes
- Assessing new medical and other developments
- Assessing changes in demography and their likely impacts
- Assessing local changes, such as new housing and new industry.

Assessing health needs

- Assessing the needs of the population served
- Considering the views of the population served
- Developing a service specification and the production of a full specification, which may be thought of as a tender.

Contracting

- Assessing the amount of money that is available for the service in question
- Given the costs of the service, deciding how much to buy and from whom
- If it is a new development, asking provider(s) for a business case
- Deciding upon the main contract currencies
- Deciding upon the quality standards to be measured
- Deciding upon the monitoring standards
- Developing the core contract
- Negotiating with the providers to reach agreement on the contract details
- Monitoring, usually monthly, the amount and quality of the service and whether it is keeping to budget
- Examining untoward events and complaints
- Feeding back needs assessment and prices information for the next round

Providers

For providers the main tasks are as follows.

Planning

- Assessing the monitoring data from existing contracts
- Deciding upon the functions of the trust: what it will and will not do
- Deciding upon a strategy regarding purchasers, for example how much time to give to each
- Deciding upon an attitude to competitors, for example with respect to high costs, high quality or low cost, low quality and new work.

Balancing the budget

- Negotiating with purchasers
- Adopting approaches to improving efficiency, such as criteria for using services and the levels of qualification of the staff required
- Expanding the services
- Managing the management costs.

Improving and selling the service

- Monitoring perceptions of purchasers, the health authority and general practitioners
- Considering patient attitudes to the service
- Monitoring public attitudes and addressing the media
- Addressing the quality control of services.

Purchasing: the first job – planning

3

THE PROCESS OF PLANNING

I believe that strategic planning at anything but the most general level is a waste of time for a time scale of over 5 years. The blocks to carrying out any form of strategic plan are:

- Policy changes
- Scientific and technological change
- Population pressure.

These would be hard to rank in importance.

Policies encouraging the development of district general hospitals have given way to an emphasis on the importance of primary care. Policies for the development of local small hospitals have been brought in just as many of the cottage hospitals have, despite great local opposition, been closed. Scientific discoveries have brought about some changes over the long term: one has only to look at the amount of money put into the treatment of tuberculosis in the 1920s, the number of gastric surgery operations in the 1960s, or the treatment of leukaemia and cystic fibrosis in the 1980s and 1990s. Population pressure has begun to make differences to the care of pregnant women and concerns about the long-term care of elderly people. The secret of good planning is to try to foresee and avoid or jump on the bandwagon of such changes to bring about the desired result.

Plans must be acceptable to the people affected. For this reason, planners have to be aware of fashions in care and the morale of the people in their services. If morale is too high, no change will be possible; if too low, no-one will be willing to take the risk of any change.

Planning has within it a paradox that must be solved. In the Ministry of Aircraft Production during the war, Ely Devons identified what he saw as

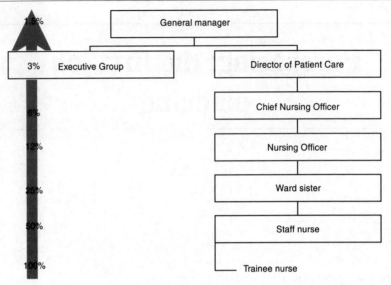

Figure 3.1   Information gathering for planners.

some of the fundamental dilemmas of planning. Every attempt at planning, he argued, revealed two problems:

- First, the need to split up the field to be covered so that each administrative unit could deal efficiently with its own sector
- Second, the need to secure that the actions of these separate units all fitted into the general plan.

These principles always lead to trouble. The first requires delegation and devolution, so that plans can be manageable and realistic. The second needs to be centralized to make sure the plans are coordinated. At each level, the coordinators regard the plans of the individual sectors as futile and wasteful because they take no account of what is happening elsewhere. Those of individual sectors regard the plans of the coordinators as theoretical, academic and unrelated to the real world.

Figure 3.1 shows part of the problem. The person who knows what is happening is the one who has to do the work, in this case the trainee nurse. For planning purposes, information needs to get up the hierarchy to the planners if they are at the top. If 50% is lost at each stage, one can see how little gets through.

PLANNING AND POLICY

Strategic planning must include the policies set by the government and higher management tiers. I sometimes feel that policy completely dominates local planning. An example over the last few years has been the subject of waiting lists. Waiting lists are curious phenomena that appear to have been of particular concern to governments and opposition parties. This seems to be a response to treating the health service as some kind of manufacturing industry, with waiting lists the equivalent of delivery dates. A survey of elderly people who had been treated in hospital showed that those who had waited for operations did no worse than those who had not waited in terms of their residual degree of disability or mortality in hospital [35]. Perhaps most importantly, waiting lists are often mentioned by patients as important measures of the quality of the health service.

For long-term effectiveness, waiting lists are obviously important if patients are in pain or die while on the waiting list when the operation or treatment they were waiting for would have reversed this. People have suggested that the government answer to these problems, the waiting list initiatives, have in the past few years in the UK reduced the number of people waiting for long periods. They have not, however, affected the average time people have to wait [36]. This appears to be because removing the tail of the waiting list encourages additions to the beginning. The way this works is not clear, but it may be because general practitioners, seeing that the list is short, send in more patients from general practice. It may also be that specialists, because patients are not waiting as long as they used to, take on more patients via outpatients who were only likely to get a small degree of benefit from their operations.

As I mentioned at the beginning of this chapter, planning needs to foresee technical innovations and use these changes. Perhaps the weakest pressure on planning is the population's view of what should happen. Sometimes, often to the surprise of professionals, a voluntary group will strongly advocate a change of direction for the service. Change in the maternity services in the past few years is a good example, changes in the service having led to more women having home births. These changes were led by women's groups despite strong resistance from obstetricians.

People who are planning must also keep an 'eye on the ball'. This is important because one sometimes cannot tell when the plans have been achieved or are irrevocably blocked. In my experience, strategic plans are never achieved or completed – they are simply replaced by the next plan, which usually has elements of the old plan. The easiest way to write a new strategic plan is to rewrite the old one and change the bits that seem especially ludicrous. Word-processors are invaluable at this stage. In the days when I had to write a strategic plan for mental illness services annually, the most depressing part was to realize how little of it had been achieved year by year.

ROUTINE DATA AS A BASIS FOR PLANNING

Routine data are those data that are collected by health service providers without a special request. In practice, they are usually required by the Department of Health, often as a statutory responsibility of the provider. A number of different public agencies collect and publish them in a variety of ways. One has to be particularly careful about whether the statistics are available for England, Wales, Scotland, Northern Ireland, England and Wales together, Great Britain (which is England, Wales and Scotland) or the United Kingdom (which is Great Britain plus Northern Ireland). The Channel Islands and Isle of Man are not usually included.

The country is the United Kingdom (UK). All international comparisons should be made with UK data. During the time that I have worked in Scotland and Wales, both have claimed to have the highest death rates 'of any country in Europe'. The statement is invalid because neither are countries. The collection of data is related to the structure of the health service. In Wales, Scotland and Ireland, for example, there is no separate regional outpost of the Department of Health. Instead, the regional tasks are split between the Welsh Office, the Scottish Office or the Northern Ireland Office and the health authorities.

The types of data available routinely that are useful for health purposes can be divided into three major groups.

- General data:
    Census
    OPCS Registers information; births, marriages and deaths
- Health services data:
    Hospital returns
    Community returns
    Notification of disease
- Non-health service data:
    Local authority
    Health and safety, etc.

General data

Census data are available every 10 years, in years ending with a 1. These data are vital for getting accurate measures of the number of people in the district and their ages. Without these data, one could not give any accurate rates to compare one area with another. Everyone must fill in the census by law. It is therefore, compared with most data sources, very accurate.

Statistics from the census are produced for the country as a whole but, more importantly, by local authority, electoral ward and other small areas. The Deccenial Supplement contains data on mortality by occupation. It is useful for checking on whether some of the local industries are associated with high death rates. Other important sources of general data are the registration of births, marriages and deaths. Births can give information on the legitimacy of babies and the place of birth. Marriage data are useful mainly for providing information on conception before marriage. This can identify risk factors for health for the well-being of children. It is not available for individuals but can pinpoint areas, such as inner cities, where there may be particular problems. The registration of deaths is important and is normally signed by a general practitioner or a consultant. Health authorities usually receive these data for their area.

Health services data

Health services data are, at the moment, in a state of some chaos related to the development of the internal market and the rapid developments in technology. Before the 1990 NHS and Community Care Act, data were collected as a requirement by the responsible government bodies. They were standardized throughout the country, each hospital providing similar returns and careful checks on accuracy. The problem was that the data gave a superficial view of what was going on in the health service. Nevertheless, the basic bed use and diagnostic data could, with a little imagination, be put to use. These data are still obtainable, but they are becoming steadily more difficult to get and there are doubts about whether they will be available in future. Some data on hospital theatre usage now appear to be impossible to obtain.

The purchaser – provider split has altered the emphasis in the health service to such a degree that the main energies of people providing information, especially those in the trusts, are now directed at providing data for the contracting process. There are considerable pressures for trusts to provide detailed financial data, much of it monthly. Many trusts, when first set up, left the information departments behind in the health authorities, so that much new training has had to be provided. Many of the computer-based systems in the trusts are also new, and these too have often had teething problems.

Providers need, most urgently, to measure their contract currencies for each specialty specified in the contract. These may be different from specialty to specialty and from purchaser to purchaser. This diversity of information may make it difficult to compare the work of one hospital with another.

In the meantime, scandals have ripped through all the health regions in England as salesmen for computer firms have captured the imagination of hapless information directors. They appear to have done this by promising them the holy grail of knowing exactly what is going on 'out there'. Doctors and nurses spend a third of their time collecting or using data directly [37]. The internal market, with its requirement for detailed monitoring data from trusts and the new liberty that trusts have to develop their own data collection system, has caused much of the confusion. Health authorities and general practitioner fundholders are demanding more and different information. However, many new data collection systems are not compatible, either in the way that they collect data or when transferring data from one computer to another.

Some attempts to bring order to the system do exist. The National Clearinghouse project collects data from trust data systems nightly and puts together comparative statistics. These are useful benchmarks against which to judge, for example, a teaching hospital with its peers. The project is still in the development stage. The NHS Network Project that collects the data backs up the Clearinghouse project.

Over the years, considerable effort and no little expense have gone into monitoring the activity of the hospital service. The returns are considerably more detailed and generally more accurate than those from the community. Several factors contribute to this, the main being that statistics in hospital are the responsibility of a records officer, who in turn has a group of staff responsible for the running of the department. Doctors and nurses are not involved in the production of the statistical returns. Diagnostic information, which has to be provided by a doctor, is the most variable in quality. On the down side, clerks responsible for the statistics from clinical records are among the lowest paid workers in the health service and among those most distant from the actual use of the numbers that they produce. They get little response about the use of their statistics or even an understanding of why they are collected. It is not surprising that the data are sometimes not very accurate [38].

Hospital data have the advantage that patients come into hospital, have something done, then go home. In the community, patients are more likely to be seen intermittently over many years. They may also be seen by different facets of the service, leading to double counting. Until recently, when patients are increasingly being given their notes to look after, it was difficult to know how many people had been to a patient at home and what they had done. Recording this centrally was often seen as a low priority.

Hospital episode statistics

Hospital episode statistics are a system for getting, for each patient admitted to hospital as an inpatient, details of age, sex, area of residence and condition treated. It also mentions operations carried out, the time the patient spent on the waiting list and how long was spent in hospital. The system collects data about the area of residence of patients, including their post code. This can be used to define the so-called catchment population of the hospital, district or region, which may be important if one wishes to look at treatment rates on a population basis. This is particularly relevant in regional centres, usually gathered around a medical school as there is a great deal of crossing of boundaries into the district by such patients. This tends to be for services that are expensive or very specialist. It is my impression that the health regions are doing less and less of this central analysis.

SH3 or QS1

These forms traditionally contained the bed-use statistics for hospitals. In future, it will not be as easy to tell the difference between the SH3, which is known as QS1 in Wales, from other data collections. The data will be collected on computer and will become one database. The SH3 has been an administrative form containing information about numbers of allocated and used inpatient beds, outpatients and day patients. The information has been extended in the last few years by the Körner data set to include data on outpatient care and specialty-based information. This is in turn being modified by the new data-collecting systems. The importance of these data is that some parts of them, for example discharges and deaths, are available in a reasonably comparable form over the last 10 years; most of the newer data sets are not.

Mental Health Inquiry

The Mental Health Inquiry relates to mental illness and developed separately, probably because of the separate development of the mental hospitals. It had the benefit of being a slightly better system in that diagnostic data were combined with administrative data. Despite this, there are considerable problems with the diagnostic data on this return, often because of genuine disagreement between psychiatrists on what is wrong with patients with mental illnesses. The Mental Health Inquiry includes a point prevalence of patients for age, sex and diagnosis and length of stay to that point; it is a census of the patients in hospital taken one evening in the year. This approach is useful where there is a large long-stay element in a hospital.

Körner

The Körner data set includes information on the different treatment specialties. There are more sub-specialty groups and more information on inpatients and outpatients who did not attend than in the pre-existing data sets. Recently, there has been a lot more information on waiting lists, especially whether the waiting list patient was classified as urgent or not, and the time patients were kept on the list. There is also information on the actions of professionals, such as physiotherapists and the pathology services, working alongside doctors. Körner data have been available for about 5 years.

Diagnostic-related groups

In the USA, diagnosis-related groups (DRGs) have for some years been a popular method of categorizing patients on admission. They have been adapted to fit in with the predetermined price schedules used by health maintenance organizations as a basis for paying hospitals. Medicare, the federal safety net for poor people, also uses them for reimbursement. Essentially, DRGs classify patients into one of around 500 categories set up in such a way that the costs of treating patients in any one category in different places will be approximately the same. Different DRGs relate to different levels of cost.

The system depends on the accurate assignment of patients to DRGs on admission. It is here that 'DRG creep' enters. There is a significant temptation to over categorize patients, in other words to assign patients on the margin between two categories to a more expensive DRG than is necessary for their treatment. There is a parallel here with some of the contracting processes in the NHS at present. One example is the pricing by hospital trusts of specialist care compared with the price of general medical or surgical care. The specialty is almost always priced higher than the general specialty. This appears, at first sight, to be sensible, but when one thinks further, the difference between specialist and generalist wards may be very little, except that the patients on the specialist wards have problems similar to each other. There is little proof that more resources are used.

The existence of specialist wards in district general hospitals is often an accident of history or to do with the area in which the hospital is placed. Hospitals in South Wales and the Potteries, for example, often have chest wards because the local industries were toxic to the lungs. There is an argument that a general ward, expected to deal with a wide range of problems, could be more expensive than a specialist ward. An example is given in Table 3.1, which shows the specialty of general medicine, medical gastroenterology and geriatrics.

The currency column consists of completed consultant episodes, and the contract level is the number of those episodes over the year in question. The trust price is the price per episode, and the marginal price the amount charged by the trust for extra cases if the trust provides more than its contracted number of cases. There is no clear, nationally agreed distinction between the definition of one specialty and that of another except an historical precedent and a general view on the length of stay of patients in each type of bed.

The geriatrics beds in this particular hospital have an integrated admission ward, so that the difference between the patients should be easy to define. Nevertheless, it is obvious that some careful redesignation of beds or a slight alteration in the admission criteria for one type of bed versus another can dramatically alter the total cost of the service.

In the USA, the countermeasure to DRG creep and other methods of circumventing financial controls has been to bring in utilization reviews, preadmission approval and other approaches. These are different types of external check on the way in which the patients are classified. To some extent,

Table 3.1 Classification of patients and costs

Specialty	Code	Currency	Contract level	Trust price	Marginal price	Contract value
General Medicine	300	Consultant episodes	4 657	£918	£246	£4 257 126
Gastro-enterology	300	Consultant episodes	356	£1 092	£273	£388 752
Geriatrics	430	Consultant episodes	2 075	£2 335	£625	£4 845 125

these checks overcome abuse of the system. However, health care spending is like a balloon: squeeze it in one place, for example hospital inpatients, and it tends to bulge out somewhere else, where there is less price restriction, for example community-based or outpatient care.

The UK government aims to develop all purchasing according to DRG-like categories in the next year or so. The reason for this is that they and the purchasers will be able to compare more closely the costs of one hospital with another for a specific intervention. It will also be possible to compare some outcomes, for example death rates, more directly by DRG categories. There is a growing tendency for more and more of this information to be published, so that patients can make their own direct comparisons between hospitals. It seems to me that this can do nothing but good as long as the data are reasonably robust. However, the origins of DRGs as a way of banding patients according to their cost must always be remembered. They are not really intended as a way of categorizing the severity of one group of patients compared with another. If outcome data, deaths or morbidity are published according to DRG to make different hospitals comparable, some careful work will be needed to validate this approach. I am not aware that any has been done so far. The relationship between outcome and diagnosis is known to be complex [39].

In England, a related system with some customization for the local vagaries of the service is known as the health-related group approach. Some categories of care, notably mental illness and forms of chronic disease, do not fit well with the DRG system. It is not yet clear how these problems will be resolved.

The problem with such detailed contracting is that it can be time consuming to work out the details of the contracts. Having said this, most providers will want to look in detail at what they are doing to improve their efficiency and possibly to sell any overcapacity to other purchasers. In other words, they will have the data readily available. Any negotiation between purchasers and providers is a time-consuming business, even for straightforward block contracts. The detailed approach can, in fact, make the negotiation easier, as it suggests a degree of openness between the two negotiators. In my experience, problems in agreeing budgets revolve around obscure difficulties often relating back to pre-internal market days. One good example is the disposal of clinical waste. The health authority had decided to centralize disposal of all of its clinical waste before 1990 at one hospital. The other trusts now have to negotiate with that trust for time in the incinerator. The authority, having set up the system feels that it has an obligation to use the new incinerator, but the trust that owns it is charging more than people outside the area are. The problem is resolvable, but this will take time.

General practice data

General practitioners now have to produce an annual report, the core of which is required by statute. This is provided for the health authority whether or not the general practice is fundholding. Basic information on prescriptions has been held for some time, but this has recently become more detailed and, indeed, prescribing data can be very valuable for looking at trends in treating patients. The annual report also contains data about patients referred to hospital, although these are often not very accurate. It does, however, allow one to cross-check the referral data held by the hospitals. People have particular problems with referral to outpatient departments, as patients who are sent but do not attend are not always recorded. These data are important as they can suggest that a department is not functioning very well if many patients fail to turn up.

Health authority general practice records are held on computer. They contain the names of the people in each practice and their address, date of birth and NHS number. The general practitioner's record is sometimes the only way of telling how many people of, for example a particular age group are present in the practice. The other benefit of the record is that it contains the NHS number. This is a unique number for everyone in the country and is used, if necessary, to trace people who may, for example, have taken part in a research project. This is done at the National Health Service Central Register in Southport. Patients of interest can be flagged in Southport, so that when they die or move, that information can be returned to the person who asked for the flagging. This is also a useful device for doctors or nurses wishing to follow up their patients over a long period.

Nationally representative information on consulting in general practice has been intermittently collected in the National Morbidity Studies over the past 20 years [40]. These have studied a large number of practices and given information on the diagnosis, number of consultations and referrals in those practices.

Community health services

Community health service information is usually collected by the person providing the service. It tends to be rather inaccurate as the people in the service see little point in filling out forms, and the feedback of the information collected is not good. In some areas, community health information is known as the Comcare system. Midwives and health visitors use it to identify new mothers from their maternity records. It also identifies children of certain ages who receive checks on their physical and mental development. A number of systems for recording the visits of community staff have been tried using microcomputers. These systems are not generally popular, although a number of new experiments are being set up. Some have made the mistake of asking community-based nurses to record large amounts of data, which look as if they are intended to check on the work of the nurses. This has been resented as a sort of spying system.

Clinics

Antenatal clinics make records of their number of sessions and who runs them; similar data are available for postnatal clinics. The number of women who attend relaxation classes and the number of attendances during the year are recorded. Outpatient clinics are generally part of the hospital episode statistics.

Child health services

People in child health clinics record the numbers of children seen, the number of sessions held and who supervised them. The school health service also gives information on medical examinations performed, ophthalmic data, ear diseases, postural defects and skin diseases. Many health authorities are trying quietly to dismantle the school health service because of criticism that their most common findings by far were head lice, virtually all the other information gathered already being known to the general practitioner. Teachers, however, are very keen to keep the service.

Immunization details

The number of persons vaccinated, including for BCG, tuberculosis and other conditions, are recorded. General practitioners have specifically been given the task of ensuring that vaccination and immunization levels are improved year after year. This has been very successful, backed as it has been with the carrot of more money for those who reach specified targets.

Communicable disease surveillance centre

The government set up the Communicable Disease Surveillance Centre within the Public Health Laboratory Service in 1977. It collates and analyses data on the incidence of infectious diseases. The registration, although legally required, is very incomplete. It is unlikely that any cases of cholera are missed, but the number of cases of, for example, food poisoning are heavily underreported.

It is easy to start an epidemic of gastroenteritis. First one says, in the papers or on TV, that there is going to be one. Following this, people will report to their general practitioners all attacks of diarrhoea. General practitioners will also remember to send in their returns on those cases. Therefore by saying there is going to be an epidemic, one can bring one about, even though the number of cases has not changed. This has sometimes been politically important. In the last months of the Callaghan government, during the winter of discontent, with rubbish piling up on the streets, a well-known Director of Public Health said that the rubbish was causing an epidemic in a provincial city in Scotland. Within days he was right.

Staff

Approximately three-quarters of NHS expenditure is on wages, about 40% overall being on nurses' wages. It is therefore perhaps surprising that many health authorities often are not clear about how many staff they employ. The returns are badly completed, partially because of a separation between the finance director's department, which pays the wages, and the personnel department that employs the people. Finance information is usually more accurate. People quickly complain if they are not paid, but the data are sometimes regarded by that department as confidential.

Cancer registration

Other information that is collected includes that on cancer registration. Cancers are registered at diagnosis, whether at post mortem or when diagnosed in hospital.

Non-health service information

Non-health service information that is relevant to health includes the local authority registration of handicapped people and the notification of industrial diseases to the Health and Safety Executive. Certificates of incapacity to work are collected by the Department of Social Security. The General Household Survey gives data on a wide variety of items, including visits made to hospital services and lifestyle factors such as cigarette smoking.

Using the data

Data about the health service can be divided into those which describe:

- Inputs to the health service
- Processes that provide the service
- Outcomes for patients.

The ultimate input variable of course is money; this buys staff, buildings and equipment. The amount of money is agreed with the purchaser. Data about its use usually relate to whether it has been used and used in the place it was intended to be. Data on staff can also be helpful. Some situations should never, without very good reason, occur: there should never be a single-handed consultant in a specialty, and there should be a minimum number of nurses to cover an acute ward. In some areas, the minimum may be just one, but that is sometimes also worth monitoring.

Process data: old-fashioned bed use statistics

There are many more process variables available. For measuring the efficiency of hospital wards or specialties, some of the most commonly employed are bed use statistics. These are:

- Average length of stay (days) $= \dfrac{\text{Average number of occupied beds} \times 365}{\text{Number of discharges and deaths}}$

- Turnover interval (days) $=$
$$\dfrac{(\text{Average number of available beds} - \text{occupied}) \times 365}{\text{Number of discharges and deaths}}$$

- Bed use factor or turnover rate $= \dfrac{\text{Discharges and deaths}}{\text{Average number of beds available}}$

The expertise of the medical staff and the severity of the patient's illness is said to set the length of stay in an acute ward. This will also obviously depend critically on the type of patient seen and whether good admission and discharge policies are in place. Long-term changes are greatly affected by fashion. Patients with myocardial infarction, the most common inpatient medical condition, stayed 6 weeks in hospital in the 1950s. Now they sometimes stay only 48 hours. Length of stay is also related to the ability of the ward nurses and social services to work together to speed up patients' discharge.

The turnover interval is a measure of the time taken for a newly emptied bed to be refilled. It is supposed to reflect the administrative abilities of staff, especially the nursing and management staff, to get another patient in after one has left. In acute general wards, these days patients are usually admitted very quickly after a bed becomes vacant. In some wards, beds are emptied because a patient is waiting, so problems with turnover interval are quite unusual in acute specialties. By tradition, it has been said that a turnover interval of more than 2 days is a cause for concern. The turnover interval is closely allied to length of stay, being the number of admissions treated per bed. Short turnover intervals, of less than 1 day, may mean that the specialty is under great stress, with wards occasionally having to close because of lack of space.

Figure 3.2 shows that the main factor influencing the average length of stay in the Welsh health authorities was the number of geriatrics doctors, suggesting a lack of staff in some places. It was therefore a meaningless measure of the effectiveness of the unit being measured, although it did reflect staff shortages. The relationship did not occur in other well-staffed specialties, for example, general medicine.

Despite these disadvantages with bed use statistics, they are occasionally advantageous. When a ward or hospital scores badly or well on the measures, there is often an explanation of why. One can combine these into an imposing-

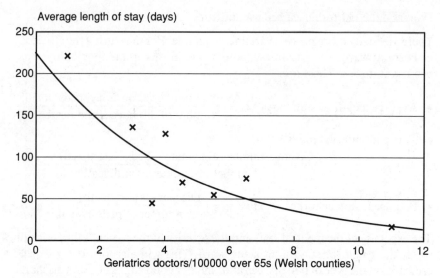

Figure 3.2 Geriatrics doctors by length of stay of patient.

looking set of data known as Barber – Johnson diagrams. These are useful for reassuring a trust that is complaining it is not receiving its fair share of the resources. Figure 3.3 shows an example, in which the hospital arrowed stated that, because of its efficiency, it should get more money compared with its neighbours. The arrowed hospital has a good bed use factor – the average number of people treated in a year per available bed. It also has a reasonably low average length of stay length, but its bed occupancy is low because of a moderately high turnover interval. This diagram shows that there is a fixed relationship between the various sets of bed use statistics. In addition, the mix of emergency or planned admissions will have an important effect upon bed use statistics. It is important for a ward that takes emergencies to have a bed available for the next emergency. The empty bed will, however, increase the turnover interval for the ward.

Admission and discharge data can confuse. Data are now collected for patients with a new line on the spreadsheet for any change of any part of the admission. A patient may change consultant, ward and specialty several times in one admission, or he or she may be transferred to another ward. Similarly, the patient will possibly require help after discharge. In a perfect world, each episode of disease would commence and be treated, the patient would get better and then leave the service. This would be counted as one episode, and the resources used and their costs would be known for each patient. This would make planning easier, but it is very expensive constantly to check that data are valid and mean what they say, and to put a price on everything that happens to a patient.

I spent a happy 6 months as a general practitioner in Canada with a full-time secretary following my every move and coding everything I did to patients.

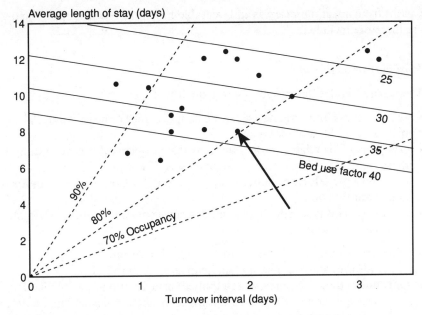

Figure 3.3 Barber–Johnson diagram for Welsh hospitals (medical specialties).

This was costed and sent to OHIP (the Ontario Health Insurance Plan) monthly and came back as a cheque. For the perfect system I mention above, each patient would perhaps need their own secretary. Incidentally, I never put two stitches into a cut in Canada: one or two was worth $5, three $8!

Outcome data: mortality and morbidity

There are two important outcomes for patients:

- Mortality or death, better described as prolongation of life
- Morbidity, or prolonged good quality of life.

Outcome information is often not quite as clear a measure of the effectiveness of the input and process as one might hope. Death rates need to take into account the age and sex structure of a population. This can be done as a standardized mortality ratio (SMR). At a population level, this measure of death rate does not fit well with measures of the effectiveness of the health service. The effects of services provided by the NHS are constantly overwhelmed by social factors, especially the degree of poverty suffered by the population being studied, as medical interventions can, even theoretically, as we saw in Chapter 2, have only a small impact on death rates or disability [41].

Another measure using deaths, specifically designed to measure the effectiveness of services, was invented by Charlton [42]. He examined deaths from causes that should, with a well-organized health service, be preventable.

Deaths from infectious diseases and treatable conditions, such as appendicitis, are therefore included.

Morbidity or quality of life

There are several different facets to the quality of life:

- *Impairment*. This is organ based, for example kidney or heart failure. There may be loss of a limb or an eye.
- *Disability*. This relates to the functions that people perform, for example their ability to walk or wash or go shopping. These are often divided into three groups: self-care, house care and mobility. Continence is another important function.
- *Handicap*. This is socially based and describes ones ability to, for example, be a parent or to do a job.

My favourite example is that of Lord Nelson, who, despite two major impairments of his arm and eye, had no handicap as an Admiral of the Fleet.

Only one of these measures, in a simplified form, is routinely available. This was a census question in 1991, the question being about longstanding limiting disability. It is especially useful, because, as it was a census question for the whole country, it is available for small areas, such as electoral wards in towns. The measure has been shown to be related to rates of admission to hospital.

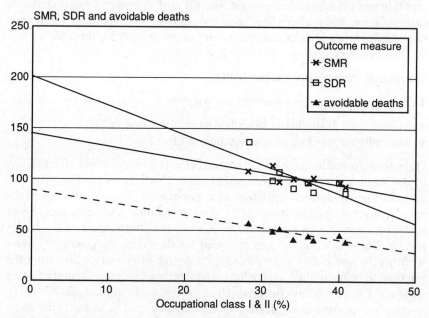

Figure 3.4 Standardized mortality, disability ratios and preventable deaths by occupational class, I & II–Welsh counties.

Figure 3.4 shows the relationship between a number of these measures, SMR, a standardized measure of disability using the longstanding limiting disability measure (SLD) and avoidable deaths with occupational class for the eight Welsh counties. One can see that there is a close relationship between all of them and occupational class, used here as a measure of wealth and poverty. All appear to be heavily biased towards the poverty of the area studied.

The Scots have been much less timid about using outcomes. They have developed a series of clinical outcome indicators and have attempted to standardize these to make comparisons between health boards and between acute hospitals [43]. Figure 3.5 shows an example for a comparison between health boards. It shows the standardized rates of admission to hospital with childhood asthma for 4 days or more by health board.

The measures that the Scots have used include:

- Health board indicators:
    Teenage conception
    Therapeutic abortion
    Cervical cancer mortality
    Suicide
    Diabetic ketoacidosis
    Inpatient stays for children with asthma
- Acute hospital indicators:
    Survival after fractured neck of femur
    Discharge home after fractured neck of femur
    Survival after myocardial infarction
    Reoperation after transurethral prostatectomy

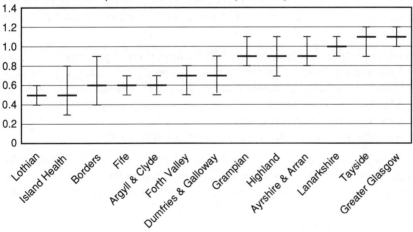

Figure 3.5   Childhood asthma: inpatient stays of 4 or more days (1992–94).

Emergency readmission soon after discharge
Survival after admission with stroke
Discharge home after admission with stroke
- Psychiatric hospital indicators:
Deaths within a year of discharge
Deaths under 65 within a year of discharge
Suicides within 1 year of discharge.

This is an impressive list.

How do managers actually use information?

A study in Scotland [44] established what information senior managers use. Over half of the managers approached said that they carried out literature searches regularly; another third said that they occasionally did so. In fact, information scientists, librarians and less commonly public health staff actually carried out the searches for the managers. Almost all the senior managers stated that they routinely consulted patients to gain information for making purchasing decisions. What they meant was that they consulted the local community health council (almost 9 out of 10) followed by population surveys (two-thirds) and consultation with consumer groups (two-thirds). Half of the managers said that their organization had set up formal liaison groups to talk to consumers.

The researchers asked the purchasers to consider what most usefully helped them when they were making decisions. Public health doctors had the greatest influence. Just over half of the senior staff thought that the information they received was of reasonable quality. Other things that influenced them, in order of importance, were local priorities, the finance available, government priorities and the opinion of general practitioners. Most of the managers felt that there were data that they would like to use which were not available.

The main areas of concern were:

- Outcome indicators that were felt to be important to patients
- Information about patients with mental illness, mental handicap and community-based elderly people, community health and general practice
- Effectiveness information
- Cost-effectiveness information
- Morbidity information, especially from general practice.

In particular, they felt a need for comparisons between providers on the quality of their services. There was also a need for financial and other economics data, especially costs and pricing. It might be thought that this is a pretty comprehensive list for managers who said that they were mostly satisfied with the information they received.

Other problems

Other problems identified by the managers were, first, the large amount of information that was minimally useful but did not exactly fill their needs. The second problem was the degree of overlap of different sorts of information. At this stage, it seems that, although some information is available and consumers are consulted, they have little influence on the way in which managers make their decisions. The National Association of Health Authorities and Trusts recently put their finger on part of the problem [45]. Both the number of information sources and the volume of information on clinical and cost-effectiveness are growing very fast. There are already some indications that this is resulting in duplication of effort. Ideally, users should have to deal with only a single access point for information on clinical effectiveness.

One can, of course, argue in the opposite direction. Medicine is not cut and dried; there are several sources of information and, by studying the interpretation of those sources, it is possible to decide where there is still controversy. It is the task of public health consultants to try to distill this information. It seems naive to suggest that there will ever be only one view on effectiveness, especially as we have not decided what the NHS is for. It may be equally naive to suggest that we will ever resolve the question.

Examples from practice: mental illness

The following example draws together data taken from inpatient, outpatient and general practitioner referral data. Many of the data have had to be estimated, but they appear to be reasonably robust.

The health services deal with a minority of the mentally ill people in any community. Many people suffer from distress caused by mental illness but do not call for help. Figure 3.6 shows data about the adult population: those over

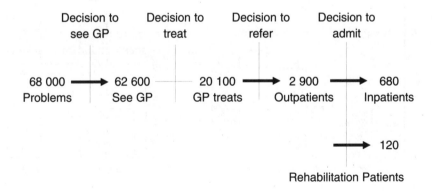

Figure 3.6 The filters to care – adults, period prevalence 1994–95.

16 and under 70 in a health authority. It shows the quarter of people who are said to have symptoms consistent with a some form of mental illness and the proportion seen by the services in a year. This uses the 'filters to care' model developed by Goldberg [46]. It highlights the difference between the number of people with problems, the number seen by their general practitioner and the proportion who go for specialist help. A number of people are admitted from the community for rehabilitation as inpatients and are shown separately. The data collected are from general practice referral rates and hospital admissions.

Disease symptoms prevalent in the community: depression

Figure 3.7 shows the estimated numbers of adults with symptoms consistent with depression in the population. The data have been calculated by multiply-ing the national rates by the numbers in each age and sex group, another common way of obtaining local data from national statistics. The national data are based on a recent OPCS prevalence survey [47]. The data have details of differences in prevalence for poor people and people of different ethnic origins; these can be used in areas where these factors are important. The prevalence is much higher in women than in men. The number in elderly women is exaggerated by the greater number of women in the over-65 age group due to the greater longevity of women. Men and women in the younger age groups are represented in roughly equal numbers.

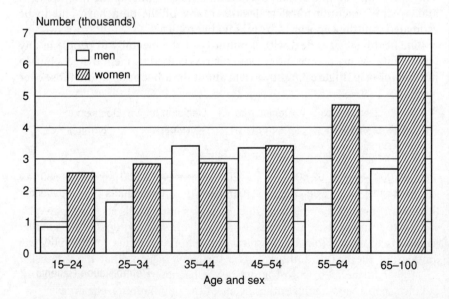

Figure 3.7 Numbers in the health authority with symptoms associated with depression – point prevalence.

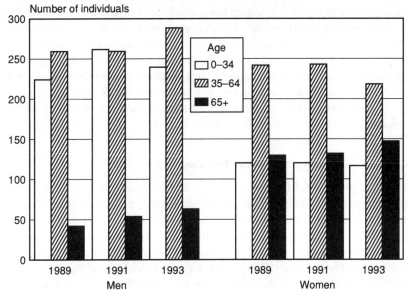

Figure 3.8   Schizophrenia–5 year period prevalence.

Schizophrenia

Figure 3.8 shows the estimated prevalence of schizophrenia for three periods – 1985–1989, 1987–1991 and 1989–1993 – based on inpatient admissions. This assumes that patients with schizophrenia in the community become inpatients at least once during a 5 year period. This assumption is becoming less tenable as improved community services develop. The figure shows that the prevalence appears to be rising in middle-aged and older men. For women, it remains fairly constant at all ages. The overall prevalence of schizophrenia in the health authority area using this method is about 3/1000 population for adults.

PROBLEMS OF PLANNING AS PURCHASERS

Obtaining unbiased advice from professionals

There have been a number of approaches for getting unbiased advice for purchasers from professionals. These usually consist of subgroups of an area-based medical committee, which is, as its name suggests, dominated by the doctors in the area. There is a danger with such groups that their real agenda is to ensure that the hospital consultants continue to dominate the strategy of the health authority. The further danger is that the dominant researcher in the area will promote his or her interests. There is a need to balance such a view against other needs of the population in the area.

Health purchasers I have known have usually tried to circumvent these problems by putting a large number of senior consultants on to a committee and letting them argue their cases between them. The theory is that this will result in more objective advice. This sometimes works, but sometimes leads to very odd results. Each of the most senior members of the committee may take over a section to press their own interest. I have been on a number of such committees. The people who are most listened to are those who espouse an interest which is not their own. A gastroenterologist pressing for more services for geriatrics or a general physician calling for more money for paediatrics is very persuasive. It is also very rare.

The relationship with public health medicine

In theory, public health physicians are able to weigh the evidence for and against new developments or the discontinuation of ineffective care. They can then advise the purchasers of these changes about how to bring them about with minimal disruption to patients. Public health consultants have their own problems. They sometimes walk a tightrope between antagonizing their consultant colleagues so much that they are hissed in BMA meetings, or they 'go native' and call for more resources for the most senior consultant. I remember one meeting of the latter type. The public health consultant, approaching the needs of the population with cardiac disease, spoke long and eloquently about a new heart transplantation unit and did not once mention smoking. I mildly mentioned the omission and was given a long talking to by the Professor of Cardiology on the error of my ways.

Purchasing: the second job – assessing health needs and service specifications

4

NEEDS, SUPPLY AND DEMAND

We use the term 'health' very loosely. We have little choice as there is no agreed definition that fits in with what the 'health' service does. The World Health Organization (WHO) definition of health identifies the 'social, physical and mental aspects of well being'. One way around the attempt to define the need for health care is to redefine it as the 'ability to benefit from health care'. In this case, the assessment of needs requires measuring the incidence and prevalence of conditions for which we have effective services. It also requires us to know which services are effective. Defining health need in this way does not allow for new discoveries or positive effects of a service which may be difficult to measure.

Need does not equate to demand for health care. The disease process can be described as:

- An individual feels unwell and wants help from the health services
- A health care professional sees the patient and decides that he or she does or does not require care
- Society generally agrees that the patient requires health care
- An asymptomatic illness that responds to treatment is discovered in an individual.

Table 4.1 shows these types of need and how to translate them into demand and supply.

Table 4.1 Need and demand: relationships

What the person feels	What the person does	Need exists	Individual demand exists	Professional demand exists	Use of Health Resources (supply)
1a Individual feels unwell	Does not wish for intervention	Maybe	No	No	Not in short term Maybe in long term
1b	Does wish intervention, approaches health service. Health professionals say no intervention	Maybe	Yes	No	Not in short term Maybe in long term
1c	Does wish intervention, approaches health service. Health professionals say yes to intervention	Yes	Yes	Yes	Yes
2a Health professional says there is need	Individual perceives no need; is compelled to accept	?Yes	No	Yes	Yes
2b	Individual perceives no need and is not compelled to accept	?Yes	No	Yes	Not in short term Maybe in long term
2c	Individual perceives need	Yes	Yes	Yes	Yes
3a Society sees a need	Compulsory	Maybe	No	No	Yes
4a Asymptomatic illness		Yes	No	No	Not in short term Maybe in long term

For example:

- 1b could occur through misdiagnosis or through hypochondria
- 2a typically occurs when a person is sectioned under the Mental Health Act
- 2b typically occurs when a person accepts screening services and an asymptomatic illness is diagnosed
- 3a indicates that society perceives a need and makes it compulsory for each person to accept, for example, fluoridation of water or compulsory immunization programmes
- 4a is apparently of minor interest or relevance to the issue of health care markets. However, asymptomatic illness can drain health care resources. For example, cancers detected early in their development may be treated with fewer resources. Purchasers decide what proportion of the budget is devoted to the early detection of illness and the eradication of risk factors. By its very nature, screening for disease is expensive and can cause considerable anxiety in the population being screened. It must be subject to strict rules [48].

Demand for health care

People express their demand for health care in a number of ways:

- Direct access to services, most notably to the accident and emergency services, general practitioners, dentists, private clinics, opticians and so on.
- Secondary referral to hospital or community services. This can be through an agency relationship in which a qualified health care practitioner (typically a general practitioner) diagnoses that further treatment may be necessary.
- Tertiary referrals when a patient is equivalent to the summation of lines 1c + 2a + 2c + 3a in Table 4.1.

These distinctions are not even as clear cut as they are set out here. A particularly demanding patient can often persuade professionals, especially busy general practitioners and consultants, that he or she needs care. My experience is that, although some patients find it difficult to describe their problems, the vast majority who have a demand also have a valid reason to report the problems to a doctor or nurse. Whether the health services can sort out that problem and turn it into a 'real need' is often the more problematic question. I often wonder why we, in public health, make quite such a fuss about the distinctions in Table 4.1; there often seems to be a sort of mean-spiritedness about the classification.

Pressures on the supply of health care

Factors that affect changes to the supply of health services have been mentioned in Chapter 1, including the ageing of the population and the demand for new technology. Other more subtle pressures include:

- *The law.* Certain forms of treatment are obligatory. Forensic psychiatric services are increasing rapidly as more care is being taken to ensure that mentally ill people are removed from or do not go to prison. There is pressure from the courts on the health service to look after increasing numbers of patients. These patients, because of dangers to themselves or others, have to be kept in secure accommodation, which is very expensive, costing about £90,000 a year for a patient.
- *Professional ethics.* Further improvements in the quality of services, which may have been felt to be adequate in the past, tend to be costly. Standards of what is acceptable rise continually. Some of these pressures seem to analyse the risks to patients in incredible ways. It has been said that it is safer for a patient to come into hospital and have a hernia operation than to go to work that morning. Fire precautions seem to become increasingly stringent in hospital year after year. In addition, there is increasing pressure for patients to have a choice where the requirements of clinical care allow it. This means that there must be some slack in the system, which is naturally more expensive.
- *Efficiency.* The more efficiently a service is provided, the less it costs to provide a specified level of service. This is brought about in a number of ways. There is a general acceptance that the majority of the work force, especially the largest group – the nurses – works reasonably efficiently. No-one has dared to question whether doctors can improve their efficiency. General practitioner lists, for example, have decreased markedly over the past few decades. People have assumed that this has led to better quality of care.

  The exception has been the lowest paid workers in the health service: the cleaners, cooks and porters whose jobs have been subject to competitive tendering. Efficiency savings for the rest of the health service have centered around reducing lengths of stay in hospital for specific conditions. There have been some moves to use less highly qualified people for undertaking a task than is traditional. There have been some moves to doing tasks in the community rather than in the more expensive hospitals. There has also been a move to reduce management costs overall in the health service. This has been a little unthinking with the percentage of the budget spent on management in the health authorities being published. The whole scheme has been bedevilled by poor definition of what a manager is. There has been no suggestion that quality should be involved when examining managers' numbers; it is assumed that less means better.

Excess demand in the health service

The market for health care has consistently suffered from more demand than has been possible to supply within the available money. In theory, a free market would cope with this by raising prices to a point where demand diminished to match supply. Even the people of the USA, the greatest believers in a market economy, have not felt able to accept such a system for the treatment of disease. Treatment has such a direct and obvious effect upon life and death that no government has felt able to leave health entirely to market forces, as this would mean that some of the poor would die of obviously treatable diseases in front of the voters.

Because demand is greater than supply, people have assumed that the result must be to ration health care. The most visible manifestations of rationing in the UK are the waiting lists for outpatient appointments and inpatient treatment. Waiting lists in other countries with a large public sector do not seem to be as much of a problem as in the UK, suggesting that other factors must play a part.

The need for treatment of varicose veins

As I have said earlier in this chapter, there is no universal agreement about what does or does not constitute a need. I have shown that the decision about who should decide what is a demand or need is difficult, at least in theory, and each patient or doctor will have different ideas. A clear example of this type of discrepancy is the treatment of varicose veins, which has traditionally been carried out by a surgical operation.

A member of the public who recognizes that she has varicose veins, without any complications such as skin ulceration, may wish to have them treated by an operation. This may be because they are unsightly and may be a source of discomfort. This individual would consider that she has a need for treatment. She would consult a general practitioner, who might decide to refer her to a surgeon. However, some doctors would not consider that the veins either needed treatment or that treatment would be effective. In this case, the doctor would interpret the person's need as a demand with no need for treatment, and would not sanction it. Those doctors believing that treatment was indicated would consider it a demand with a need and would sanction it. If the health service purchaser involved, either the health authority or general practitioner fundholder, had decided that varicose vein surgery was a low priority, it would consider that the demand the patient was making was not justified. In other words, her demand was not accompanied by underlying need.

Decisions of this type were made for about one-third of the population of Oregon, where it was decided that the evidence for benefits from some treatment was not good enough for the State to invest in these services. A doctor who thought that the patient had a reasonable demand, in this situation, would have to stifle it, since there would be no means of meeting it. In the UK, she would probably kick up a fuss and call the papers and the local opposition Member of Parliament, both of whom would kick up a fuss in turn. Chances are that the patient would get the treatment she wanted. So much for theory.

HEALTH SERVICE PROVISION

Ideally, those who have needs and only those who have needs should use the NHS. As I have suggested, this does not happen. Articulate and persistent patients are more likely to have their demands met. This is probably why well-off people are more likely to receive non-emergency treatment than poor people [49].

Providing more services will not necessarily mean that people will use those services to meet previously unmet needs. If more services become available, patients and doctors react by resetting the thresholds of what is a need and what a sanctioned demand. It is important to note that positive rather than negative feedback can occur. If the service meets more demands, patients may respond by making even more, rather than less. If fewer demands are met, fewer demands rather than more may be made. If general practitioners become more available, it is likely that patients will feel that doctors have more time for them. They may then convert both unexpressed needs or likes into expressed needs or likes, which they present to the doctors as demands. General practitioners may well react by sanctioning more of the patients' demands. If more consultant time is available and outpatient waiting lists shorter, general practitioners may be more ready to refer patients as their threshold for referral falls. It has been suggested that the increase in demand for emergency medical beds in 1995 and 1996 was largely due to oversupply of acute general medical beds [50].

Selecting priorities for health care

Health services will need to indicate priority areas so that work can develop most rapidly on the most important things, whether this means overt rationing or simply ordering the work that needs to be done. Criteria for this include:

- Problems with high mortality
- Problems with high morbidity
- Problems that are local needs due to poor access to services or inequity in the way they are provided
- The views of public and professionals
- Complaints or satisfaction surveys
- Services where there is a necessity or an obvious opportunity to use an alternative provider
- Services where the purchaser has reason to believe that a very good value service is not being provided or that a poor value service is offered
- Policy guidance or instruction from the Department of Health or region.

I have not made this list exhaustive. Purchasers will debate which problems should have greatest priority and then discuss the implications.

PRINCIPLES OF PURCHASING

A number of different sources have suggested principles for purchasers. In England, the *Health of the Nation* document [51] emphasized the need for purchasers to plan health care. It recognized that the main concern of the UK health service is with illness rather than health. The service spends the great majority of its time trying to satisfy the immediate demand of patients for treatment. The document stressed the importance of influences that are not within the health service, such as poverty and poor housing upon health and the importance of working with organizations trying to tackle these.

Maxwell, some years ago, also suggested a series of principles that should underlie any service [52]:

- Access to services
- Relevance to the needs of the whole community
- Effectiveness for individual patients
- Equity
- Social acceptability
- Efficiency and economy.

THE PROCESS OF PURCHASING

Purchasing health care within the health services divides naturally into a number of processes:

- The assessment of the needs of the population served
- The development of a service specification, which is a type of tender
- Negotiation with the purchaser for a price for the tender
- Agreement of the contract
- Once the contract is under way, it will be monitored, and feedback from the monitoring process is used to develop new service specification data

ASSESSMENT OF NEED IN PRACTICE: LONG-TERM CARE

When studying the need for services for people with long-term health problems, epidemiologists would, for preference, start with data about the degree of disability and hence dependency of people in the locality. They would continue with data about the known responses of families and friends to this dependency. They would try to take into account the degree to which relatives in a particular area, whether inner city or village, can cope with a given degree of dependency. A further factor would be the extent to which relatives should contend with difficulties.

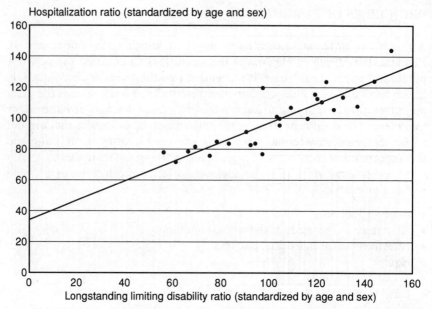

Figure 4.1 Hospitalization rates by longstanding limiting disability for Cardiff electoral wards.

Few such data are locally available. The best that we can do in most health authorities is an estimate, using national data, such as the OPCS survey of disability in the UK [53] or the 1991 census data on limiting long standing disability. These indicate differences between areas and may be a useful indication of the need for care in one small area compared with another. Figure 4.1 shows that, for small area data, in this case the electoral wards in Cardiff, the data for long standing disability standardized by age and sex relate to emergency hospitalization rates. There appears to be a degree of consistency between the two measures of need in the small areas.

Assessing the need: background

The problem with long term care is that everyone sees themselves as being on the shores of the Styx, either as boatman or passenger [54].

The mid-1970s saw the private sector becoming for the first time an important force in the care of elderly people in the UK. Voluntary organizations found that social security officers would pay benefits to a residential home on behalf of residents unable to afford their fees if local authorities were unable to foot the bill for these people. This process became widespread and in 1983 was formalized by the Conservative government. One-third of pensioners were already receiving supplementary pension, which later became income support. This automatically entitled them, as long they had only a

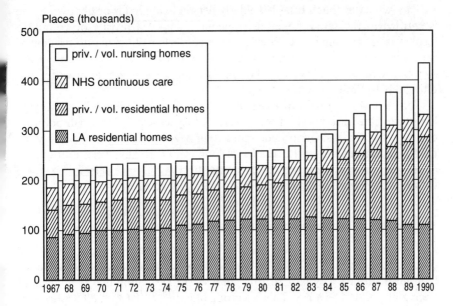

Figure 4.2 Nursing and residential care places – England.

small amount of capital, to extra benefits after admission to a residential or nursing home. Two-thirds of elderly people who needed such care were eligible.

The availability of this income support, together with a booming property market, encouraged a rapid expansion of private residential and nursing homes. Figure 4.2 shows the growth of the private and voluntary residential homes from 1968 to 1990. It shows the increase in private nursing homes and the reduction in local authority and NHS long-stay facilities.

Almost one-third more elderly people entered long-term care establishments than would have if the rates for different age groups had remained unchanged from 1981 [55]. Long-term care became effectively free on demand for about 30% of the elderly population for a while in the mid-1970s. I feel, given this background, that the number of people entering care overall did not increase very dramatically.

Evidence of this resistance to residential long-term care in the UK is found in the low rates of usage of residential homes compared with most European countries. France has 1¼ times more places than the UK, whereas some countries such as the Netherlands have 2–3 times the number per head of population. Whatever the reason, as private residential care began to develop, with demand increased by geriatricians who saw an easy way of discharging their long-term disabled patients, the costs of such care to the government began to soar. The NHS and Community Care Act 1990 was partly born out of the worries engendered by these soaring costs.

The Act states that a disabled elderly person living in his or her own home is entitled to the same money as someone living in a private or voluntary residential or nursing home. People on the borderline of going into residential care can use the money to support themselves at home. The Community Care Act uses social services personnel to monitor the costs of community care and ultimately to limit the amount available.

The 1990 Act brought in more regulations for maintaining the quality of long-term care, notably the Social Services Inspectorate. It is worth pointing out that, both in this country and most other developed countries, notably the USA, regulations about the quality of long-term care have been in force for many years. It may be argued that the situation would have been much worse without regulation, but it has not been especially good with it.

Reasons for the anomalous position of NHS long stay

Long-term care wards in NHS hospitals still tend to have very poor facilities, often in long, open, 'Nightingale' wards. They are particularly unsuitable for long-term care as they lack privacy and, with their communal facilities and open plan, tend to be noisy. This is a group of patients that specially appreciate quietness. The wards make it difficult for elderly people to do anything for themselves. They were designed for young war-wounded men in the early 19th century, and that is what they were good for. They look very similar to, and are often in the same buildings, as the workhouse, which people of the older generation can remember.

Purchasing long-stay health care

I have described the principles applied for purchasing care earlier in this chapter (p.59). I will use the Maxwell criteria on the facilities available for long-term care to clarify which best meet the criteria.

Access to services

Elderly people may have some problems with obtaining services to assist them at home for a number of reasons, the most immediate of which is that many older people do not know of the existence of some services. The older the person is, the more likely this is to be the case (Figure 4.3) [56].

There are many people unaware of the existence of services that have, for years, formed the mainstream of facilities provided for elderly people. Especially worrying in this regard are day centres and sheltered housing, where the impetus to take up the services often rests with elderly people themselves. However, people know of and understand some of the basic services. General practitioners, chiropodists, home helps and meals on wheels are well known, as are their functions.

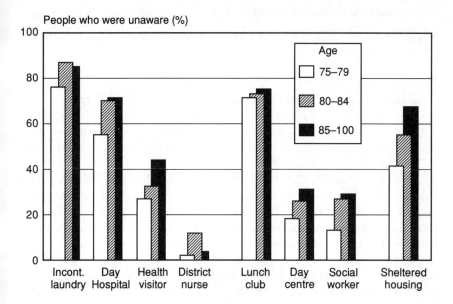

Figure 4.3   Elderly people unaware of services.

Relevance to the needs of the whole community

Long-term care for elderly people is an essential part of the care of old people who become impossible to treat at home because of the burden of the caring needed on their families. In addition, some elderly people have no family and need virtually continuous help at home. This may sometimes be more reasonably given in long-term care.

General acceptability

It seems self-evident that the long-term workhouse-based hospital ward is not acceptable. No purchaser of services who had ever visited one would choose it if there were any other options. Health authorities will be looking for cost-effective alternatives, and the simplest approach for most will be to use voluntary and private sector nursing homes or extra care sheltered housing.

Acceptability to family and other carers

Once the elderly are admitted to residential care, some studies have shown that carers feel that their elderly relatives are being well cared for, whereas others seem to suffer considerable guilt. The lives of carers in some studies have often been changed immeasurably for the better as a result of the elderly person being admitted to institutional care. One thing that must make the difference is the support available to help people who care for dependent elderly people. The support available at present in many places is stereotyped and limited, in both quality and quantity.

Effectiveness for individual patients

There are two aspects to effectiveness: whether the service prolongs life and whether it prolongs the quality of life.

Prolonging life

Researchers have published figures on annual survival for different forms of long-term care. These depend upon the initial degree of illness of the patients. To avoid this, the data have been published according to the initial severity of disability of the patients, measured as an activities of daily living (ADL) score [57]. Figure 4.4 shows the data.

Those with little disability (0–2) show a considerable difference between the chances of an elderly person surviving in an NHS psychiatric home and private nursing home on the one hand, and an NHS geriatric ward on the other. For moderate and severe degrees of disability, the private nursing home comes out best. We may expect the NHS acute sector to do badly as many elderly people will have acute illnesses, not necessarily shown up by a long-term disability score. There may also be differences, even within the disability score, between those in one form of residence compared with others.

Despite these possible reasons for the differences, a naive purchaser would need to be persuaded that it was not the poor environment in the geriatric hospital that led elderly people to die in larger numbers than elsewhere. The

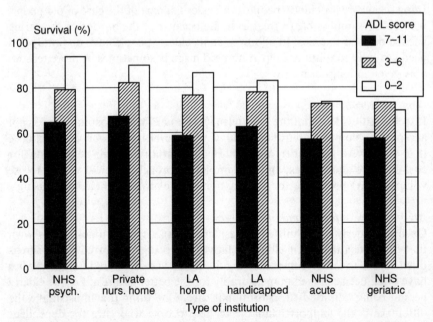

Figure 4.4 Annual survival in long-term care by place of residence and disability.

old-fashioned NHS wards have considerable problems of cross-infection from chest complaints, and often a generally depressing atmosphere.

Death rates have been measured in alternatives to long-stay hospital, although these studies have been small and have not used randomized trials [58]. A study set up in Darlington looked at patients given supported home care instead of long-term hospital care [59]. There was a dramatic increase in the number who remained at home in the project group compared with controls at both 6 and 12 months. Unfortunately, there was an equally dramatic difference in death rate at 6 months, favouring those in hospital. This difference had disappeared by a year later. The researchers explained this by making the point that a much higher proportion of the project group than the control group was receiving care for terminal illness. The major difficulty with this, apart from invalidating the deaths data, is that it suggests that the two groups may have been different in other ways.

Prolonging the quality of life
The authors of the Darlington study also measured quality of life. The high early death rate meant that fewer than half of the patients were available at 6 months for measures of their quality of life. Patients cared for at home had a higher quality of life compared with those who remained in hospital. The measure of physical disability was no different, but social activity levels were greater for the group at home. There is no doubt that some long-term hospital facilities discourage social activities for patients, often due to the physical layout of the ward.

Equity

Elderly people with the same problems that need long-term care are treated differently in different places in the UK. Those who are judged to need health care, according to the joint criteria drawn up by each health authority and social services department, are given it free without a separate test of their physical or financial status. Those who are judged to need social services may be cared for in private or voluntarily owned nursing homes, and social services may support such people at home. Their physical and financial needs must be assessed by social services before they are able to receive the facilities. Local health authorities and social services departments have to agree detailed criteria for a need for health care and whether the person is sufficiently disabled to warrant assistance. This decision depends upon a multi-disciplinary assessment of the needs of the patient [60]. These criteria are different for each health authority.

Work in Newcastle has shown that people in residential homes, NHS wards and private nursing homes show considerable overlap in the severity of their disability [61]. The inevitable differences between areas in the definitions of the need for care will mean that some elderly people with the same problems will be disadvantaged compared with others. The Newcastle researchers suggest that disability measures are not a good way of separating people who need health care from those needing mainly social care.

This is not surprising. Disability measures, commonly used to assess the need for health care in this context, were developed for work with large populations. They are useful for comparing reasonably large groups of people but were never intended to be used for judging the physical state of individuals. The measures are incapable of uncovering the sort of detail needed for making clinical decisions.

Social acceptability

A group of 75 year olds were asked under what circumstances they would consider going into some form of institutional care. Only one-third could think of a situation in which they might consider it. Half of the people claimed that they would not think of entering a residential home if they were incontinent and unable to get out of bed! Virtually all the people questioned said that they had a relative who would be available to help them and that this person or persons would look after them, allowing them to remain at home.

One of the main reasons for elderly people wishing to be treated at home is the poor image that they and many other people have of hospitals and nursing homes. Elderly people have suggested that geriatric units, in particular, lead to a loss of dignity and self-respect. Whilst many elderly people accept

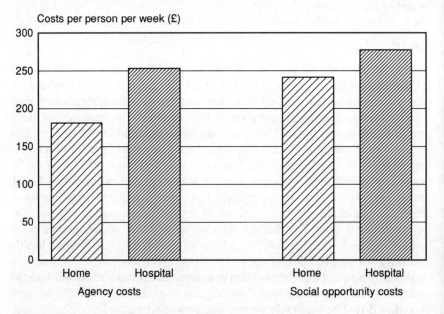

Figure 4.5   Long-term hospital versus home costs.

the need for hospital care for specific ailments, they are much less happy to be part of geriatric care, especially long-stay geriatric care. They clearly feel labelled and wish to avoid this by being admitted, if they have to be admitted, to general medical or surgical wards in hospital [62].

Efficiency and economy

A number of researchers have studied the costs of different types of long-term care. Donaldson [63] looked at the costs of NHS-based nursing homes and compared them with the costs of long-term hospital wards. Data on costs show that they are very similar. The costs of home-based and hospital-based care have also been compared. (Figure 4.5). The group treated at home had an average agency cost, that is the costs to the service providers, much below that of the hospital-treated group. The social opportunity cost figures, that is the costs to the family, were also lower for the home-managed group.

Government advice

A case in Leeds of a disabled 64 year old discharged from hospital in 1993 led to a ruling by the Ombudsman, and there was subsequent government direction that health authorities should make available long-term care places. Authorities were told to agree the criteria for entry to these places with other interested parties. In fact, authorities were required to do this 3 years before as part of the development of the Community Care Act. The methods to be used were not prescribed as closely in 1990, but similar work has been carried out by most health authorities.

Groups covered by the eligibility criteria and policies

The government advice arising from this case showed that a large number of different groups are involved in long-term care:

- Rehabilitation and recovery
- Palliative care
- Inpatient continuing care
- Respite health care
- Specialist or intensive medical or nursing support
- Community and primary care (at home or residential homes)
- Specialist transport.

As I have mentioned above, in practice standardized measures of dependency are used. These should only be used with the opinion of a specialist in the problems of the patient, either a doctor or a nurse, to estimate whether any intervention will have an effect upon that person's health.

Health authority policy

One health authority, in response to these changes, set up a series of new approaches or developments of existing ones:

- Rehabilitation:
    Comprehensive stroke services
    Head injury service improved
    General practitioners and young people in secondary care to have access
      to day hospitals
    Combined rehabilitation for children
- Palliative care:
    Assess increased numbers
    Give choice to nursing home patients
    Develop inpatient respite beds
- Inpatient care for elderly and younger disabled people:
    Review the existing provision
    Review the needs of adolescents with mental illness
    The majority in NHS facilities
    Some to be managed in independent nursing homes
    Learning disability places funded
- Respite care:
    Extend to young adults and children
    Provide at neighbourhood hospitals
    Examine needs for children
- Support for nursing home, residential care or community:
    Targeted specialist care
    Equipment loaned to nursing homes
    Specialist medical and therapy services
    Patients on ventilators, etc. supported
    Agree policy for nursing homes to keep some equipment
- Home-based continuing care:
    Policy to be developed.

Review procedure

Patients no longer considered to need inpatient health care but who need continuing care must be given a written care plan. They must also have a named person to whom they can talk if they or their family are unhappy with the arrangements for their discharge. If they still disagree about being discharged, there will be a review. This is explained in a leaflet that outlines the whole procedure.

A designated officer will take on the review procedure, and an independent review panel will carry this out. The panel will consist of:

- An independent chairman
- A health authority representative and deputy
- A local authority representative and deputy.

A decision will be reached within 2 weeks.

The future

There is no obvious best buy when choosing how to set up long-term care, nor is it easy to decide the number of places required [64]. Full analysis suggests [65] that, whatever system proves to be best, the present approach, using large hospital wards, is not in the running. There is increasing pressure on independent nursing and dual-registered homes as a result of the development of home care in the Community Care Act. Health authorities might well, in the medium term, find it best to purchase places for long-term care in voluntary or private nursing homes. This will change the nature of these nursing homes as, although nursing homes have individuals as sick as any in the NHS wards, the overall average degree of dependency is greater in the NHS.

The NHS will have to have closer control over the management of such places than they have with private homes, as the NHS will still be responsible for the care given. An interested and closely involved consultant is likely to maintain the necessary quality of care in such small units. This has the added advantage of ensuring that the consultants will have a close say in discharging patients from acute and rehabilitation hospital beds into long-term care.

An alternative, as tried in Darlington, is for augmented home care. This holds out promise for the future, and a carefully controlled study would give valuable information on the further development of such an approach. A third alternative – extra care beds in grouped housing – is being carried out at present in a number of places. The monitoring of such development is, so far, largely descriptive but seems to offer a reasonably quick and cheap way of providing the buildings. The great benefit of not having an obvious 'best buy' for patient care is that a number of options are possible at the same time, thus increasing patient choice.

SERVICE SPECIFICATIONS

A service specification uses the needs assessment work to specify more closely the type of service that the purchaser requires. One or more providers will respond to the service specification with business cases. One provider may be asked to respond in a relatively informal way to the specification if that provider has been giving satisfactory service for some years before the advent of the internal market.

Example of a service specification: cardiology services

Purpose

To provide a comprehensive service, including the prevention, diagnosis and treatment of cardiac disease.

Aims

The overall aims for cardiovascular disease are:

- To provide good resuscitation services, accurate diagnosis on admission to hospital, prompt pain relief, anti-ischaemic therapy and thrombolytic treatment for people with early myocardial infarction.
- To coordinate and develop an intensive health prevention and promotion programme, which has been agreed at local level, to reduce the incidence of heart disease.
- To ensure a rapid and effective response to patients with a suspected heart attack.
- To provide a coordinated approach to opportunistic assessment in primary care.
- To provide rehabilitation after a heart attack or heart surgery.
- To achieve increases in the quality of life of those suffering the consequences of cardiovascular diseases.
- It is anticipated that by 1997 a paramedic will be present on all emergency ambulances and in addition that defibrillators will soon be available in police cars.

Targets

To contribute to the achievement of these aims, the following targets have been identified according to the needs assessment for cardiovascular disease:

- Through prevention and health promotion, to reduce the prevalence of cardiovascular diseases by 15% by the year 2002 compared with the rate in 1988.
- Through prevention and health promotion, to reduce the rate of premature deaths from coronary heart disease and stroke among those under 65 by 15% by the year 2002 compared with the rate in 1988.
- To reduce by at least 30% the percentage aged 15–16 who regularly smoke cigarettes by the year 2002 compared with 1988.
- To reduce by at least 20% the percentage aged 17–64 who regularly smoke cigarettes by the year 2002 compared with 1988.
- To reduce to 30% those aged 17–64 classified as overweight or obese by the year 2002.

- To reduce the numbers of sudden deaths of those under 65 in which cardiovascular disease is the main cause, by 10% by 1997, and 15% by 2002, compared with 1992.
- To reduce by 15% the deaths from heart attacks and sudden cardiac arrest by 1995, and by 30% by 2002, compared with 1992.
- To achieve a 20% successful discharge from hospital of patients found with ventricular fibrillation on the arrival of ambulance services by 1995.
- To reduce the number of patients having a second heart attack within 3 years of the first by 15% by 1997, and by 20% by 2002.

General service requirements

The service is expected to operate within the terms of the contract and according to the general quality specifications and needs assessment. Services provided by cardiologists and cardiac surgeons are also provided by other specialities, and other service specifications such as those for general medicine and paediatric cardiology should also be noted.

Population served

Residents of health authority area.

Location of Service

Emergency medical care
The current service provision of accident and emergency care is located at provider A.

Inpatient care
This is presently purchased from coronary care units, situated at provider B and provider C. A small number of residents receive treatment at provider D.

Outpatient care
This is presently purchased from outpatient departments at provider B, provider C and provider A. A small number of residents are treated at the outpatient department at provider D.

Scope of Service

A description of the activities required for the management of patients with cardiac disease within the health authority is as follows:

1. *Preventive services*:

- GP clinics:
   Screening

Blood pressure
'Well-person'
- Health promotion activities
- Lipid clinic
   For high cholesterol (medical biochemists etc.).

2. *Emergency care*:

- Coronary care units
   Provider B
   Provider A
   Provider C
- Emergency admissions
   To CCUs
   To general wards
- Ambulance service
   All emergency vehicles to have defibrillators
- CPR programmes.

3. *Diagnostic services*:

- Outpatient referrals:
   Cardiology
   General Medicine
   Paediatrics
- Chest pain clinic or heart failure clinic
   Provider C (open access)
- Inpatients
   Beds for inpatients and day cases
- Cardiac catheter facilities
- Outpatients (none are open access)
   Echocardiograms:
      24 hour ECG recording
      Exercise testing
      12-lead ECG (partly open access).

4. *Cardiac surgery (cardiothoracic surgeons)*:

- Coronary artery bypass grafting (CABG)
- Valve replacement or repair
- Cardiac transplantation (Harefield, Papworth and others)
- Operations for the correction of congenital heart disease.

5. *Interventional cardiology (cardiologists and paediatric cardiologists)*:

- Percutaneous transcoronary angioplasty (PTCA)
- Balloon valvotomy
- Congenital heart cases

- Intracoronary stents.

6. *Pacing etc. (cardiologists)*:

- Permanent pacemakers
- Electrophysiological studies
- Automatic implantable defibrillator (provider E)
- Radiofrequency ablation (provider E).

7. *Rehabilitation:*

- Provider B and provider C:
    Rehabilitation courses (nurse run):
      Post-surgical patients
      Some post-myocardial infarction patients
      Leisure centres, i.e. self-help group (paid for by patients)
- In addition:
    health review in outpatients department
    health review at general practitioners.

8. *Research and training*:

- Basic science
- Clinical research
- Health care evaluation and audit
- Training:
    Medical students
    Nurses or postgraduates
    Ambulance crew, etc.

Detailed service requirements

This service specification does not seek to provide explicit detailed direction for improvements in the management of cardiac disease or in the maintenance of those high-quality services that already exist. However, the service is required to provide effective interventions to patients with suspected and proven cardiac disease, to increase the integration of primary, secondary and tertiary care, and to reduce waiting times wherever possible.

Emergency care

A person presenting with chest pain should be taken to the nearest hospital with an accident and emergency department and then to the coronary care unit if necessary. Adequate and appropriately manned ambulance services should be provided for the residents of the health authority, including paramedic services manned by 'extended skilled ambulance persons' or paramedics. These personnel are skilled in endotracheal intubation, intravenous access and peripheral venous lines; they are not trained in central venous lines.

Paramedics are also trained in emergency domiciliary obstetric services (EDOS).

Cardiopulmonary resuscitation (CPR) programmes
Provision should be made for CPR training schemes for the residents of the health authority.

Stable angina
Guidelines regarding the management of stable angina have been published recently by the British Cardiac Society and the Royal College of Physicians of London. They have suggested monitoring requirements for primary, secondary and tertiary care, i.e. general practitioner, general medical, cardiological and surgical care. Not all patients with angina are referred to cardiologists; some will be managed in general practice if they respond well to medical treatment. There are no written protocols yet identifying which patients should be referred for more specialist investigation and treatment. These will be developed.

An open access chest pain clinic should provide rapid specialist advice to general practitioners about patients presenting with chest pain (possible angina), with the aim of treatment to improve quality of life and prolong life.

Unstable angina
Adequate and appropriate provision should be made for the management of unstable (unpredictable) angina, necessitating urgent admission to hospital, preferably on a coronary care unit, for intensive drug therapy and monitoring. Many patients will stabilize on this regime and can be discharged from hospital. Some, however, will continue to have symptoms and are in danger of myocardial infarction. Therefore invasive investigation (e.g. coronary angiography), with a view to angioplasty or urgent cardiac surgery, should be provided.

Heart attack
Guidelines for the management of patients with suspected heart attack have recently been published and endorsed by the British Heart Foundation. A local protocol based on these national guidelines has been developed. Following acute myocardial infarction, patients should be offered cardiac rehabilitation courses (run by nurse practitioners).

Heart failure
The majority of patients are managed without admission to hospital. The cornerstone of investigation (to exclude surgically correctable causes of heart failure) is the echocardiogram, which currently requires referral to a cardiologist or general physician. An open access heart failure clinic seeks to provide

rapid diagnosis and investigation to patients who have been referred by their general practitioners for the investigation of breathlessness. Some patients with severe heart failure are referred for possible cardiac transplantation. Guidelines for the management of heart failure are drawn up by local physicians and provide a basis for clinical practice.

Referral and discharge mechanisms

The patient should not be discharged from hospital before arrangements have been made to meet any continuing health or social care needs. The arrangements for meeting these needs will be agreed by the hospital with agencies such as community nursing services and local authority social services departments before the patient is discharged, according to the Patient's Charter.

Specific quality standards

The needs assessment states that:

- Ways of coordinating and implementing an intensive prevention and promotion programme must be agreed at local level
- Rapid assessment must be available to people with suspected coronary heart disease, with speedy treatment where required
- A rapid and effective response to a heart attack is vital
- The service must be responsive to an individual's need for rehabilitation after a heart attack or heart surgery
- There must be a sensitive system of review for people with chronic disability resulting from cardiovascular diseases.

These measures will be specified and given numerical values, for example the time between calling and receipt of care, in consultation with providers.

Monitoring and evaluation

The quality of the monitoring and evaluation of cardiology and cardiac surgery services has a high priority and we recommend that attention is paid to the health authority quality specification. Clinicians and providers are encouraged to consider measures of effectiveness for cardiology and cardiological services during 1996.

The following measures, among others, should be monitored:

- Delay in receiving thrombolysis for myocardial infarction: percentage whose call-to-needle time is within 90 minutes
- Length of time on waiting lists
- Deaths on waiting lists

- Perioperative mortality
- Survival, including both in-hospital and 1 year survival following myocardial infarction
- Percentage of myocardial infarcts that receive thrombolysis
- Percentage who return to work.

The purchasers expect that a regular clinical audit will be carried out and reported.

Purchasing: the third job – contracting

5

FINANCING THE HEALTH SERVICE

NHS funds are decided after the government's annual public expenditure survey round and are announced at the autumn statement of the Chancellor of the Exchequer. Spending on the health service is in two main sections: hospital with community health services, and family health services. At health authority level, these are brought together in one budget. Each is divided into revenue and capital spending. Another area of spending is the central health and miscellaneous services budgets, which the government administers centrally. They include the administrative costs of the Department of Health.

Traditionally, finances are divided into revenue and capital. The reasons for this are that some capital projects in the health service, such as a new hospital, are very expensive but quite rare. A trust's spending in the years of a new project is not comparable with that in years where no such project is happening. A cynic might maintain that, with a centrally funded health service, the government need is to control where expenditure is channelled to avoid upsetting certain parts of the electorate; some spending could thus be deferred without danger that the electorate would take its revenge. It certainly gives the central government a degree of control over major spending programmes.

Whatever the reasons, capital spending on the UK health service has always been poor, resulting in very old and poor-quality buildings. Visitors from the continent and the USA are constantly appalled by the number of Victorian and Edwardian hospitals that people in the UK continue to use. I have known a group of German visitors leave in embarrassment at the state of services to which they had come to, supposedly, learn from. Even people in the service continue to be horrified by the time it takes to plan and build new, quite modestly sized hospitals.

Allocations to health authorities

The Department of Health gives money to the regional offices in England according to the number of people resident in those regions. The capitation rates are then weighted to take account of different factors such as age groups, as elderly people use more health services than younger ones. SMRs and a factor that assists areas with a scattered population are added into the equation. The SMR is intended to be a proxy for differences in the basic health of the population.

Some geographical supplements are added. The Department of Health gives money for staff working in the London area to reflect their increased costs. They also pay an allocation to reflect the variation between regional offices in staff costs apart from London. Regional offices of the Department vary slightly in the way in which they allocate their money to their health authorities and general practitioner fundholders. The general practitioner fundholders are given funds, which would otherwise have been available to their health authority, to purchase specified services.

Capital expenditure

The definition of capital expenditure is the purchase cost of an asset that generates benefits over more than 1 year. It includes the purchase of land for building, the cost of those buildings and the adaptation of existing ones for health purposes. Capital spending by NHS trusts is financed through the depreciation of existing capital work, surpluses and borrowing. For the remainder of the NHS, a separate capital allocation continues to exist. This is allocated between the regional offices on a formula similar to that for non-capital money. Regional offices of the Department of Health allocate capital allocations to the health authorities depending upon their building and other programmes. The capital allocation is split into:

- Major building schemes
- Medical equipment costing more than £50 000
- Ambulance services
- Priority services such as learning disability and mental illness.

The regional offices delegate a proportion to health authorities for items of medical equipment, vehicles, minor building alterations, fire precautions and staff housing. Medium-sized schemes may be delegated to the district, but overall financial management is at regional level.

Revenue expenditure

This covers the costs of services in the current year and includes:

- Paying staff
- The cost of goods and services
- Hotel services for patients
- Accommodation for staff
- The cost of drugs appliances
- Fuel
- The repair and maintenance of buildings.

DRAWING UP CONTRACTS

There are three basic types of contract in the health service:

- *Block contracts*. The provider receives a fixed payment for the services given. The number and type of cases treated under the contract are not specifically designated.
- *Cost and volume contracts*. Providers receive a fixed sum for a basic level of treatment and receive extra payments for treating patients beyond this level.
- *Cost per case contracts*. Providers receive an agreed price for each case treated.

The term 'contract', normally associated with a legally binding agreement, is a misnomer [66], as these contracts do not have the protection of the courts. Indeed there is a tendency in some parts of the health service for purchasers and providers to pay scant regard to the contract other than as a basis for renegotiation half way through the year. The reason for this is that health authorities and their provider units worked this way in the first 40 years of the health service; these old habits die hard.

Block contracts are useful where the number of patients using the service alters hour by hour and day by day but where the service has to be available at all times. The classical situation is accident and emergency services. Block contracts are relatively simple to describe and are therefore said to be cheap to transact; that is at low cost in the time of the people trying to agree to the contract.

Contract currencies

Cost and volume contracts need to specify what volume is being measured: the contract currency. There can be problems in agreeing these. In some specialties, there is evidence that too many outpatients are being seen many times without any benefits to the patients. Purchasers may purchase only first outpatient visits, costed to take into account a smaller proportion of revisits, which aims to urge the providers to reduce the number of revisits that patients make. There is a tradition in long-stay wards of setting the contract currency according to the number of bed-days used up during the year. This urges the providers to use up their bed space to its maximum. It also has the effect, of course, of discouraging people from discharging patients. Most contract currencies will have up and down sides of this sort.

Problems sometimes arise between purchasers and providers when purchasers wish to have complicated measures of quality or contract currencies that are not routinely used. They also arise, of course, when the purchaser wishes to reduce the quantity or value of the contract, but the reason for the disagreement is more open in that case. Changes to quality or currency measures can sometimes cause problems for a trust. This is not usually to do with the quality standard itself but because of the re-tooling needed to collect the data. In addition, changing currency measures may have an unknown effect on the contract, either increasing or decreasing the quantity provided. This makes it difficult for the trust to estimate its coming year's budget. One way around this is to collect the new currency in 'shadow' form for a year so that the health authority can compare the old and new currencies directly. Quality measures are more difficult. Collecting the data may be simple or may be extremely time consuming. These problems are increased if the contract is altered every year instead of being agreed for several years. There is a belief current in health authorities that good-quality data should be based upon data that the trust is already collecting for its own use. I worry about this as it assumes that trusts have data that are relevant to their needs; this is not, at present, true.

Extracontractual referrals

Extracontractual referrals are purchased by the health authorities or fund-holding general practitioners for occasional cases they wish to purchase from a trust that does not have a standard contract with the health authority or fundholder. These may be to take advantage of a special service provided, or there may be particular reasons why that patient may not want to be treated in the trust where the contract is set. Consultants in one trust will sometimes refer a patient on to another specialist: so-called tertiary referrals. The health authority cannot refuse to pay for these tertiary or emergency referrals, although they may demur for normal referrals if the cost appears to be very great for a service that could be provided locally.

How contracts are developing

In the early days of the internal market, contracting between health authorities and trusts tended to use block contracts based on Körner specialty definitions, the routine data collected for central government. This method is often insensitive to the differences between groups of patients, especially the severity of the patients with a particular disease in one hospital compared with another. Even within one hospital, this broad-brush approach may cause problems for the provider. Several purchasers, especially general practitioner fundholders, may wish to buy what is ostensibly the same service, but one group of patients may be considerably more severe. They will therefore require more services for the same money due to differences in case mix.

One way of reducing this danger is to cut up specialty-based contracts into a smaller range of services, based on diagnosis. This, if used carefully, should make more homogeneous the group of patients being treated and the services they need. This approach needs to be well understood before it is used a lot. Where there is uncertainty about the severity of patients' diseases, a widely based contract allows one to offset the 'peaks' of one element of case mix against the 'troughs' of another.

Contracting models for complex cases

A wider range of contracting models is developing at the same time as a move towards contracting for smaller and more focused groups of patients. This will be particularly relevant to contracts for tightly defined groups of patients with highly specialized services. These are often provided by one or only a few trusts in a region. A number of health authorities and general practitioner fundholders may purchase them.

We must take a number of things into account when we select a particular model:

- *Critical mass.* Can a case mix be found for a contract that is predictable for its volume and costs no matter how many purchasers might be involved?
- *Instability in the overall number of cases.* In some services, there is wide variability in the total number of patients referred from one year to the next, or even month by month. This may be due to the rarity of the disease. Other examples are when the treatment is new and the service is only beginning to grow. It may be a problem in some superspecialist areas, such as heart transplantation. Another area that often gives trouble, owing to the problems of caring for dangerous patients, is forensic psychiatry. Services that deal with problems highly affected by environmental factors or which care for infectious diseases will also have this problem of fluctuating numbers.
- *Doubts by the purchaser.* A purchaser may not wish to commit to a contract because of a lack of trust in the hospital, or because the purchaser may wish to encourage a new approach to the problem. Examples may be a paediatric service that is very inpatient orientated when the purchaser wishes to encourage a joint community and hospital approach.

- *Instability in the severity of successive cases.* Even if a contract is defined for a specific condition, this type of case-on-case variation will cause marked alterations in the cost of treatment despite the similarity of diagnosis or treatment. This creates difficulties in predicting the overall annual cost of a contract. Patients with severe mental illnesses are examples of these problems.
- *Provider vulnerability.* The provider is vulnerable to collapse or major financial instability if one or more of its services is reliant on cost-per-case or Extra Contractural Referral (ECR) income to cover most of its costs.
- *Purchaser vulnerability.* A purchaser may be vulnerable to major financial instability or liable to curtail other investment if it is reliant on cost-per-case or ECR finances to purchase a particular service. This can also occur with health authorities when major reorganizations are occurring. General practitioner fundholders may be vulnerable especially as capitation payments for fundholders take over from the original historic approach. I mention this in Chapter 6.
- *Complicated services.* This is for those conditions where the treatment invariably entails either a clear choice between a few alternatives or certain subsequent treatments. Contracting for 'a basket of procedures' to treat the condition may be preferable to contracts for the separate parts of the treatment. This may be useful for diseases where rehabilitation is a large part of the treatment, such as for stroke victims. People with long-term disabling diseases, for example cystic fibrosis, also fall into this category.
- *Multiprovider services.* Some conditions require a programme of specialist treatment, which may involve a series of linked but separate episodes of care from different providers. This may be contracted for by the purchaser as a programme rather than as individual elements. This may be the case for cancer services, where radiation therapy may be in a different trust from surgical services.
- *Shared contracts.* It may be possible for groups of purchasers and providers to get together to review contracts for a single service simultaneously provided to several health authorities. Health authorities may work with each other or with general practitioner fundholders, having agreed the contract between them
- *Financial economies of scale.* As the internal market develops, health authorities will negotiate a better price by purchasing for several years together, entailing less risk to the provider. The government could help here by giving general long-term indications of what funding they will give over a number of years. This, given the pressures on them and the size of the health service budget, is unlikely.
- *Other sources of finance.* One may look for elements of the service that may be a legitimate charge against other sources of finance, such as research and development or waiting list allocations, or other contracts.

Table 5.1 shows an outline of some of the possible models and their uses.

Table 5.1 Models of contracting and their applicability

Contract model	Features of the model	Notes on current applicability
Supraregional finance	• High-cost or low-volume services meeting rigorous criteria • National or cross-regional catchment area • Services centralized in a few providers • Subject to overall workload HAs have guaranteed 'free' access • 'Insurance premiums' paid via top slicing of RHA allocations	• Heart and lung transplants • Liver transplants • Neonatal and infant cardiac surgery
Cross-regional insurance or contracts	• High-cost or low-volume services centred on few hospitals with cross-regional catchment area • For services that do not meet supraregional criteria or are awaiting designation • Volatility of referrals such that 'risk pool' needs to cover several regions • Can be simple block contracts collectively financed by HAs in several regions or more, or sophisticated insurance arrangements between the HAs and the hospital. (In both cases, hospital would get some or all of its costs covered in advance and participating HAs would get some or all costs incurred by referral 'free' at point of use)	• Forensic psychiatry (especially court referrals) • Head injury or severe brain damage • Neonatal extracorporeal membrane oxygenation • Haemophilia (very high cost cases) • Prolonged high-cost intensive care and other 'big' ECRs
Intraregional insurance	• High-cost or low-volume services centred on a few hospitals in region with a regional catchment • Volatility of referrals such that 'risk pool' is sufficient within the region • Can be simple 'as required cost sharing' agreement between several HAs (where hospitals have reassurance that cash will be available if required), **or** • Can be more sophisticated insurance payments in advance by HAs to the hospital (where hospital has cash 'up front' and HAs have assured access 'free at point of use') • Arrangements need to be explicit on how much of the costs or excess costs are borne by (a) the hospital's contract income, (b) the HA of residence, (c) other HAs, and (d) regional brokerage	• High-cost haemophilia cases • Out-of-region referral by courts for forensic psychiatric assessment and treatment
Regional purchasing	• High-cost or specialist services centred on a few hospitals in region with a regional catchment • Subject to overall workload, all HAs in region have guaranteed access 'free' at point of use	

Table 5.1 *Cont.*

Contract model	Features of the Model	Notes on current applicability
	— HAs 'insurance premiums' paid by top slicing of their allocations by RHA	
Region-wide block contracts	• High-cost or specialist services centred on a few hospitals in region with a regional catchment area • Subject to overall workload, all HAs in region have guaranteed access 'free' at point of use • HAs 'insurance premiums' paid by contributions made by each HA (e.g. on basis of weighted population) to a lead purchaser who negotiates or runs contract on their behalf • Hospitals have guaranteed income for much of their costs and economy of effort in negotiations • Hospitals may also have separate contracts/ECRs from non-participating HAs for the service	• Spinal injuries • Regional rehabilitation service • Communication aid centre • Regional genetics service • Secure/semi-secure facilities for learning difficulties and mental illness • Supraregional or regional assay service (for hospital both within and outside the region) • Neonatal high-dependency care (with consortium of hospitals)
Co-ordinated contracts	• High-cost or specialist services centred on a few hospitals in region with a regional catchment area • Separate contracts negotiated by individual HAs or consortia • To ensure (a) consistency of service, (b) economy of effort in negotiation, (c) common approach, and (d) avoidance of differential access and standards, all contract negotiations co-ordinated by a steering group representing all HAs and the hospital	• Regional radiotherapy centre • Neurosciences
Sub-contracting	• HAs contract with a primary provider who then subcontracts elements of the service to other providers • High-cost or specialist services centred on a few hospitals in region with a subregional catchment area • Particularly useful to cover (a) outreach or disparate elements of a service provided in local units (b) specialist elements of a service (e.g. diagnostic support) provided by another hospital (c) services in transition from one location and/or type of care to another	May have applications in e.g. • outreach clinical • sub-contracting of specialist diagnostic support (e.g. MRI, assay services) • management of the relocation of a service from one provider to another

Table 5.1 *Cont.*

Contract model	Features of the Model	Notes on current applicability
Consortium contracts	• High-cost or specialist services centred on a few hospitals in region with a subregional catchment area • HA groups collectively negotiate contracts for (a) economies of scale or effort, (b) bulk purchasing, (c) develop purchaser expertise, and (d) 'insurance' against modest volatility of each HA's referrals	• Specialist psychiatry • Cardiac surgery
Umbrella contracts	• Useful for HAs or general practitioner FHs for small volumes of referral in several specialties from a single hospital • Referrals (often of similar cost) in several specialties grouped together under a single 'umbrella' • Flexibility between the specialties involved for purchaser; stable income for hospital	In some regions, used by HAs buying cases from remote hospitals and general practitioner FHs purchasing a package of small individual volumes
Individual contracts	'Lowest' form of contract between a single HA and single provider covering one specialty or subspecialty	

What goes in the contract

As a minimum one should specify the following.

Duration

The duration of a contract varies according to the type of contract. It will be most critical with block contracts. Providers do not want to provide a blank cheque but will want to make sure that there is continuity of care for all contracts, most especially block contracts. It is important that too much detail does not reduce the flexibility of the service. Three years should be a minimum length of contract for block contracts once the organization has settled.

Having said this, only a tiny proportion of 3 year contracts has been given by any of the organizations I have worked for since the internal market came into being. The main reason for this has been that every year, for the past 4 years, a very large part of the organization has undergone radical changes to its top management in response to government policy. The main provider with which I work has developed its contracts with an entirely different team each year for the past 4. The one exception was one of our finance directors, who was present in years 1 and 3. He was running a unit that was working up to being a trust in year 2. It has been impossible for purchasers and providers to develop close working relationships it this situation. These changes have also considerably hindered the development of best practice, as contract negotiations have always been started late because of organization changes, by which I mean that they have often started after April, when the aim was to complete contracts by the first of that month.

Quality

The point of contracting is to improve the quality of services as well as their efficiency and cost-effectiveness. This will cover both the clinical and non-clinical parts of the contract. They should try to guarantee:

- Appropriate treatment and care
- That the optimum clinical outcome is achieved
- That complications and other preventable events are minimized
- That patients are treated with dignity and as individuals.
- That the environment is conducive to safety, and reassurance and contentment of patients
- That the speed of response to patients' needs is reasonable and that there is minimum inconvenience to them, their relatives and their friends
- That patients have some say in their care.

The difficult part of these standards is obtaining relevant information about them. The most effective way is to ask patients specific questions when they are away from the service being monitored. This can be quite costly. I have mentioned above the useful advice that general practitioners can give the health authority.

One may check quality using one or more of the following measures:

- Legal standards and national codes of practice. These are often checked by outside bodies, such as the Royal Colleges.
- Methods for assuring quality, such as medical audit, nursing audit and surveys of patients' opinions. These should be routinely provided for the purchasers, but often are not.
- Specific performance measures as part of the contract or Patient's Charter.
- Assessing clinical outcomes. This may be possible for condition-based contracts as, for example, for stroke, fractured femur and myocardial infarction (see the Scottish experience outlined in Chapter 3).
- An assumption of standards that can reasonably be expected from the service. General practitioners may be especially helpful with this aspect.

EXAMPLE OF A CORE CONTRACT

Draft service agreement between yyy Health Authority (The Purchaser) and xxx NHS

Trust (The Provider)

Services Covered:	*to be completed as appropriate*
Contract Duration	1 April 199X to 31 March 199X
Total Contract Value:	£ xxx
Party 1	Name of Purchaser – yyy Health Authority
Party 2	Name of Provider – xxx NHS Trust

For and on behalf of the Purchaser ....

Designation...

Date:...

For and on behalf of the Provider: ....

Designation:..

Date:...

Introduction

This document sets out the requirements of yyy Health Authority for the health care services it wishes to purchase and includes specific proposals for monitoring the amount and quality of the service to be provided. It is the link between the Authority's requirements, as set out in the Purchasing Intentions and Business Planning Guidelines, and the provision of services.

Objectives

The objective of the agreement is to enable the Purchaser to secure a comprehensive health service for the residents of yyy Health Authority. This will be achieved through the provision of a range of high-quality and timely health care across defined specialties, with reasonable skill and care being exercised.

This agreement is underpinned by the mutual commitment of both parties to the overall objectives set out in the Secretary of States' document *Caring for the Future* [Welsh example] to achieve:

- Ever-improving health
- Cutstanding service and real choice for patients
- First-class stewardship.

Both parties agree to build on existing good contracting relationships and to continue the dialogue in the development of services. Both parties also agree to work together to seek to achieve the highest quality of health care and to incorporate priorities for maintaining and developing services that take account of:

- Local health strategies
- Needs assessment

- Clinical effectiveness
- Ease of access to appropriate health care
- The quality of the environment within which patients are treated and cared for
- The standard and level of communication with patients and relatives
- The mental health strategy
- The resettlement plan for learning disabilities
- Social care plans.

Duration

The duration of this agreement is x years from 1 April 199X

If it is the intention of either party to discontinue the agreement in part or in whole, adequate notice must be given in writing to the other party. This will minimize any disruption to services. Where changes proposed by the Purchasers will affect the Providers' overhead costs, 6 months notice will be given.

Services to be provided

Details of services to be provided for the residents of yyy Health Authority include: [To be completed as necessary].

Health promotion

The Provider is requested to take advantage of all incidental opportunities for health promotion that arise in providing these services and generally to seek to promote the health of the community in which it operates.

Pharmaceutical services

Provision of services by access to the drug information centre, clinical pharmacy, pharmaceutical quality assurance and community service pharmacy at the levels set out in the service specifications.

Prescribing

All prescribing and costs associated according to WHC(91)94 [Welsh example] for patients initially treated by the Provider will be absorbed by the Provider within the agreed contract price. General practitioners will not be asked to prescribe high-cost drugs unless agreed shared care protocols exist and all regularity, statutory and ethical issues have been satisfactorily resolved.

There should be a clear mechanism in place for the review of new drugs, drug utilization, costs and prescribing.

The service agreement does *not* include:

- The emergency ambulance service
- Activity associated with waiting list initiatives
- Tertiary referrals from this provider to other providers
- Referrals made by a general practitioner fundholder that are chargeable to the general practitioner fundholder
- yyy Health Authority residents who have elected to become private patients.

The Provider shall not assign any of its rights or responsibilities under the contract without the agreement in writing of the Purchaser.

Priority of treatment

The Purchaser expects priority of treatment to be determined according to the clinical need of the patient and the need to fulfil Patients' Charter guarantees. The Purchasers' patients are to be treated with similar priority to those of other purchasers.

Patient's Charter guarantees

The Provider is required to accept the responsibilities laid on it by the Patient's Charter and to meet the Charter Standards.

Management of waiting lists and waiting times

The Provider will be held responsible for the efficient management of waiting lists and the achievement of the Patient's Charter total waiting times guarantees. To monitor this, information will be required as described in the section on monitoring. The Provider should follow both the best practice guidelines for the management of lists [67] and, in so doing, perform routine internal and external validation of lists. A named senior manager should be responsible for waiting list management.

For non-urgent inpatients awaiting treatment, details of potential Charter breaches should be forwarded to the Health Authority at least 2 months before the breach date. Should breaches occur, details in writing should be immediately forwarded to the Chief Executive of the Authority and the patient's general practitioner. An explanatory letter should also be sent to the patient.

Where monitoring information indicates that

- Waiting time targets are not being met, and
- Resources and contracted activity are not being used to take corrective action,

the full cost of treatment for those patients outside the standards will be withdrawn from the contract price to enable treatment by another provider.

Non-attendance

The Provider is required to have mechanisms in place that identify which patients fail to attend for a booked clinic appointment. Unless exceptional circumstances or patient care dictates, the Provider will be expected to return such patients to the care of the relevant general practitioner for reassessment.

Service specifications

Service specifications have been developed for inclusion in the agreement starting 1 April 199X and to help to inform the development of condition-based outcome measures.

Performance review and quality

The Health Authority will focus its quality monitoring activities on the key areas, set out in the monitoring section.

Emergency and contingency plans

The Provider will be expected to have, maintain in a state of readiness and exercise all relevant emergency plans.

The plans that the Health Authority has to ensure are in place are as follows:

- Major incident plan
- Arrangements for dealing with accidents involving radioactivity
- Arrangements for dealing with incidents involving chemicals
- Civil defence in the NHS
- Control of communicable disease.

The Provider is expected to be involved in planning for and dealing with such incidents. This is required by the Purchaser's senior accountable officer or the director of public health medicine or consultant in communicable disease control.

In the interests of protecting patients, visitors and staff, the Purchaser will expect the Provider to have in place an appropriate range of other contingency arrangements. Examples include plans to deal with a serious breakdown of utilities or services, withdrawal of labour, extreme weather and evacuation of buildings.

Untoward incidences and accidents

The Provider must notify the Purchaser immediately of any untoward incident occurring which has resulted in death or serious consequence for any patient, visitor or member of staff.

Volume and mix

The volume and mix of activity to be provided under this agreement are set out below as appropriate. [Details follow.]

Pricing methodology

The Purchaser recognizes that the Audit Commission has the responsibility for auditing costing for contracting. However, the Purchaser will also audit costing standards, and the Provider will be expected to provide relevant information relating to this process. The relevant information will be agreed and will identify the costing approach and methodology for treating costs within the trust and will not include the disclosure or detailed costs attributed to the Purchaser.

Price

The contract price for the work undertaken regarding this agreement is £xxx. This price represents last year's cost quantum plus the relevant cash increases as well as the present year's productivity agreement. The reconciliation to the contract price is outlined in Appendix X and is further enhanced by details shown for individual services.

Variances in activity

The provider is required to pace contracts in line with the agreed activity levels to ensure that all emergency and urgent cases are accommodated within the contract levels. The balance remaining will form the level of elective cases to be undertaken by the Provider, which should be directed towards the achievement of Patient's Charter guarantees and Purchasers' targets. The forward planning of elective cases should take into account the Provider's overall capacity as well as previous years' experience of the incidence of emergency and urgent admissions. This should avoid cancelling booked admissions.

It is a requirement of this agreement that the Provider will manage the agreement without additional funds. Any proposed increase in elective cases above the agreed levels must be discussed and agreed with the Purchaser before the treatment takes place, and should be related to achieving Patient's Charter guarantees. Increases in activity that have not been agreed in advance will not be funded. The exception may be emergency or urgent cases occurring in the last month of the agreement that the Provider could not have reasonably be expected to foresee. Where the monitoring reports and performance reviews indicate an underachievement, the Process for Resolving Disputes will be brought into action.

Variation of agreement terms

There may be exceptional circumstances during the year that are beyond the reasonable control of either party that prevent the discharge of the agreement. When this becomes apparent, both parties must discuss any proposed changes and agree a timetable leading to the resumption of normal contractual arrangements so that full performance can be achieved.

Data definition and technical standards

All data sets should comply with central Department of Health definitions. Similarly, all technical standards, including those for electronic data interchange, should comply with those agreed and adopted.

Monitoring information

General monitoring arrangements were outlined in the Purchaser's Business Planning Guidelines. This information should be directed in the agreed format (normally electronic) to the Director of Information. The basic principles underlying these requirements are:

- Openness and the sharing of information
- Timeliness of submissions
- Quality and consistency of data
- The derivation of data from operational systems
- The provision of data in electronic format
- The provision of patient-based minimum data sets where possible, to allow analysis by small area and general practitioner and data audit exercises
- The provision of residential and local general practitioner catchment datasets, the protection of patient information, that is to fulfil the requirements of the Data Protection Act, Medical Records Act, Patients Charter and agreed NHS confidentiality and security protocols [68–70].

The Provider will be expected to develop information technology systems within the framework of the All-Wales Strategy. A key issue is the need to have procedures in place for the new NHS number by xx.xx.xx.

Monitoring visits

A programme of visits will be agreed with the Provider to include unplanned visits at any time of the day or night. This will have due regard to the care of patients and may include executive and non-executive directors. Health Authority representatives will always carry identification.

Invoicing and settlement

The Purchaser agrees to make payment to the Provider by the 15th working day of each month, subject to the timely receipt of the associated monitoring reports and supporting documentation for the prior month.

Penalties and incentives

Patient's Charter

Breaking Patient's Charter waiting time guarantees will result in money being withheld from the Provider. For each patient who breaches one of the guarantees, the value of that patient's treatment will be withheld. This action will take place at the end of every month. The Purchaser will be allowed access to facilities to allow the information to be audited.

Monitoring returns

The submission of the monthly hospital activity and waiting times information after the deadline laid down will be monitored and reviewed against the performance of other providers. Performance league tables will be published on a monthly basis. Failure to achieve the agreed standards of timeliness and quality of data will result in an appropriate response from the Health Authority, following discussion with the Provider.

Non-performance

Following a monitoring visit, or following receipt of any other indication that the terms of the agreement are not being met, the findings will be discussed with the appropriate level of management. If the Purchaser or Provider is not performing according to the terms of the agreement, the following procedure will apply.

Where one party considers that the other party has breached its obligations, that party will instigate a meeting with the other within 14 days. Following the meeting, the party that has not performed adequately will be given 2 weeks to resolve the issue to the satisfaction of the other party. It is assumed that there will be joint discussions to reach an acceptable outcome. Where the problem has not been sorted out within the agreed timescale, the other party will have the right of recourse to arbitration.

Process of resolving disputes

When an issue has been identified as a potential dispute, either in the process of negotiation or in the operation of an existing agreement, the guidance in Contracts: Resolving Disputes will apply.

Renewal of agreement

The provision for annual renewal in full will be subject to the satisfactory performance of the agreement. It will also be subject to the submission of the Provider's capacity plan and provisional prices in response to the Purchaser's purchasing intentions by 30 November each year.

Nursing and midwifery education practice and advice

It is expected that Providers will comply with the standards of the United Kingdom Central Council for Nursing, Midwifery and Health Visiting on the Code of Professional Conduct, including:

- Education and competence for continuing practice
- Specialist health care
- Midwifery practice and supervision
- Continuing registration status
- Clinical supervision
- Effective supervision of support staff.

Providers should maintain the level of support and advice of specialist nurses, midwives and health visitors to the commission and undertake statutory responsibilities with the health authority. These are:

- statutory responsibilities for child protection in midwifery
- statutory responsibilities for midwifery and midwifery specialist advice
- specialist nursing and midwifery advice including:
    infection control
    diabetic care
    breast care
    continence care.

Occupational health service

It is a requirement of this agreement that the Provider furnish an occupational health service for the staff in its employ. This service must be consultant led, the consultant being accredited in the specialty of occupational medicine.

Estate management

The Provider will be expected to manage the estate according to the objectives, principles and methods of estate planning and management. These are established in Estate Code and demonstrate the most efficient use of capital and overheads.

The Provider should be expected to forward a certificate to the Purchaser verifying compliance with guidance on the hot water temperature by 1 June 1996 as identified in WHC(96)27 [Welsh example].

Monitoring

In 1996/97 yyy health authority will give priority to monitoring the following quality issues:

- Discharge policies
- Use of emergency beds
- Developing a general practitioner focus
- Waiting list and waiting time management
- Availability of timely and robust data.

Monitoring specifications for the above (excluding data requirements; see Appendix X) are set out below and will be developed with the relevant commissioning team throughout 1996/97.

Discharge policy

- That a single discharge policy ratified by the trust board, which includes quantifiable standards and monitoring procedures, is agreed with local general practitioners and social services departments.
- That monitoring systems are agreed to demonstrate implementation and compliance with the eligibility criteria for continuing health care.
- Monitoring of Patient's Charter standards.
- That patients should not be discharged before arrangements have been made to meet any continuing health or social care needs.
- That general practitioners should be notified of patient discharge within 24 hours (target = 100%).
- That inpatient care should avoid readmission measured as a percentage of patients who have unplanned readmission within 30 days of discharge.

Use of emergency beds

Evidence of a written policy on contract management that should encompass detail on management of an emergency workload in medical and surgical specialties. The policy should include:

- Admission policy (including assessment unit)
- Each patient to be seen by a consultant within 24 hours
- Monitoring procedures
- Discharge planning
- Evaluation of policy.

The trust should be able to present this policy to the commissioning authority by June 199X.

Quarterly data providing information on:

- Bed numbers (availability)
- Length of stay (LOS) by specialty: average LOS
- Number with LOS≥ 7 days
- Number with LOS<24 hours.

Weekly data providing information on:

- Number of admissions by general practice
- Number of emergency on-take closures.

General practitioner focus

Waiting list management information available to general practitioners by consultant and referring general practitioner:

- Reports of first outpatient appointment to be sent within 5 working days
- Named community psychiatric nurse for access to community mental health team
- Named community health workers
- Clear emergency admissions policy published following consultation with general practitioners.

Management of waiting lists and waiting times

Waiting list data to be provided to the Authority on a monthly basis within 10 working days from the end of the month:

- Providers will provide evidence of regular audits of their waiting list, including regular validation to ensure accuracy, and targeting those patients waiting over 4 months for an outpatient appointment and 12 months for an inpatient treatment.
- Trusts should provide evidence of local policies for dealing with non-attendance at outpatient clinics and patient-cancelled appointments.

Evidence that local programmes for reducing waiting lists are being implemented at an agreed pace. Examples might be reducing new to old outpatient ratios, increasing the proportion of procedures carried out as day cases, preadmission review clinics and general practitioner referral protocols.

6

General practitioners as purchasers

FUNDHOLDING GENERAL PRACTITIONERS

Figure 6.1 shows the number of general practitioner fundholders over time. Table 6.1 shows the number of fundholders in England in spring 1996, where the greatest proportion of the population were covered by fundholding general practitioners. It shows the increase in the proportion of the population served by fundholders in the 1996 round of applications. Over 3000 general practitioners applied in 1996 in over 1200 practices, to make over half of all the general practitioners in the country fundholders. In this round, the government reduced the maximum list size for standard fundholding to 5000. It also extended the scheme to cover virtually all elective surgery, outpatients and specialist nursing services. A new community fundholding scheme for practices with over 3000 patients was also introduced. General practitioners will be responsible for the funding of staff, drugs and most of the community health services but not inpatients or outpatients, in the community scheme.

Most health authorities have schemes for including general practitioners who are not fundholders in the purchasing of services. These take a number of different forms.

Applying the responsibilities of purchasers to general practice

General practitioners acting as purchasers of services will need to follow guidelines similar to those used by the health authorities. The problems with applying them are different for general practitioners, whether they are general practitioner fundholders or working through a local purchasing system. It will be possible to get an idea of the problems by looking at the Maxwell criteria in the six sub-headings used previously (p.59)and applying them to general practice.

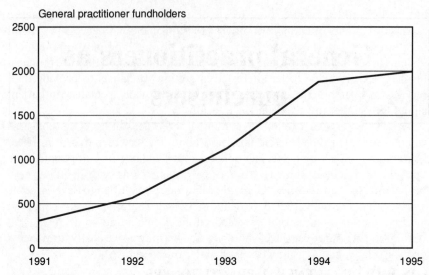

Figure 6.1 Number of fundholding general practices in England.

Access to services

Services given in or near to the general practitioner's surgery are likely to be more accessible to patients than those given at a single point for a large population, such as in a district general hospital. Some groups of patients,

Table 6.1 Applications for general practitioner fundholding in 1996

FHSA	Number of general practitioners applied	% of population served
Rochdale	47	45
Sunderland	62	44
Lancashire	241	34
Barnsley	36	30
Brent & Harrow	71	29
Devon	91	28
Hillingdon	34	28
Northumberland	48	26
Coventry	38	26
Bradford	65	25
Dorset	112	23
Barnet	42	23
Cumbria	64	22
St Helens & Knowsley	36	22
Walsall	32	22
Ealing, Hammersmith & Hounslow	67	20
Wiltshire	66	20
Croydon	32	20
City and East London	50	19
Wirral	36	19

especially disabled people, find access difficult, especially to older practice premises. Patients often have another type of problem with access to general practitioners when they try to find their way through complex appointment systems to see their practitioner. General practitioners, when they are purchasing services, are likely to be interested in getting specialists to provide their services in their practice premises. They often provide specialist outpatient clinics, physiotherapy or social work locally.

Access to services can mean a number of other things. One concerns whether people or the professionals know about the service in question. There is little point in having a special clinic for a particular group of people if the publicity for it is bad. Hidden costs may exist, such as long or difficult journeys for patients or their relatives. General practitioners may wish to develop some services that are delivered to patients at home. There has been a marked increase in the treatment of severe disabilities, including some people on ventilators, at home over the past few years. This may prove costly for patients or their family, acting as an effective barrier to the service.

Relevance to the needs of the whole community

The whole community may mean something different for general practitioners than for a demographer or epidemiologist. The tradition for general practice has been the concern for the patient presenting to them at that moment. Having said this, general practitioners have awareness of the social background and pressures on the area in which they work. These insights are not available to doctors, nurses and therapists working from a large central point. UK general practitioners almost totally decide which patients should receive non-emergency hospital and community services. They have been particularly effective in keeping down the demand for these services, compared with countries where patients have open access to hospital care. It may be this parsimoniousness which has kept the costs of the UK health service so low compared with other countries. The UK has managed, despite this, to have reasonable measures of health overall, such as a low infant mortality ratio.

Effectiveness for individual patients

General practitioners work in primary care, where the evidence of effectiveness for most of the interventions is untested [71]. This makes effectiveness-based work when purchasing primary care services very difficult. There is also a lack of knowledge in general practice about what effective interventions do exist. To counter this, people are increasingly aiming data on effective purchasing at general practitioner purchasers [72].

Equity

Equity is difficult for general practitioner purchasers to ensure, with a tradition of managing one patient at a time. The more expensive treatment regimes that general practitioners will need to buy are also rare. For example, each general practitioner may see only one or two patients on haemodialysis a year. This makes it difficult for a them to decide whether their patients are being treated equitably compared with patients in other practices.

Social acceptability

In theory, general practitioners should be aware of the social acceptability of the treatment that they give or purchase for their patients. However, general practitioners are not always as aware of their patient's social conditions as might be wished [73]. General practitioners need specifically to ask their patients about the acceptability of the treatments that they receive, from both secondary services and their own provider services.

Efficiency and economy

General practitioners in the UK are, albeit unconsciously, aware of the need to restrict costs to the health service. I have mentioned that general practitioners, acting as gatekeepers to the expensive hospital services, have, for many years, referred a relatively small proportion of their patients to specialist care compared with other countries [74].

Accountability of fundholders

General practitioner fundholders purchase services, including their own. They are therefore able to short circuit both the internal market and the planning mechanism. In theory, they are able to bypass government policy as long as the health authority, in its guise as their paymaster, does not notice. Health authorities have the job of monitoring the claims for payment from general practitioners, opticians and pharmacists. These claims individually cover small amounts of money but large numbers of items. They are therefore extremely difficult to check.

Management accountability

In response to these concerns, the government produced a series of requirements for management accountability from general practitioners [75]. This proposed four basic requirements:

- Advanced announcement of major purchasing shifts
- An annual practice plan
- A performance report
- A performance review.

Accountability to patients and the wider public

- Publishing information (e.g. annual practice plan and performance report)
- Involving patients in service planning
- Ensuring an effective complaints system.

Financial accountability

- Preparation of annual accounts for independent staff
- Providing monthly information for monitoring by the health authority
- Securing health authority agreement to use of savings
- Stating the plan's contribution to local efficiency targets set by the NHS Executive.

Fundholders have not been particularly good at keeping within their budgets, about one in five overspending [76]. This has been at a time of relative plenty for them. It seems likely that this will change, especially as the central funding of general practitioners is likely to change: in future, they will be paid on a *per capita* basis. In other words, their pay will be according to the number of patients that they have. There will be adjustments for greater probable demand, rather than on historical precedent as at present. It should be said that I, as part of a team of purchaser of services for a population of three quarters of a million people, with a budget of half a billion pounds, would not like to attempt to predict the demands and consequent costs of a population of 10 000 people. A very small number of unusual problems could easily throw any predicted costs completely off track.

Further measures of accountability for general practitioners include:

Clinical and professional accountability

- Participating in clinical audit of general medical services of activities
- Ensuring appropriate clinical audit of purchased hospital and community health care.

These points about accountability do not examine fundholding in detail and do not clarify who is supposed to check on general practitioners. It is not clear whether the job belongs to the regional executive, the health authorities or the patients. The health authorities are best placed for this.

EFFECTIVENESS OF FUNDHOLDING

Prescribing costs

The government hoped that general practitioner fundholding, with its emphasis upon general practitioners paying for their drugs, would reduce prescribing costs. Traditionally, UK general practitioners are conservative prescribers. In the management changes, general practitioner fundholders were given the drugs budget and the power to reinvest any savings that they could make in other services for their patients.

At the same time, the government set up an indicative prescribing scheme for general practitioners who were not fundholders to help them to control their costs. The health authority sets a financial target for each practice based on their previous prescribing costs, together with an estimate for inflation. No penalties are imposed on practices that fail to meet their targets. They are given information on their prescribing pattern compared with the pattern in other practices.

A group of researchers set up a study to look at the prescribing patterns of the practices taking part in the Oxford region fundholding groups [77]. In both the fundholding and non-fundholding practices, the cost of drugs and the number of items prescribed rose steadily over the 3 years of the study. A group of non-dispensing fundholding practices was found to have the highest costs at the end of the study. Paradoxically, this was the group who had the greatest incentive to keep its costs low. In the initial stages of the study, a year after fundholding started, fundholding general practitioners seemed to have been more effective than non-fundholders in controlling their costs [78]. Three years later, however, the pattern reversed and the difference between the types of practice decreased.

Inflationary influences on prescribing costs caused both groups to increase their costs despite the cost-control measures. Heavy marketing of some new anti-depressants and other drugs led to an increase in their prescribing, even though they were no more effective than those already available. This pressure from the drug companies appears to have been more powerful than government policy. This is not really surprising. Pharmaceutical companies put very large budgets into persuading general practitioners to buy their goods. This publicity grows increasingly sophisticated and is very effective.

Outreach services

One of the features of fundholding practices has been their ability to set up specialist services in practice premises. The evidence for the effectiveness of these is generally poor. Some services, such as direct access physiotherapy, are untested [79]. Others, such as outreach consultant clinics, are of dubious efficiency and cost-effectiveness [80]. The cost of outreach ophthalmology services has been shown to be three times greater than its hospital equivalent because of lower throughput [81]. This may, to some extent, be overturned if the social costs to patients are included in the equation. A study in East Sussex [82] questioning fundholders in that area showed that general practitioners felt that community psychiatric nurses gave a good value service but there was no objective evidence. There needs to be much more testing of the effectiveness of this type of work.

Referral to hospital

The government intended to cut down the number of referrals which general practitioners made by giving fundholders the non-urgent hospital in-and outpatient budget for their patients. There is some suggestion from research that general practitioner fundholders are, because of their fundholding, becoming more critical in their decision to send patients to different surgeons [83]. General practitioners mentioned that, when choosing a surgeon to whom to refer patients, they were most influenced by their confidence in the consultant's ability, short waiting times and informative feedback from the providers. The costs of the treatment and the convenience to patients were less important. The majority of referrals from these fundholders were sent locally. Another study suggested that referral patterns to hospital were no different for fundholders and non-fundholders [84].

Patient care

Another detailed before and after study suggested that, after becoming fundholders, general practitioners were less good at giving time to people with subtle sociomedical problems and more effective at treating the traditional medical problems seen in general practice [85]. This group examined the way in which fundholders and non-fundholders managed people with joint pain and found that the fundholders were maintaining their times for consultation with patients at much the same level as before becoming fundholders. They were, however, less likely to refer patients for investigations or to hospital [86]. Patients showed less satisfaction latterly than formerly with their care. There is no objective evidence of whether they were more or less successfully treated.

Two-tier problems

In the early stages, while the methods of payment for fundholding general practitioners depended upon their historic usage of services, there is some evidence that such practices received more than non-fundholding general practitioners. A study in North West Thames looked at the amount *per capita* allocated to patients in fundholding and non-fundholding practices for inpatient and outpatient care [87]. This suggested that the allocation of money for inpatients belonging to non-fundholding practices was between two-thirds and nine-tenths of that allocated for inpatients from fundholding practices. The costs for each episode of care were similar, so there was no inherent difference in the type of patient referred for care.

Evaluating fundholding generally

Most recently, a National Audit Office survey has looked at the effect of general practitioner fundholding. The setting up of fundholding with decisions made closer to the needs of the population gives family doctors considerable freedom to innovate. This has led to some improvement in existing services and the development of interesting new ones. In May 1996, the Office published the results of its main investigation [88]. The report suggested that many fundholding practices have improved communication with hospital services, with open access to pathology and radiology. They also had practice-based services for many groups, including those needing physiotherapy, dietetics, chiropody, psychiatric nursing and psychology. The fundholders spent less on drugs than did non-fundholders.

However, fundholders, as purchasers of hospital services, have not bought services according to the best evidence of effectiveness. They have not taken the opportunity to use or develop guidelines for the best treatment of complicated diseases. Very few have tried to assess the needs of their practice population before purchasing services. The survey, a simple comparison between fundholders and non-fundholders, cannot separate the effects of fundholding from those general changes which were happening in general practice.

Fund managers, compared with the skill and resources held by health authorities, are very undertrained. The report suggested that much of the advice and training needed by fundholding general practitioners was available in the public health departments of health authorities. Fundholding has brought about some minor improvements in the care given to patients, but it has not altered the way in which doctors practice. I feel that the Audit Commission was a little naive to expect doctors, trying to learn the new skills of purchasing, to have time to overhaul their old skills at the same time.

ASSESSING NEEDS IN GENERAL PRACTICE

Researchers have looked at different methods of defining health needs for general practice. General practitioners and community nurses have the advantage that they are able to observe patients' health, both physical and mental, over long periods of time. They also know their family backgrounds and the environment to which they belong. This should make it possible for people working in the area to get hold of data for defining and measuring health needs. They should also be able to consider how their needs can be met and monitor the performance of people providing services outside the practice.

Commissioning in this way needs to take into account the social, educational, employment and housing aspects of health care [89]. Methods of assessing health needs from general practice have not been very much developed in the past. Community profiles built up over time have been the exception [90] rather than the rule; there has been a mistaken view that simply looking at a practice profile is the same as looking at the needs of the population. People have done some work looking at illness rates using estimates [91]. They have suggested that a combination of practice-based and centrally held information in the same area would provide a more complete picture of needs than either could separately [92].

One research project has attempted to compare different methods of needs assessment in general practice [93]. The four methods of assessment used were:

- Rapid participatory appraisal
- Postal survey
- Routinely available local statistics
- Practice-held information.

Rapid participatory appraisal originated in developing countries to gain insight into the community's ideas about its needs. In the cited study, a team consisting of the general practitioner, health visitor, two social workers and a community education officer collected data from three sources. They looked at existing documents about the neighbourhood, interviewed a range of people and observed the neighbourhood directly. They built a profile of nine aspects of the community as an information pyramid (Figure 6.2). The bottom layer defines the composition of the community, its organization and its ability to act. The second has socioecological factors, and the third is about the services provided for it. The top layer is concerned with policies that involve the community. The point of this approach is that data collected from one origin are rejected or validated by comparing them with at least two other sources. Informants for this process are people with professional knowledge of the community, community leaders and people who are well placed because of their work.

Figure 6.2   Information pyramid constructed for rapid participatory appraisal.

The study in question also took a small sample of residents in the area and interviewed them in groups. Two focus groups were set up to discuss and decide the importance of the problems uncovered. A postal survey involved sending questionnaires to all the people in the practice. The idea of this part of the study was to assess their need for primary health services [94]. The questionnaire included questions about.

- Chronic illness
- Acute illness
- Symptoms
- Health status, including data that were built up into the Nottingham health profile
- The use of health services
- Social and demographic characteristics
- Long-term health problems.

Finally, the researchers collected routine statistics about outpatients, obstetric episodes, inpatient care, births, deaths and census information.

The information already held in the practice included some about the prevalence of chronic disease, repeat prescribing and data about screening and health promotion. The researchers examined a sample of 100 medical records to get an idea of the extent of acute illness, prescribing and psychosocial problems. Information from the patients' records about referral to hospital was recorded. They reviewed deaths over the past 4 years and data about surgery consultations, house calls and out-of-hours visits. Patients registered as drug addicts or having human immunodeficiency virus (HIV) were examined, and the health visitors, district nurses and practice nurses were asked their views.

Table 6.2 shows 4 conditions of the 20 looked at in the study, and the information gained from those conditions by the four methods used. Asthma or chronic bronchitis had a high prevalence by both the postal survey and the review of practice data. There were few outpatient referrals but quite a large number of admissions and several deaths.

In the survey, 18% of the respondents reported they had trouble with stress, depression or bad nerves, although these were documented in a lower proportion of the medical records. The census data gave information about high unemployment, many single parents and other potential reasons for this stress. All four methods gave information about drug misuse, HIV infection and smoking.

Comparative prevalences of problems

Table 6.3 compares the prevalences of the conditions using the different methods. The postal survey yielded a higher prevalence than did the review of practice data. For example, the number of people who thought they had a

Table 6.2 Results of different assessment methods

Condition	Practice data	Local statistics	Postal survey	Rapid appraisal
Asthma or chronic bronchitis	6.5% prevalence 6% taking bronchodilators 3% taking inhaled corticosteroids	Few outpatient referrals, 13% of all admissions 3 deaths	14% prevalence 9% saw doctor in past 6 months for this	'Many toiling for breath' Damp housing causes asthma in children
Stress or depression	12% (medical records search) Medical records of 100 non-respondents to the postal survey reported stress or depression in 20, drug misuse in 8 and alcohol problems in 6	Census revealed many potential stressors: high unemployment; many single parents	18% prevalence of being anxious, depressed or bad nerves. 10% saw doctor in past 6 months. 72% requested help or advice 16–44 age group scored highly on health profile, emotional reaction, social isolation. Helpline suggested	Stressful environment and lifestyles Regular citizens' advice, a course about alternative therapies, and a creche suggested
Drug misuse or HIV infection	Many patients receiving methadone substitution lived in Dumbiedykes High turnover of drug addicts Several children with needlestick injuries Moving out of Dumbiedykes was the solution some patients gave for their drug problem	HIV carrier was fifth most common reason for adult hospital admission in 1991 Many indicators of socioeconomic disadvantage revealed by census	6% wanted help or advice about illegal drugs 26% wanted help or advice about HIV 'Would like HIV test without documentation'	Interviews revealed some young families isolated single parents misusing drugs Drug users received prescribed substitutes and bought extra drugs from suppliers. Drug misusers not concerned about HIV; not using condoms. Domestic violence common. Residents knew drug misusers.
Smoking	50% current smokers; many smokers had died of smoking-related diseases	Frequent admissions for disorders of circulatory and respiratory systems High smoking-related mortality	47% current smokers; 50% of smokers want help or advice about giving up Opportunistic advice is most popular method of health promotion	Smoking perceived as cause of ill-health but a necessary coping mechanism or just a habit. More young girls smoke. 30% of local shop's turnover was for cigarettes

Table 6.3 Estimated prevalences measured by different methods

	Assessment method		
	Routine statistics (%)	Postal survey (%)	Practice data (%)
Arthritis		31	12
Stomach problems		20	12
Stress or depression		18	12
Asthma or chronic bronchitis		14	7
Hypertension		13	3
Heart disease or angina		10	4
Upper respiratory tract infection in past 6 months		46	20
Limiting long-term illness	20	22	17
Repeat prescriptions		46	27
House ownership	20	34	
Car ownership	15	25	
Household with telephone		81	67

heart problem or angina was over twice the number recorded by the doctor. The conclusion of the survey was that participatory appraisal was the only method to cause change during the data collection. The authors give as an example alterations to the local bus route to run into the council estate, with a 30% increase in passengers. The district council housing department provided fenced-off playgrounds, and a company intends to construct a local supermarket. Otherwise, the four methods appeared to be good for different things. The authors suggest this and that the following model is useful:

- Start with practice-based knowledge and experience of working in the local community.
- A public health physician joins the assessment team to draw up a practice profile including mortality, morbidity and demographic data.
- Conduct a rapid participatory appraisal to identify broad areas of perceived health need.
- Conduct a survey to clarify specific issues.
- Help to implement and review the changes.

They conclude that for a general practitioner realistically to be involved in commissioning, he or she will need protected time. The authors suggest that combining public health and general practice skills by getting a public health-trained person involved in the practice is a valuable start.

GENERAL CHANGES IN APPROACH IN GENERAL PRACTICE

Movement of services into the community and primary care

Countries with more highly developed systems of primary care tend to have lower health care costs [95]. Attempting to shift the balance from secondary to primary care has therefore been a popular catchphrase in developed countries. This has not been simply a cost-cutting exercise. Primary care is said to be 'first-contact, continuous, comprehensive, and coordinated care provided to populations undifferentiated by gender, disease or organ system'. In that case, a health service dominated by secondary, tertiary and emergency care will tend to be fragmented, discontinuous, uncoordinated and costly.

Out-of-hours working

Few issues have aroused as much fervour among general practitioners as their commitment to provide a 24 hour service for their patients. There has been a growing clamour, particularly among newer recruits, to opt out of it. To help with this problem, they have launched a network of emergency treatment centres.

Researchers have looked at such approaches in Greater Glasgow and Lothian. In Greater Glasgow, the great majority of general practitioners have signed up to use six centres, scattered throughout the city, which close at midnight. General practitioners staff the centres on a rota basis, as well as with specially recruited nursing and reception staff. Early indications are that one-third of patients still need home visits and two-thirds come to the centres. Preliminary findings from the evaluation of a similar general practitioner out-of-hours centre, piloted by Lothian Health Board, show that a local children's hospital has reported fewer accident and emergency admissions from the local area since the centre opened. There has also been a dramatic fall in general practitioner home visits.

Another study [96] showed that there was a great variation, between one-tenth and one-half of the calls, in the acceptability of the centres to patients. The attendance rate dropped with increasing age. Overall, 4 people out of 10 said that they did not have transport, and one-third said that they were too ill to attend. There appeared to be no difference between those who agreed or did not agree to attend. This was measured according to whether they received a prescription or attended hospital as a result of the call. The authors conclude that the organization needs to do a great deal of selling of the idea to people before the centres will cover a high proportion of patients.

Problems of paying general practitioner fundholders

I have mentioned that general practitioners originally received budgets that were set according to the work that they had done in the 2 years before their application for fundholding status. This often involved one of the partners, usually the one who was most keen on fundholding, going through the patients' notes. His or her task was to find out who had been seen at the relevant outpatients and who treated in hospital for nonemergency care.

The money for the general practitioner fundholders is taken from the allocation to health authorities for secondary care. This consists of a specified set of elective inpatient and day case procedures and community services [97]. In future, the money given to fundholders is likely to be based on a formula based on the number of patients in a practice. It is likely to be similar to the way in which the money is currently allocated to the health authorities [98]. There has been recent new guidance from the Department of Health suggesting a compromise between the two systems [99]. Some of the historical usage data can be used in conjunction with a capitation formula to reduce the impact of a sudden change from one system to the other.

People have tried to use routine data to make up a sensible capitation formula [100]. In the quoted study, the authors developed what they described as a statistically robust, theoretically sound and intuitively appealing model for the acute activity [101]. Despite this, they could not come up with a sensible model for the effect of health and socioeconomic indicators on what fundholders buy for their patients.

RELATIONSHIP BETWEEN GENERAL PRACTITIONERS AND HEALTH AUTHORITIES

Assistance of general practitioners by health authorities

Commissioning services by general practitioners, both fundholding and non-fundholding, is likely to develop in three tiers. The first of these will be for regional services. The rarity and expense of these services means that a small number of extra cases could completely upset the budgeting of a group of general practitioners. Indeed, they are known as regional services because their small numbers and high cost meant a great difference in the numbers of these patients year after year. This meant that they were capable of destabilizing the budget of the health authorities with populations of about half a million. This effect will be even greater on a group of fundholding general practitioners covering a population of about one-tenth of that.

There are a number of conditions that fall into these categories, for example people who need renal and cardiac transplantation, those mentally ill people who need regional secure accommodation and children with rare genetic disorders. The population base for such services in the past has generally been about two million people, although this will, of course, vary with the condition. Even the health authorities with about a million in population may be too small for purchasing such services. Most of the commissioning will therefore need to be led by the health authorities or even by consortia of several authorities.

The second group of services are those which total fundholder general practices currently manage. These are the day-to-day emergency services that are usually needed at short notice, often without the general practitioner seeing the patient. Examples of such patients are those admitted to accident and emergency departments and those with emergency surgical or medical conditions, such as appendicitis or a heart attack. Some general practitioners will wish to buy these services directly, as total fundholding practices. Total fundholding practices work with populations of about 50,000 people, so this will help to smooth out the year-on-year variations in numbers. However, quite common diseases, such as fractured neck of femur, occurring in about 0.1% of the population each year, will still be quite rare for such practices with only 50 a year. This number is likely to vary from year to year between 35 and 65, the normal statistical variation, without external influences, such as a long spell of icy weather, having an effect.

The health authority may work with non-fundholding general practitioners by grouping together general practitioners in similarly sized geographical areas, sometimes known as localities or, in London, zones. This allows the general practitioners to have a say in what goes into the contracts and gives the health authority an opportunity to point out the national policy implications of contracts. They will also wish to develop long-term strategies for different parts of the health service with the general practitioners in this type of forum.

General practitioners are likely to lead the third type of commissioning. Once indicative budgets for each practice have been set up and tried for a few years, they may be left to do this type of purchasing for themselves, even in non-fundholding practices. In the case of fundholding general practitioners, this rests entirely with the general practitioners at present. The sort of services purchased this way include those for patients who require non-emergency surgery or medicine. These are often services that have waiting lists, and part of the aim of the purchasers will be to try to reduce these lists as far as possible. The population base for such work will be as low as 5000 people. Smaller practices are already allowed to be fundholders, especially 'mini-fundholders', who can purchase community-based services, their drugs budget and staff costs with a population of only 3000 people.

There is increasing pressure by fundholding general practitioners to have a seat on the board of health authorities, and it will be interesting to see how this progresses. Non-fundholding general practitioners will have to be closely involved in commissioning in future. It seems unlikely that fundholders will be represented without non-fundholders.

Not all general practitioners want to be fundholders

The reasons why general practitioners have chosen to become fundholders have been the subject of detailed research [102, 103], but people seem to have paid less attention to the reasons why general practitioners have chosen *not* to apply for fundholding. One study conducted interviews to find out why some general practitioners and practice managers had decided against applying for fundholding. The practices varied greatly in many ways, including the extent of fundholding already going on in their area.

General practitioners and practice managers most often objected to fundholding on philosophical grounds and gave this as the reason why their practice had not applied for fundholding. Twenty-four general practitioners stated clear or strong objections. More detailed reasons included a dislike of producing a two-tier system. There was also unhappiness about general practitioners' greater responsibility and the feeling that this would lead to their having to ration care. The second most commonly given reason for not applying was an objection to the extra workload and time needed. Several reported satisfaction with the way that their authority purchased services for them and saw no reason to change it. The region involved had developed several different models of practice-sensitive purchasing as alternatives to fundholding [104].

The opposition of these general practitioners is not, however, necessarily an obstacle to the recruitment of new practices. Almost half of the general practitioners said that if other practices locally became fundholders, they would have to apply. Another third said that such developments would possibly lead them to apply for fundholding. These findings suggest that peer pressure and pragmatism are strong among general practitioners and are likely to be important determinants of how fundholding develops.

LOCAL WORKING AS A MEANS OF COORDINATING HEALTH AUTHORITIES AND GENERAL PRACTITIONERS

I have mentioned that, in some areas, health authorities have given general practitioners notional budgets to work with, even though they are not fundholders. A notional budget consists of the funds for which the practice would be responsible if the health authority purchasing budget was divided between all the practices in the authority area. One health authority calculates the budget using a formula that weights the allocation according to the regional referral patterns, increased or decreased according to the local authority standardized mortality ratio (SMR). The budget includes most, but not all, of the acute services purchased by the health authority.

The main purpose of the scheme is to increase general practitioners' involvement in purchasing health care. The health authority mentioned designed a notional budget to allow practices to compare their rate of referrals with their colleagues and for them to see the financial effect of the referrals. The general practitioners can use these data with the drugs usage data they already receive. I anticipate that general practitioners will eventually take the lead in all purchasing, and this scheme is seen as a useful introduction. Where there are savings on the total budget, the practice qualifies for a reward from the fund created by the health authority.

The basis of the scheme is a set of five reports giving information about the notional budget and the practice activity, especially their referrals to hospital in-and outpatients. The reports are a series of graphs that illustrate the budget performance of the practice, comparisons with other practices and the practice patterns of activity compared with others. Someone from the authority discusses with each practice how useful might be other, more detailed data, held within the computer monitoring system. To make the data in the report as understandable as possible, the authority has included the same data for the fundholding practices and has given a combined analysis of all the practices in the area.

The notional budget-holding scheme follows the established and successful prescribing incentive scheme. The scheme works at two levels. The first level is almost a direct copy of the prescribing scheme. The health authority allocates a notional budget to the practice for the year. There is also a target for reduction in the total amount spent. If general practitioners hit this target at the end of the financial year, the practice qualifies for a reward. This reward will be based on the amount of cash that can be recovered from the contracts already agreed with provider trusts. The general practitioners can spend the reward on equipment or services that will benefit patients directly.

At the second level, the authority can free up a greater proportion of its budget if changes can be identified before contracts are agreed. The general practitioners have to identify important changes to contracts up to 12 months before these are included in the authority's purchasing intentions. Practices agree the changes they would like to see and discuss with the authority how to do this. To fit in with the contracting process, the general practitioners write these changes up in a practice health plan for inclusion in the authority's purchasing intentions. The authority then incorporates these changes in contracts with providers.

Health authority support

The health authority recognizes that this scheme will be completely new to some practices. It also requires a different way of thinking about how clinical practice is linked to making the best use of resources, so practices will obviously need to be supported. This approach contrasts starkly with the process faced by the early fundholding general practitioners. They had to learn the process of purchasing with no help and sometimes some hindrance from the health authorities.

Liaison general practitioners

In each borough, the authority has identified one or more liaison general practitioners to work with practices and the local health planning teams. Their role is one of explanation and encouragement to help all practices to make use of the information the scheme provides. They will represent general practitioner interests in wider discussions with other agencies, such as social services, and help to set up and run local general practitioner-led purchasing teams.

General practitioner development unit

The general practitioner development unit has responsibility for the success of the scheme and monitors its running. The unit helps practices to understand the clinical aspects of changing referral patterns. They identify and discuss areas of interest or concern and discuss how the authority might assist general practitioners. The unit uses annual and other regular practice visits to talk to doctors. The unit is responsible for setting and agreeing the targets and keeps an eye on how savings are used. This is similar to the fundholding scheme.

Practice reports

The notional budget-holder schemes produce practice reports, which include details of the budget used compared with the target budget and how the practice got on compared with the other practices in the area. It also tells each practice about their activity levels for inpatients and outpatients compared with others. Figure 6.3 shows the comparative activity for one practice, the average for the locality and the health authority. The practice can choose to use other comparative data. The authority gives further information about exceptional or low usage of a particular service. If the practice purchases more than or less than 5% of the average for the local authority area that contains

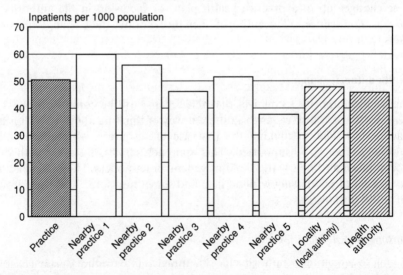

Figure 6.3 Data given to practices in notional budget-holder scheme – inpatients.

the practice, this is reported and can be commented on. The last section of the report contains data about the providers that the practice used during the year.

THE FUTURE FOR GENERAL PRACTITIONER PURCHASING

At the time that I am writing, the Labour parliamentary opposition say that they will abolish fundholding when they get into power, although it seems unlikely that a Labour government would reverse the move to give primary care the main say in what goes on in the health service. General practice, with its close contact with the general population, might be thought to be more natural allies of a socialist party than are hospital consultants.

Despite being given a great deal of potential power within the health service over the past 5 years, general practitioners are not happy. This shows itself most obviously in the extreme difficulties general practice trainers have had in recruiting trainees. There is also a growing tendency for many young doctors to work, in effect, as salaried practitioners by working full time for locum agencies. In this way, practitioners appear to be opting for a life where they can work with patients within hours that they control. This also means that they do not have to take on the burdens of managing the service, or at least their part of it, as well.

There have been marked changes in the way in which general practitioners provide out-of-hours care in a number of places; I have mentioned some of these schemes above. This trend is becoming the norm in one form or another throughout the country. Part of the discontent that general practitioners feel has even led some to advocate that the service should become a salaried service, with practice lists being discontinued. A contracts manager would have the task of finding a service provider, be it an NHS general practitioner or a privately paid one. Patients would register with the management system rather than the general practitioner.

It may within this scenario, be that community or hospital trusts will provide the managers and will hire general practitioners to do, initially, out-of-hours work. This may evolve into a primary care service provision, general practitioners being tempted by a steady salary with defined hours and conditions of work. They will also be able to give up their management duties to the management of the trust or their own managers, if in a total fundholding consortium. The managers may become the employers within the practice instead of the employees.

Conclusion

Talking to large numbers of general practitioners one reaches the conclusion that some of them relish needs assessment, service specification and setting contracts. The majority simply wish to treat patients, one to one. Even the carrot of being able to cash in one's stake in a new surgery at retirement is not enough inducement for many to take on the job of the modern general practitioner. This entails purchasing, or at least having a hand in, the purchasing of, services for 50 000 people. At the same time, they have to try to balance a complex budget and be responsible for deciding which new developments should be supported in the local hospitals. They simultaneously have 24-hour-a-day, 7-days-a-week responsibility for about 1500 patients.

If total fundholding continues to enlarge and eventually becomes the norm, its management will also develop. This may be as groups of such managers coming together in an *ad hoc* way or becoming part of an existing private network. Some American-owned companies might wish to be involved in this management. I have mentioned above the option for general practitioners to decide to be managed by the trusts, especially the community trusts who are used to dealing with community nurses and health visitors. This has begun to happen in a small way [105].

Whatever occurs, the resulting organization will begin to look something like the health maintenance organizations (HMOs) in the USA. These guarantee a core package of care, both primary care and acute care, for a set premium. In the UK, the premium may be set by the government as a limit on the cash available rather than a stated amount for each person in the HMO. One of the least-noticed effects of general practitioner fundholding has been that primary care has now, for the first time, been given a fixed budget rather than an open-ended one. There is a danger that, by handing over the management of the service to professional managers or a special cadre of general practitioners who wish to become full-time managers, primary care will lose its present ascendancy. General practitioners may give up their new birthright to lead purchasing for a good night's sleep.

The general practice fundholding scheme is the most comprehensive attempt to date to shift the balance of power, and hence to shift resources, to primary care in the UK. Some fundholders have made savings in their hospital budgets, but their rates of outpatient referral and hospital admissions are as high as those of their non-fundholding colleagues and are still rising [106,107]. The investment by fundholders in new practice-based services has not reduced the demand for specialist care. It is too early to say whether the fundholding experiment is effective. It may be, in some years time, that it was the spur for further changes.

Whatever happens, primary care is unlikely ever to be the same again. Despite the promises of more influence and power, young doctors are less happy about going into general practice than ever before [108]. This lack of enthusiasm for the subject has increased more in men than in women and despite considerably more exposure of medical students to general practice as an academic discipline during their training.

Providers: the first job – planning

7

PROVIDERS

The term 'provider' covers a wide variety of different services in the health service. The providers may be hospital trusts, community health services, integrated hospital and community health service trusts, mental health service trusts or combined community and mental health services trusts. In addition, there are specialist units or hospitals, such as ambulance trusts, dental hospital trusts and specialist cancer trusts. Besides these NHS-based trusts, there are private hospitals and some private community nursing services. General practice is a special case in which general practitioners and their primary care teams provide a wide range of services. Voluntary organizations are also providers.

The main aim of all of all of these providers except for the general practice-based ones is to win contracts to provide their services. These groups measure their success by their ability to retain and obtain new contracts. There are a number of things which contracts contain and which will cause them to be, or not be, successful:

- Quality
- Price
- Whether it is a local provider
- Serving a niche market
- A high demand for the services offered.

Quality

Success depends on the quality of the service being high. Most health service providers will claim high quality, and it will be necessary for a provider to give evidence of this. One way is to try to obtain a British Standard for the service, or some other nationally recognized accolade. The provider may have developed special quality standards, externally validated. People believe that quality and costs have to be balanced against one another. If this were entirely true for consumer goods, the Consumers Association would not sell *Which?* to a quarter of a million people monthly.

My impression is that this lack of balance between quality and cost is exaggerated for health services. Where I have been involved with competitive tendering for clinical services, the cheapest service has, almost without exception, been the most innovative and able to provide the best quality. This has had something to do with the provider defining from scratch what the service does for patients and working out the simplest way of doing it. This contrasts with the traditional method of assuming that a service requires to be given in the way it always has been. An excellent example has been a rheumatology service in a local health authority. Here, assumptions that the service needed a central hospital base, needed consultants to do the majority of the work and needed to maintain a long waiting list were all overturned.

Price

The contract is likely to be successful if the price is average or low average. If it is too low, no-one will believe it, as the fixed costs for most providers are likely to be similar. The service may have special characteristics, such as using nurses to perform a function normally carried out by doctors. An example may be the use of psychiatric nurses instead of consultants to assess patients who have taken an overdose of drugs.

Local provider

One-third of the patients involved in a waiting list initiative in Cardiff refused to travel 10 miles to a nearby hospital for their operation. This may have been because they preferred to be treated at the University Hospital, with the kudos and suggested high quality that that name portrayed. It may have been the difficulty of travelling to another place for treatment, that the alternative hospital had a bad reputation, or that people just do not like to travel for their hospital care.

Serving a niche market

Some providers give a particular service that is difficult to obtain elsewhere. This may be a specific service provided by a dental hospital, or radiotherapy as part of a cancer service or, for example, magnetic resonance imaging (MRI) scanning. Some specialties such as paediatric pathology, are quite rare or difficult to obtain.

High demand for services

Some services, because of changes in demand and, often, the poor status of the specialty, have a low supply and high demand. A particular example of such a service is forensic psychiatry. People see the patients as unpleasant and dangerous. Hospitals often have to admit patients by order of the courts, so that purchasers cannot refuse to pay for them. They are also very costly. Facilities are insufficient for the demand, partly at least because of the poor development of the service, and partly because of an increased demand, fuelled by pressure to move people with mental illness out of gaol.

FUNCTIONS OF TRUSTS

Any organization that hopes to provide goods or services will, according to Henri Fayol in 1916 [109], have five main functions:

- Planning
- Organizing
- Command
- Coordination
- Control.

In planning, the leaders of the organization have to decide the objectives of the business and how they carry these out. Plans of some type or other are necessary, if only to decide what business the organization will follow and where it will be based. Generally, planning can be divided into three main parts: strategic, tactical and operational.

Strategic planning

- What business is the organization in, and not in?
- How will it be financed?
- What organizational structure will it have?
- What geographical area will it cover?

Tactical planning

- What products should the organization produce and how should they be altered?
- What investments need to be made for the future?
- What should the prices be?

Operational planning

- How should the trust be laid out, for example hospital or community services?

- What equipment is needed?
- How many people are needed, and with what skills?

BOARDS OF DIRECTORS

Ten things boards of directors of a trust should know; well, eight is enough surely?

1.   How to express what you value in the health service

Questions to be answered
What are your values? Is the effect of your trust on death rate and quality of life (outcomes) of greatest value to you? Is there always a trade-off between deaths and quality? The relative importance of keeping the balance sheet right and patient care. Do the economists have an answer? Where does patient choice fit? The interaction between the health needs of people and what they want.

How to answer them
Get the trust to measure these parameters. Describe the shortcomings and strengths of each for the trust.

2.   How to identify and understand the first 10 things you need to know about the patients in your trust

Questions to be answered

1. The population of the area covered by the trust.
2. The numbers and proportion of old people and young people.
3. The effects of the mix on health.
4. The overwhelming effect of poverty on morbidity and death rate. What about premature deaths or avoidable deaths: are they any better? The infant mortality ratio and what it means.
5. What are the differences between measures of quality of life: impairment, disability and handicap?
6. Are 'quality-adjusted life years' an answer, or are they too simplistic?
7. The difficulty of influencing remaining health margins by health services.
8. What are the main diseases?
9. What proportion of those diseases reach the services? What happens to the rest?
10. Which diseases are being effectively managed in terms that a patient would understand?

How to answer them
Take examples given from different trusts or health authorities. Given data on these parameters, have them displayed and explore their meaning. Look at

data on poverty, time and place and their overwhelming influence compared with the health service.

3. How to be illuminated rather than dazzled by data

Questions to be answered

What do you want to know about the organization? What are the inputs, processes and outputs in the organization? Where are the raw data collected, and by whom? What is their training? Is what you get now relevant to those questions? Are financial data integrated into the information service or set up differently? Is data collection cost-effective? Who needs the data, and who uses them? How do you know?

How to answer them

Set up a method for collecting data you need to know and no more. Go through the data given to you by your organization and work out which of these made a difference to the last five times you made a decision. Develop a scoring system for deciding the value of data at any one time.

4. How to identify, fight and interpret jargon

Questions to be answered

Why do people use jargon? Who in your organization uses most? Is it important to feed back the jargon produced by government departments? Does it make them feel good? Does it make your documents more acceptable to that department?

How to answer them

Use a clarity index. Test some government and trust documents using the index. Compare with novels and newspapers. Calculate the number of times a noun is 'verbed'.

5. How to reduce the cost of quality

Questions to be Answered

How much do you pay for quality in each part of the organization? When is quality too high? What methods can be used to reduce costs while maintaining or improving quality? Does 'making quality everyone's business' work? Who should be and who are the final arbiters of quality in your organization?

How to answer them

Examination of the *Which*? philosophy. Test a particular service or set of services by suggesting seven ways of giving the same service more cheaply:

- Substitution of people
- Substitution of place
- Substitution of organization
- Substitution of time: earlier or later
- Substitution of method
- Ignore the problem
- Delay answering the problem.

6. How to win when dealing with health professionals on their ground

Questions to be answered
What do professionals uniquely provide? Why? Who certifies them? Which part of their job is performed solely by them? What other tasks should professionals perform which they do not at present?

How to answer them
Examine a service that is highly professionalized. Examine where their contribution is essential and where it is not. Suggest alternative approaches. Suggest other areas where professional expertise would be useful because the professional is already present, for example counselling or identification of non-health problems. Suggest training to allow professionals to carry these out.

7. How to recognize the opportunities presented by policy changes

Questions to be answered
What is the reason for the policy change? What are the hidden agendas? What are the side-effects? How can these be used?

How to answer them
Look at a major policy shift, for example to community care. Describe the political, economic, social and industrial aspects, for example new discoveries being the reason for the development. Analyse these pressures by the time they are likely to continue. Suggest and test developments that fit into these changes. Describe the side-effects.

8. How to decide whether a new idea is marketable

Questions to be Answered
What are the new fields of research and development? Do they work? Do they have to be accepted for now because of political expediency? For how long? Is it an attractive subject? Does it fit in with the present social ethos?

How to answer them

Suggest a means of testing a number of new ideas. Decide the criteria for success and failure. Develop a likelihood test for each. Decide what limits can be changed to make it more or less acceptable. Decide.

INFORMATION FOR OPERATIONAL PLANNING

Using routine data: providing acute inpatient medical care for elderly people

Several specialties deliver acute hospital medical care of elderly people in the UK: general medicine, its sub-specialties and geriatrics. The proportion and type of elderly patients seen by these groups vary from place to place. All of them need to monitor the care that is given, to make sure that it is of good quality.

I examined all the patients admitted to geriatrics or general medicine locally during the year 1993/94. Figure 7.1 shows the number of people who were discharged from the wards during the year by the specialties. The trusts involved had an age-related policy for the care of elderly people, the figure clearly showing the effect of this. At the age of 75, there is a marked fall in the number of patients admitted to general medicine and a rise in the proportion admitted to geriatrics. Overall, there is a dip in the number of admissions at that age that is difficult to explain, but seems to relate to the age cut-off.

Figure 7.1 shows that geriatrics patients are more likely to die than those in general medicine from an early age, the difference increasing as patients get older. Many of these in geriatrics were readmissions with chronic disease who will have a high mortality. This theory is backed up by the fact that if only

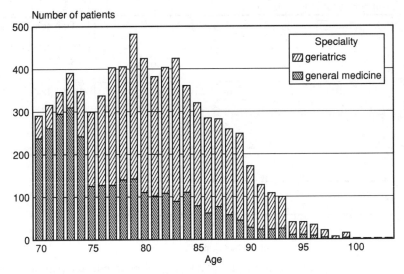

Figure 7.1 Admissions by age and speciality.

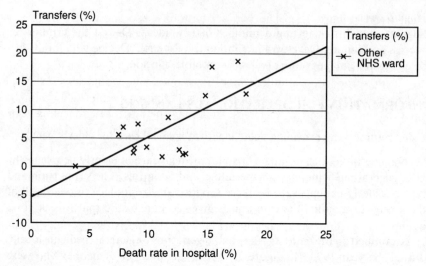

Figure 7.2   Relationship between death rate and transfer rate for patients – by general medical consultants.

emergency admissions are examined, the excess death rate for geriatrics increases. Non-emergency admissions would be likely to have a specific problem for which they were to be treated.

I looked in some detail at the way in which consultants in general medicine and geriatrics worked. Figure 7.2 shows that those general medical consultants whose patients had a higher death rate in hospital also tended to transfer more patients to other consultants. Geriatricians, on the other hand, showed no

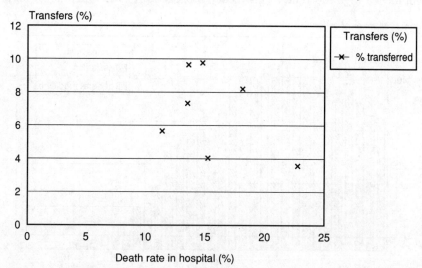

Figure 7.3   Relationship between death rate and transfer rate for patients – by geriatrics consultants.

such trend (Figure 7.3). The two scattergrams also show that there is a considerable difference between consultants in their hospital death rate.

I then looked at the number of times during the year that each specialty admitted patients. Interestingly, there was little difference between the specialties in the proportion admitted more than once: one would have expected geriatrics to have a higher readmission rate. Perhaps even more interestingly, the rate does not change much with age. I have held the view for many years that readmissions are not a particularly useful measure, except of the tendency of some illnesses to recur [110]: they are not a measure of poor therapy.

Lengths of stay were quite different between the specialties, with general medicine showing an average length of stay of about half of that in geriatrics. This presumably reflects the greater degree of severity of the patients admitted to geriatrics, which is not routinely measured. It also goes some way to explaining the difference in death rate between the specialties, as if people are discharged, they obviously cannot be counted as hospital deaths. The consistency of the difference, especially about the cross-over at 75 years, does make one wonder why, if the change at that time is largely administrative, the lengths of stay for those age groups are not closer than at earlier ages, when the difference in severity is more pronounced. It suggests that geriatrics may be less efficient than general medicine.

Figure 7.4 shows the number of days spent in hospital for each patient in geriatrics. The geriatrics data have a long tail, presumably those patients with multiple pathology and chronic disease, in which they specialize. The spikes at weekly intervals suggest that patients are being discharged at these intervals preferentially. It looks as if the consultants are holding on to patients until

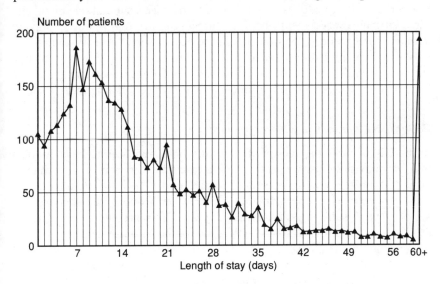

Figure 7.4 Length of stay for emergency admissions – geriatrics only.

their next admission day, a week later. These spikes are not due to planned readmissions because I have used data only on patients who were emergency admissions. It seems likely that some consultants are deliberately blocking beds for their next on-take day. If this is the case the trusts need to investigate it closely.

Provider data: differences from purchasing data

Trusts need to be more aware of what processes are likely to be effective than do health authorities and purchasing general practitioners. In theory, the trust is in a better position to tell whether the services it is providing are likely to be effective, based on national data, or whether the service is working well locally. The reason for this is that the trust will have a cadre of experts providing the service in question, who should be aware of new developments and critical analysis of the field. Oddly, this often seems not to be the case.

All departments and units have a history in the way they were set up and developed, which often seems to dominate the way the service continues. Virtually all departments work hard and are busy, but most are not keen to examine their results. There are many exceptions, but providers often seem not at all keen to look at their work objectively. It may be that the main effect of the internal market will be for providers to give their managers an objective view of the work that they are doing.

Using provider data for developing audit measures: fractured femur

Fractured neck of femur is a useful condition to use as a marker for others. First, virtually every patient with a fracture is admitted to hospital, so that the number closely reflects the numbers in the population. This is in contrast to most of the common diseases that bring people into hospital. For these, a large and unknown proportion of the patients either do not notice that they have had an attack, or general practitioners treat a proportion at home.

Background to proximal femoral fractures

In the UK in 1980, the age-specific fracture rates were seen to have doubled over the previous 25 years [111]. The increase was greater in women than in men, and by 90 years of age 32% of women and 17% of men had sustained such a fracture. Thus approximately 113000 women and 34000 men over the age of 50 years suffer a hip fracture each year. This represents a cost of about £500 million annually. A change in the cause of these fractures must have been responsible for the increase. Since the 1980s, age-specific rates have levelled off [112], but the increasing number of very elderly people suggests that the number with fractures will continue to rise.

There are three known variables that appear to cause fractures of the neck of the femur in elderly people, but which of these is responsible for the changes in incidence is not clear.

They are:

- The subjects' neuromuscular state, for example their balance, muscle tone and reaction to toppling, which lead to falls
- The fragility of their bones
- The nature of the environment in which elderly people live.

Falls
Falls in elderly people are very common and increase proportionally with age [113]. The single most important cause is accidental tripping, which occurs more commonly in the younger elderly, probably because they are the most active [114]. Drugs, particularly night sedation, are probably a cause of falls [115]. Muscular weakness and the loss of neuromuscular response with increasing physical or mental frailty can be important in people resident in old people's homes and those who are housebound. Many people have published data to show that frequent falls are important, even when they do not result in fractures [116]. They cause many elderly people to remain housebound rather than expose themselves to falling and can therefore have a major effect upon mobility and confidence [117].

Fragility of bone
Another possible cause of the number of fractures in elderly people is the decrease in quantity and quality of bone. Patients with a fracture of the femoral neck have a reduced bone density compared with matched elderly people without fractures [118]. Loss of bone with ageing appears to be the norm in Western industrialized countries. Poor calcium or vitamin D intake also affects the quality of bone structure [119,120]. Some factors other than diet, for example smoking and lack of exercise, also increase the fragility of bone [121].

Environment
Old people, compared with younger, are more exposed to poor housing. Trailing wires, loose rugs, outside lavatories and poor lighting are more common in households for this age group than for the rest of the community. In addition, they are less able to perform routine improvements and maintenance to their houses than are younger people. A randomized controlled trial aimed at reducing the impact of these environmental problems on people, using a health visitor, was set up. It was unsuccessful at reducing the number of fractures that occurred, although it did reduce mortality in the intervention group [122].

Strategies for improvement

Prevention

A recent review has described several strategies for reducing the number of people with fracture of the proximal femur [123]. These could help to reduce the loss of bone density that underlies hip fracture. Of these, evidence suggests that physical activity is the most important and it is a method of prevention that can be both enjoyable and sociable. Regular exercise, in theory, would reduce the risk of hip fracture by at least half. This comes to 30 000 cases of hip fracture each year in the UK. Stopping smoking is also important. A woman who stops smoking before the menopause will reduce her risk by about one-quarter.

Postmenopausal oestrogen replacement, sometimes called hormone replacement therapy, appears to halve the risk of hip fracture, but the people lose this protection within a few years of stopping treatment, so this limits its use. People need to continue oestrogen replacement almost indefinitely if it is to do more than reduce the incidence of hip fracture in younger age groups, in whom hip fracture is uncommon and recovery generally uncomplicated.

Treatment

The death rate following treatment for fractured neck of femur varies from 10% to 40%. People have worked out possible treatment options by trying to predict which patients are likely to die. Ions [124] indicated that people who had dementia and were of advanced age were likely to have a poor outcome. They used a simple 10 question test and showed that patients who scored low were generally unfit for operation and rehabilitation. The consultants therefore treated them without operation.

In another study, the most dangerous conditions for people with these fractures were again, dementia, postoperative chest infection, neoplasia, age and wound infection. Three-quarters of demented patients over the age of 85 years were dead within 6 months, compared with 20% for similar patients over 75 years of age. However, for those under 75 years the death rate was only 7% [125].

Management of patients

Preoperative

Initially, people thought that delaying surgery for more than a day or so would have a bad effect on patients with femoral neck fractures. This may not always be the case, at least for high fractures. It is certainly helps patients who need it to spend a short time improving their general medical condition to make them as fit as possible before surgery. In those patients in whom this medical treatment is necessary, the operation becomes one of semi-election rather than a true emergency.

Nonetheless, the aim should be for the majority of patients to have surgery within 24 hours of their fall. The medical management for the remaining patients should be performed quickly. In a survey by Gilchrist [126] nearly 8 out of 10 patients received surgery within the first 24 hours after the fall without complications. Sikorsi has published even more impressive figures [127].

Postoperative

Current practice is for therapists to mobilize patients out of bed within a day or so of the operation. However long it takes patients to be mobilized is of no consequence; what really matters is that the patients are up and mobile.

Rehabilitation

There is increasing evidence that home-based rehabilitation has many advantages for these patients. One of the most successful hospital-at-home schemes in the country has a team that concentrates on the care of people with fractured neck of femur [128]. This is likely to be the most successful approach for the future. Knowledge of the mobility of patients before they fracture their femurs is essential, and careful monitoring of the mobility of patients is also essential to decide when the optimum result has been achieved. Work on the function of day hospitals suggests that much of the rehabilitation effort can be wasted on trying to attain the impossible [129].

Late consequences

About 5% of people who fracture one neck of femur fracture the other. A number of ideas, including wearing hip protectors, have been suggested for such people to reduce the rate of fracture of the other hip [130].

Routine provider data

We can use routine data to examine the effectiveness of the trust at treating these patients and to monitor their auditing. Figure 7.5 shows patients treated for fractured femur and the number who died under the care of different consultants over 3 years. We must take these trends with caution, especially as a number of consultants had not been working for all the time. Nevertheless, consultants who show a trend tend to show an increase in the proportion of patients who died under their care over the 3 years. During the same period, the proportion of patients not operated on after emergency admission has

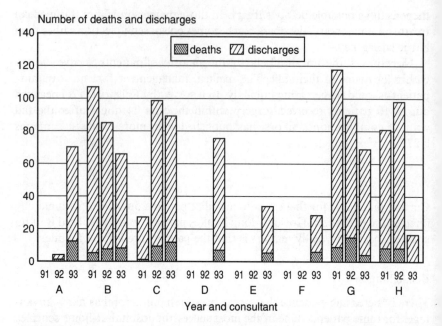

Figure 7.5 Deaths by consultant. Fractured neck of femur – emergencies, 1991/2–1993/94.

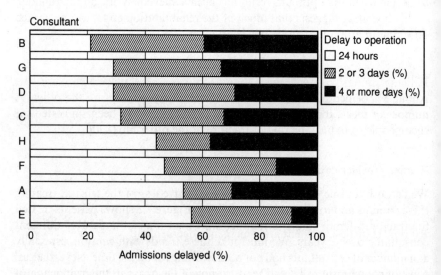

Figure 7.6 Delayed operations. Fractured neck of femur – emergencies only, 1993/94.

decreased from 18% to 8%. It may be that the higher mortality is due to an increased tendency to operate on high-risk patients when they would have been better left alone.

Figure 7.6 shows data on delays between admission and operation by the different consultant firms. There is a marked difference between consultants in the amount of delay their patients experience, and the present delay between admission and operation is not acceptable. On speaking to the people involved about why this is so, there is a tendency for anaesthetists to blame surgeons and surgeons to blame anaesthetists for the delay. The following guidelines attempt to bring together the data presented so far. Preventive services will need to be developed for others.

SUGGESTED AUDIT STANDARDS FOR CARE

Inpatient care

Patients, from their earliest contact with services, including the ambulance service, will be kept as free from pain as is possible. Transporting patients must be kept to a minimum to reduce mobilizing the fracture, and to restrict blood loss from the site and further displacement of the fracture. Where complex medical factors are present, advice should be taken with the minimum of transfer of patients. This should not involve transfer from one hospital to another. Any triage should occur in the accident and emergency department.

Problem 1

Pressure sores as a result of lying on a hard trolley in accident and emergency.

Guideline
Patients should wait no longer than 1 hour before standard pressure sore preventative measures are instituted.

Standard
100%.

Exceptions
None.

Monitoring
Routine statistics: accident and emergency department:

Compliance
Lack of compliance will result in discussion of the case with internal management. Three cases will be discussed by the trust multidisciplinary audit committee. Five cases will result in financial penalties from the purchaser.

Problem 2

Poor management of the case, especially analgesia and immobilization of the fracture owing to a delay in accident and emergency.

Guideline
The patient will be cared for in an acute inpatient ward within 2 hours of admission

Standard
100%.

Exceptions
None.

Monitoring
Routine accident and emergency statistics.

Compliance
Lack of compliance will result in discussion of the case with internal management. Three cases will be discussed by trust multidisciplinary audit committee, and five cases will result in financial penalties from the purchaser.

Problem 3

A delay in operating, causing excessive pain, fluid loss and immobility to the patient, the increased length of stay also increasing the cost to purchaser.

Guideline
Primary fixation within 24 hours of admission to the accident and emergency department.

Standard
100%.

Monitoring
Routine inpatient data.

Exceptions
Those in poor physical condition. Criteria are by routine monitoring of all patients admitted but not operated upon within 24 hours by the consultant in charge or the senior registrar. Quality of these data are to be monitored as part of internal audit, and is not expected to be more than 20% of total.

Compliance
Lack of compliance will result in discussion of the case with internal management. Three cases to be discussed by trust multidisciplinary audit committee, and five cases are to result in financial penalties from purchaser.

Problem 4

Rehabilitation of patients.

Guideline
Patients with poor prognosis due to immobility before admission or a poor state on admission assessment are to be given special attention.

Monitoring
A review and suggestions for improved methods of rehabilitation for such people are to be put to the providers as a report.

Problem 5

The need for an overview of the effectiveness of the service.

Guideline
The measurement of Barthel and AMT scores on patients on admission, an estimate of preadmission state, and on discharge and at the end of rehabilitation phase or at 6 weeks, whichever is the earlier.

Standard
100%.

Monitoring
Availability of the scores to purchasers.

Exceptions
Deaths as an inpatient.

Compliance
Lack of compliance is to result in discussion of the case with internal management. Ten cases will be discussed by the trust multidisciplinary audit committee. Twenty cases will result in financial penalties from the purchaser.

Conclusions

Hip fracture is an important cause of morbidity and contributes considerably to the cost of health care. Several strategies could help to reduce the loss of bone density that underlies hip fracture. Among these it is suggested that physical activity is the most important, and it is a method of prevention that can be enjoyable and sociable. Stopping smoking is also important, a woman who stops smoking before the menopause reducing her risk by about one-quarter. These policies can be adopted by both sexes and continued into old age.

The everyday care of frail patients with acute fractures of the femur needs to be overseen by a consultant with general expertise in medicine. I consider it preferable that that person should be an 'orthopaedic physician', within the orthopaedics department and with contacts with medicine than for the development of a separate unit. Their position as consultants means that orthopaedic surgeons should have at least a joint responsibility for patients who come into their care.

The present acute treatment and rehabilitation of fractured neck of femur in the health authority need to be considerably improved. Rehabilitation, just now, revolves around inpatient care and day hospitals. I believe that home rehabilitation therapies need to be extended for this group.

8

Providing: the second job – balancing the budget

RULES OF COSTING AND PRICING IN THE NHS

There are three rules of pricing the services that trusts provide:

- Price must equal cost.
- Cost must equal the total cost.
- There must be no cross-subsidization between activities.

Trusts may, if they have satisfied the demands of their main purchasers and have spare capacity, sell their services at marginal cost, i.e. without taking account of fixed and semi-fixed costs.

TYPES OF COST

Figure 8.1 shows the three types of cost that trusts must meet as they vary the amount of work they do. Fixed costs are those which remain, such as the cost of buildings, no matter how many patients are treated. Semi-fixed are those which change only when a certain proportion of the patients increases or reduces in number, such as because of the closure or opening of a new ward. Variable costs alter directly with the number of patients seen, such as dressings and treatment costs. Staff costs are often semi-fixed in the health service because many of the professionals have medium-or long-term contracts of employment. Whenever I am involved in trying to alter the way a service is working, especially moving patients from one hospital to another, the trusts try to suggest that about 90% of their costs are fixed. This is one of the main blocks to changing services for the better.

Three cardinal rules

All provider trusts within the NHS have three basic rules:

- To break even
- To give a 6% rate of return
- To meet their external financing limit (EFL) for their capital expenditure, their borrowing limits.

Most trusts rely heavily upon a single health authority for purchasing most of its services – often about 80% – with general practitioner fundholders forming the next most important group at 10–15%. Other purchasers and extracontractual referrals form the remainder. The proportion of funding from their general practitioner fundholders is likely to increase as more total fundholders come into being. At present, it seems unlikely that this will be more than half of the budget in the future.

Besides the basic rules the financial arrangements for provider trusts are that:

- they receive no direct funding from the Department of Health and must earn all their income from contracts
- they can borrow funds, within annually approved limits, for purposes such as acquiring or replacing assets

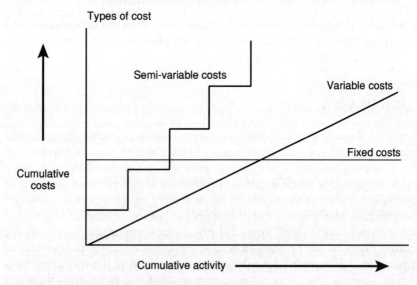

Figure 8.1 How costs alter with increasing activity.

- They usually retain depreciation and any surpluses after meeting financial obligations and can use this money to repay loans, to invest or to spend on capital projects
- Their accounts are commercial in style, following Companies Acts requirements where appropriate.

Contracts

Trusts earn the greatest part of their revenue from contracts to provide health services. They make these contracts with the health authorities, general practitioner fundholders and, where applicable, private patients. They also obtain a small amount of money from extra contractual referrals for occasional cases where the patient belongs to an area that does not have a contract with the trust. These may be patients travelling some distance or taking advantage of a special service provided by the trust. Some money is also given for supporting medical and dental education and research, for education and training of other health care professionals and from income-generating activities.

The rules do not allow trusts to cross-subsidize services between different contracts. Trusts must only use marginal costing when they have unplanned spare capacity arising during the year. Trusts should not plan to achieve more than 6% rate of return on their assets when contracting with the NHS. The reason for this is that such an increased rate would take the money out of the system for the current year. This would in turn reduce the amount of patient care purchased by health authorities. Trusts working with the private sector are not subject to this restriction, and services can be priced at a level that the market will bear. There must be a minimum of 6% return on assets, but if a higher return than 6% is made, this can be used to reduce the prices charged to NHS purchasers.

Assets and capital debt

Each trust owns its assets: land, buildings and equipment. The value of the net assets (assets less liabilities) is transferred to a trust when it is set up. This amount is matched by a capital debt that is owed to the Department of Health. There are two parts to the capital debt:

- The interest-bearing debt, which has defined interest and repayment terms
- The public dividend capital, which is a form of long-term government finance on which the trust pays dividends to the Government.

The dividend capital has no fixed repayment period, but in the long run the return on it is expected to be no less than a loan for the same amount. Trusts need not pay dividends annually, only when the unit makes a surplus after meeting its fixed interest obligations. The Secretary of State sets the balance between these two for each trust.

Trust assets are valued as:

- Land and buildings held for operational use are valued by the district valuer at their open market price for their existing use. If land and buildings become surplus to requirements, they are valued at their open market value for alternative use.
- Other tangible fixed assets, for example medical equipment or furniture, are valued at their current cost.
- Intangible assets, such as intellectual property, are valued individually.
- Current assets, for example stocks and debtors, are valued according to normal accountancy principles.

There are two sources of finance to enable a trust to maintain and expand its facilities and to obtain working capital:

- Funds generated by the trust itself from depreciation and retained surpluses, or from sales of land, buildings and equipment
- External borrowing from either the Secretary of State or the private sector.

External borrowing

Trusts are able to borrow from the Secretary of State or commercial sources. Trusts, as all parts of the public sector, have to show they are getting good value for money from their borrowing, whether from the public or the private sector. Borrowing must therefore be on the best terms available. The Secretary of State can guarantee a trust's loan from the private sector, which reduces borrowing costs. In seeking such a guarantee, the trust has to demonstrate advantages over borrowing from the Secretary of State.

Unguaranteed borrowing from the private sector is likely to be more expensive than borrowing from the Secretary of State or guaranteed commercial borrowing. Trusts may borrow on an unguaranteed basis only if they show that it is cheaper than other forms of borrowing. A trust has to demonstrate its ability to pay interest on, and repay, loans. These rules cover borrowing money under the Private Finance Initiative (PFI), which has recently been strongly backed by the government.

It initially seemed that the government were not at all keen for trusts to borrow money privately. They seemed, with their comments about borrowing from the Secretary of State always being cheaper, to be encouraging trusts only to borrow publicly. Recently, the government has cut the amount of available money for capital and requires trusts to look at the possibility of private finance before the Secretary of State will consider funding capital schemes. Curiously the private finance initiative seems to involve, if it were possible, even more government checks and balances than does borrowing from the Department itself.

The Private Finance Initiative

The government in the 1995 autumn statement reduced markedly (by 17%) its capital financing and put this into the revenue allocation. Its view is that the trusts should make this up by going to private companies to finance new large projects. This Private Finance Initiative (PFI) is carefully monitored at all stages by the Department of Health. A trust that wants to borrow money to build a new hospital or other capital development has to consider the possibility of a deal with private industry. The trust has to show that the project can be completed more cheaply this way. As borrowing money from private companies is always more costly than borrowing directly from the government, a number of ingenious deals have been struck. St James's Hospital in Leeds for example, has, agreed to allow its financer to build a hotel on the site. The *quid pro quo* is that patients are allowed access to 60 of the beds as a patient hotel. The aim of this is to reduce the pressure on acute beds by keeping patients in the hotel who have travelled some distance or who are convalescent but not ready to send home.

Most such deals involve borrowing the money over, say, a 25 year period, the private financier being given the contract to provide cleaning and other hotel facilities for the building. The disadvantage for the health service is that the deal may tie the trust into a contract for 25 years, without guarantees that the facility will be needed at the end of that time.

Annual business plan

Trusts must prepare an annual business plan covering 3 forward years. The business planning cycle for trusts needs to be in line with that of health authorities because of the inter-relationship between trust finance and that of purchasing authorities. Business plans must be linked to the annual Public Expenditure Survey (PES) timetable to allow the total external financing requirements of trusts to be considered.

In preparing plans, trusts need:

- To estimate how much money is likely to be available from their main purchasers over the period of the plan. Mostly trusts know there will not be much, if any, more; there may be less money available. Even general elections do not necessarily ensure more cash these days, although they are a better bet than most.
- To make clear the likely impact of inflation over the period of the plan. This usually has to do with what the nurses are asking for and liable to get in the annual pay negotiations. They form about 40% of the revenue costs of most trusts, more for community trusts and much more if one includes nursing auxiliaries.

- To set out clear, justified plans for capital developments and their funding.
- To provide sensitivity analyses based on different assumptions. These 'best and worst case' scenarios can often turn a fairly grey non-executive completely grey in an afternoon.

The NHS management executive compares each trust business plan with a number of financial criteria:

- Achievement of financial targets and duties
- Satisfactory capital investment proposals, particularly to ensure that the trust can recover total costs, including capital costs, from its contract income
- Consistency with the trust's strategy and with the health care strategies of regional offices and health authorities
- Control of working capital
- Satisfactory borrowing and investment strategies
- Non-NHS income
- Sensitivity to key assumptions, especially risks.

The internal market was originally intended to make the relationship between the health services, especially the trusts, and the Department of Health more 'hands off'. The amount of reporting that trusts have to do does not suggest that the grasp is releasing yet.

The external financing limit (EFL)

The EFL is a cash limit on the net external financing for a trust, usually used for developing new capital projects, especially buildings and equipment. External finance is the difference between agreed capital spending by a trust and its internally generated resources. Put simply, an EFL consists of:

- New loans taken out by the trust; less
- Repayments of loans during the year; plus or minus
- Net charges in deposits and other liquid assets.

The government determines the national total for trust EFLs. The NHS Management Executive sets an individual EFL for each trust within the national total, taking account of its plans for capital development. The point of the EFL is to make sure that trusts use their capital wisely. Because of the separation of revenue and capital spending in the health service, there has been a tendency for capital developments to go their own way. They then often drag revenue spending along behind when the building is completed.

The EFL is a means of making trusts stop and think about whether they really do need to spend capital before going ahead with their plans. It also puts trusts on an equal footing with private providers who will have long-term charges on their capital spending. I am not convinced that it has really worked yet in either case. It may be that, as trusts look more closely at their spending in future, they may take into account the knock-on effects of their capital spending. It is my impression that, for example, closing an old hospital and opening a new one involves an enormous amount of work. Problems are especially great for obtaining agreement from the local population to the closure of the old one. The next greatest problem appears to be getting agreement from the local authority planners (and the local population) to open a new one. The knock-on effects of the capital costs on the EFL pale into insignificance as a problem. The time scales are such for a large project that the revenue consequences will probably not be a problem to the incumbent finance director.

A trust may have an EFL that is positive, zero or negative:

- A positive EFL is set where the NHS Management Executive has agreed capital spending for a trust that exceeds its internally generated resources. This results in the trust needing to borrow or reduce investments to finance its spending programme.
- An EFL of zero is set where the agreed spending programme equals its internally generated resources.
- A negative EFL is set where the agreed spending programme is less than internally generated resources. In these circumstances, a trust is not able to use all its surplus or depreciation on capital spending. Trusts must use some or all of this money to repay loans or invest it. The trust normally holds the investments and they may be available to finance future planned spending.

Most capital projects planned by trusts require funding over a period of up to 25 years. In these cases, agreement to a trust's business plan means that the Department gives a provisional commitment to funding in future. However, trusts must seek approval annually for the planned spending on major projects.

Borrowing to maintain the EFL

Each trust must keep within its EFL each year. However, there is some flexibility in that a trust may borrow extra funding in the last quarter of the year, with Department approval. This may be up to 1% of the sum of its total turnover and fixed asset spending. This additional borrowing is deducted from the following year's EFL.

Financial duties of trusts

As mentioned above, each trust has two financial duties besides staying within its EFL:

- To achieve its financial target. This is a real pre-interest return of 6% on the value of net assets, essentially an average of the opening and closing assets shown in the accounts.
- To break even on its income and expenditure account, after paying interest and dividends, taking one year with another.

There is also a general obligation for trusts to ensure that their activities achieve the best value for money.

Where a trust has a cash surplus considerably greater than its reasonable need for funds, for example from the sale of land or buildings at a price reflecting development gain, the Secretary of State may make the trust pay the government all or part of its reserves.

Keeping accounts

Each trust must keep proper accounts and present them annually in a specified format, which is based on the requirements of the Companies Acts, with variations to reflect the special circumstances of trusts. The accounts must show a true and fair view of the trust's financial affairs. The trust must follow the relevant standards of accounting practice.

The trust submits these accounts to the Secretary of State. They are the corporate responsibility of the trust board, but the trust's chief executive, advised by the director of finance, is responsible for ensuring, on behalf of the board, that all accounting and financing matters are in order. This includes ensuring that:

- All public funds are properly managed and safeguarded
- Standing financial instructions are complied with
- The accounts of the trust are properly presented.

The director of finance is responsible for ensuring that financial systems and controls meet the requirements of good financial management. The chief executive, advised by the director of finance, is responsible for answering, on behalf of the trust board, any questions about the accounts of a trust. He or she is also responsible for informing the NHS Management Executive if, at any time, the long-term financial viability of the trust is at risk. It is astonishing, given the foregoing that trusts do, fairly regularly, manage to go bankrupt.

Auditing

The accounts of each trust are audited by the Audit Commission. The National Audit Office (NAO) is responsible for auditing the accounts of all NHS trusts and laying them before Parliament. The NAO has right of access to papers and other records relating to each trust's financial, accounting and auditing matters. Both the Audit Commission and the NAO may conduct value-for-money studies in trusts.

Negligence claims

Where costs arise from clinical negligence, trusts meet the cost of any settlement. Where the costs are above a specified amount a trust may borrow against its EFL to cover the excess costs and repay the loan, with interest, over a defined period. The repayments of the loan, with interest, are included in the trust's costs each year. Trusts may make their insurance arrangements to cover risks other than those arising from clinical negligence. These arrangements are normally a mixture of self-insurance and commercial insurance.

Trusts are not liable for losses from actions arising before their operational date. Regional offices of the Department of Health meet and handle such losses as they think appropriate.

Trusts and information

Trust boards must have full and up-to-date information, including financial information, to make effective decisions, and trusts need to have good information systems to support their operations. All trusts need systems for payroll and personnel and for financial management, including costing services, invoicing and handling accounts. Hospitals need systems which, at a minimum, enable them to manage inpatient and outpatient services, and waiting lists and times. Community trusts need to collect basic Körner data, for example counts of contacts by age, sex and location. Trusts are free to develop the systems they need for their work, and the level and sophistication of these information systems will vary between trusts. Each trust decides whether to run and manage its own systems, to participate in regional information systems or to contract out to use other systems.

Trusts have to provide information to other bodies, for example data to purchasers, both health authorities and general practitioner fundholders, about the services they have provided. These are known as contract minimum data sets. It is for each trust and its purchasers to decide, within the contracting process, whether any extra information should be provided. Trusts also have to provide some information to the NHS Management Executive, either directly or through the regional offices. This includes data for national registers, such as the Cancer Register, manpower returns, annual accounts and information on their financial position.

Cost centres

Trusts, apart from ambulance trusts and some based on specialist services, such as cancer hospitals or dental hospitals, provide a wide range of services. Most trusts therefore divide their services into groups known as directorates. In a hospital, there may be directorates of medicine, surgery and child health. These groups are usually managed by a clinical director, who is often a senior consultant but may come from any of the professions involved in the service, including management itself.

For financial purposes, the trusts divide into a number of subgroups known as cost centres. The cost centres are often the same as the directorates, so that each clinical director is also responsible for a budget to run the directorate. There is a growing tendency for directorates to deal directly with purchasers for particular services. Any contracts agreed will need to cover the costs of the directorate itself and will have a share of the central management costs of the trust. This is often a delicate manoeuvre as no cost centre wants to support the centre. There is also a tendency for each cost centre to feel that it pays more than its fair share.

Cost improvement programmes

The government have, over the past few years, set targets for health authorities to provide cost improvement programmes. The point of cost improvement programmes is that they are intended to improve the value for money given by the service. Health authorities may retrieve the money in a number of ways. It may be either 'cash releasing', i.e. the budget of the trust is simply reduced, or by transferring the money from existing services into new developments within the same overall budget. Trusts find the latter much easier to deal with as internal changes can be labelled as new developments without any loss of income.

The cost improvement programmes are, not surprisingly, very unpopular with trusts. For the past few years, the government have set these at 3% of the health authority budget. The authority can ask for 3% from all of its trusts or can ask for different percentages from each one. This is often difficult to justify as most trusts believe that they are already very efficient. There are, of course, no generally agreed measures of efficiency, so it is difficult to make objective decisions. As a result, most authorities ask for 3% from all of their trust providers.

Cost improvement programmes have the advantage of being centrally fixed by the government. Purchasers, when trying to speed up a new development or improve its finances, can blame the government for them. Trusts therefore have little option but to re-engineer their services as new developments. Such programmes are, by their nature, unfair and crude, but they do help to overcome some of the inertia in the service.

SETTING THE FRAMEWORK FOR NEGOTIATING CONTRACTS

The starting point

Contracts are obviously heavily influenced by the existing pattern of services. The purchaser's starting point is a specification of the services needed. This specification will develop year by year, altered by the information that purchasers and providers get from the operation of their contracts. General practitioner fundholders will also have a view on the ways in which services should be provided.

Core services

Health authorities will need to decide which services are core. This is not a description of its importance; they are those to which patients need guaranteed local access and where there is no sensible alternative available. The core services may be different for different areas of the health authority's population. In the early days of contracting, most health authorities and general practitioners assumed that NHS community services should be given to the provider at or near the patient's home. Since that time, a number of general practitioner fundholders in particular have decided to use managers of community services from outside their area. The people working with patients, district nurses and health visitors have often remained the same people, but they have been appointed and managed by a different management group.

General practitioners appear to be more critical of community services than hospital services. It is my experience that they are more likely to change their preferred provider for community services than for hospital care. This may reflect the greater expertise that general practitioners have for judging community-based services, or it may be that community services, by their very nature, are more difficult to provide at a proven high standard.

Selecting alternatives for non-core services

Non-core services are those for which health authorities can choose between two or more options and where the people living in the health authority area might benefit from that choice. This allows health authorities or general practitioner fundholders to look at a range of potential providers. In this, they take into account the nature, range, quality and price of the services on offer.

The responsibility for placing contracts lies with health authorities and general practice fundholders. Health authorities need to be sure that non-fundholding general practitioners can refer to their preferred provider unless there are very good reasons for not doing so. This will include arrangements for referrals by general practitioner fundholders, which involve a procedure not covered by their practice budgets, or which exceeds the cost limit for a single case of £5000.

Joint purchasing

An advantage of the contractual relationship between providers and purchasers is that it forces health authorities and general practitioners to work together to obtain the best treatment for their patients. Despite improvements, general practitioners still say that they do not have sufficient information to make sure that they improve the quality and speed of treatment. They have little experience of that type of work. In future, health authorities and general practitioners will be better placed to coordinate their contracts with hospitals. Monitoring the existing contracts will improve health authorities' and general practitioners' ability to assess how well providers are spending the contract funds.

Health authorities have the problem that they are the paymaster for general practitioners on the one hand, and partners in purchasing services on the other. This makes the relationship a difficult one, answered at the moment by having health authorities with an odd split down the middle separating the two jobs. Inevitably, the two functions clash. General practitioners who feel aggrieved about their allowances may be reluctant to help an authority with the next health plan. The fundholders are often resistant to agreeing contracts with providers when they are in dispute with the health authority over their funding.

Extracontractual referrals

Sometimes patients need emergency treatment and their general practitioner is unable to secure a bed in a contracted hospital or decides, for clinical or social reasons, to send the patient elsewhere. In that case, general practitioners can refer to non-contract hospitals and the health authority will meet the cost from its budget; the health authority cannot refuse to fund an emergency referral. Having said this I, when confronted with such an extracontractual referral, will always ask the general practitioner why he or she made that decision. This information may be vital for the development of new contracts in the future. It probably also dampens down the number of extracontractual referrals, as the general practitioner will know that a request for more information on the case will follow.

The government expects the great majority of non-emergency referrals to be to trusts with which the health authority has made a contract, but some exceptions are bound to be needed. This may be because it was not practicable for the health authority to contract with all the hospitals potentially able to treat its residents. It may be because of one-off cases or particular circumstances that make it necessary or preferable for a patient to be treated at another hospital. The needs of all patients can never be foreseen. Some trusts can find useful niche markets for such extracontractual referrals.

General practitioners are also free, when necessary, to refer non-emergency cases outside the area. As for emergency cases, there is a contingency reserve available in the health authority. The health authority will not challenge the general practitioner's choice of provider unless the proposed referral is unjustified on clinical grounds. They may ask whether an alternative referral would be equally efficacious for the patient. Many extracontractual referrals are made because of a patient's wishes.

In any event, when a trust receives an extracontractual referral, it will need to discuss with the patient's health authority financial arrangements and other terms. The hospital is responsible for informing the general practitioner how quickly it can provide treatment. The health authority monitors these procedures to see whether they provide any general lessons for placing future contracts, and to reduce the costs of such referrals in the future.

WRITING A BUSINESS CASE

A business case is a formal proposal that presents the case for a change in investment, usually by a trust, or a voluntary or privately funded provider. The type of business case will depend on the type and size of the project. A business case consists of a suggestion for increased or decreased investment in a specific project, and it may also be a way of bidding for allocations from the NHS Executive or regional offices. A business plan is different. It is most commonly the annual plan for the trust describing its proposed activities in a coming year. More uncommonly, it may be a major piece of work containing a number of new cases for investment in a trust that is making considerable changes to the way in which it works.

Some trusts have developed their own form for business cases, but the general outline is similar. A business case is about a new investment. The aim of the case is to satisfy the trust and health authority that the investment will cost-effectively benefit patients. Business cases for large investments, particularly capital schemes, will require support from the board of directors of the trust, the health authority, the government or regional offices. For smaller projects, the business case may be an internal document. The complexity of the health service means that clinicians need to be closely involved. In practice, managers often construct the business cases for their specialties, which are then modified by clinicians. They also contribute to cases for trust-wide projects, but they will need a great deal of advice from doctors, nurses and therapists.

Unless there are significant changes to a service, small projects paid for from revenue will not normally require a business case. Any scheme that will change the quality of a service or the risks attached to it should have one, even if it is quite a small scheme. Larger projects that are funded by the trust are usually identified in the annual business plan. They should be supported by an outline business case, and a business case must be produced for large capital projects.

Contents of the business case

The business case should consist of the following:

- *Executive summary*. This is a synopsis outlining current service provision, trends and demand changes and the case for investment.

- *Introduction.* This need be only a description of the purpose of the document and the methodology used.
- *Current services.* This is an outline of current service provision describing the main characteristics of the service being considered, which should include:

    size

    purpose and function

    costs

    resource utilization

    patient throughput

    accessibility

    clinical or other services available

    performance against contract and quality targets.

- *Trends.* An analysis of trends describes the benefits of the service and the factors that affect its growth. Account may be taken of:

    national, regional or local health strategies

    purchaser requirements

    Charter standards

    referral patterns

    social change

    population movement and demographic changes

    developments in technology, techniques, therapies and clinical standards

    changes in demand and expectation.

- *Demand.* An analysis of future demand for the service. This should include the effect of demography, epidemiology and social change. It must show that there is a difference between the service needed and that provided. It must be clear whether this gap represents unmet need at present or in the future. A response to the gap might offer:

    delivery of increased or decreased volumes of services

    new services or new ways of delivering existing services

    improved clinical outcomes

    improved financial performance

    improved value for money through productivity or improved resource use

    improved quality of delivery, such as environment or waiting times.

- *Option appraisal.* This section should outline the possible responses to the gap between delivery and demand for the service, and should include the following elements:

    define the objectives of the project

    identify a range of possible solutions that meet those objectives

    compare the costs, benefits and risks of each option

    focus on the choice of the best affordable solution.

When comparing options, it is essential that comparisons are valid. One should set costs at the base year, using prices at a given time. Comparisons of costs have to use similar criteria, so there must be a similar set of assumptions between staff costs about grading, on-costs and absence rates. One should state all of these assumptions.

Some NHS trusts use a scoring method for option appraisal. They award points against each option for such things as capital cost, access, compliance with safety regulations, compliance with long-term plans, etc. The score suggests how well an option meets each factor. The health authority may give each factor its own weighting, and the score is multiplied by that weighting. The number and nature of factors and the weighting applied may be published. This helps trusts preparing business cases to know the basis on which comparisons will be made.

For example, I might wish to assess a scheme to provide improved access in a waiting area. This may be considered against bids for money the trust has set aside for quality improvements. The weighting includes the factors listed in Table 8.1. For simplicity, I have assumed that these are the only factors, and that the scheme scores 70 out of 100 against each factor. The scores are multiplied by the weighting, so that for meeting Patient's Charter standards, the total would be 70 (score) x 6 (weighting) = 420. Thus the total for this scheme would be 1540 points. One may apply additional rules so that purchasers can select the best schemes. The highest of a number of scores is not necessarily enough. In this example, the schemes have to score at least 50 against every factor and have a grand total score of at least 1500 points.

One must approach such models carefully. People sometimes suggest that the use of such a weighting approach makes the whole process more objective. This is nonsense for the factors and the weightings are both subjective. The benefit of the model is that the rules can be agreed before the bids are in. The fundgiver, whether a health authority or the executive of a trust, is required to agree in some detail on the objectives of the new scheme. There is less likely to be any real or perceived fixing of the results.

The process of weighting factors needs people to make a subjective judgment, but if they agree to this the measure may be 'less subjective'. On occasion, it might be easier to make a judgment about which is the best scheme when they are all in. Often, the process is mainly useful for teasing out the best and worst points of a new service. One can then take care to assist it with its

Table 8.1 Factors to be considered in bid for money

Factor	Weighting
Compliance with specific trust or health authority objectives	2
Meeting Patient's Charter standards	6
Improving quality standards not specified in the Charter	3
Capital cost (the lower the cost, the higher the score as more schemes can be implemented)	3
Revenue cost	4
Ease of implementation	4

weak aspects when it is completed. The process can also be instructive for showing the way that decision makers are biased within the committee.

- *Risks.* One should include a detailed risk appraisal of the options, describing the sensitivity of the options to things in and outside the organization's control. This section should consider best and worst case scenarios.
- *The preferred option.* This section includes a more detailed appraisal of the selected option, including:
    time scales
    source(s) of funding
    resource requirements
    capital requirements
    revenue consequences for both income and expenditure
    cashflow projections
    manpower implications
    information requirements and reporting implications
    contractual implications.
- *Conclusion.* This would summarize the position as laid out in the business case, explaining concisely why the particular proposal is being brought forward.

Sometimes one scheme is so innovative and likely to be effective that the whole process can, with the agreement of the committee making the decision, be abandoned. In my experience, trusts often sometimes fail to produce a business case at all, even when the result is quite vital to them. It is also common for trusts that already have the contract to underestimate the work that they are already doing and forget to bid for vital parts of the existing service. Sometimes trusts that already run the service appear to feel that setting up a business case is a waste of time and put in very little effort. This was more common when the internal market was a new concept, although it occasionally still happens.

COSTING A CONTRACT

In costing a contract, it is important to check a number of points:

- Can the NHS afford the service at all? People have suggested that we can afford to spend £30 000 per person per annum on saving a life or avoiding a major disability. So no one effective treatment can, with equity to all, cost more than £30 000 if the aim of the health service is simply to save lives or avoid major disabilities. Many standard treatments presently used cost more.
- Is the service effective? If so, is it sufficiently more effective than the standard treatment to make re-tooling worthwhile?

- Does it have hidden costs? Do we know all of its impacts, for example on the family or the environment?
- What is the aim of the service; which of the aims are you trying for? – for example, cervical screening aiming to save lives or reduce anxiety? A community-based mental illness service trying to reduce suicide or maintain quality of life in chronic schizophrenics? Different aims will require quite different approaches. Some aims may be untenable with our present state of knowledge.

Types of cost

- Public sector resource costs: the direct costs to the service.
- Personal costs: costs and benefits provided by the service to patients and staff.
- Environmental costs: costs and benefits to the community at large.

One can compare these costs with those of any industry. Companies making shoes or cars have all of these costs: they have production costs, and costs and benefits to the population and environment. Environmental costs to manufacturing industry in these days of environmental awareness can be very important indeed. Services need to be costed because any provider will need to tell purchasers what they will get for their money. This will be necessary for them to make a reasonable bid when purchasers are trying to place contracts.

Reducing costs

Reducing costs is important. The health service is given a finite amount of money so that any reduction in costs in one area will potentially allow that money to be used in other areas. A first approach to cutting costs is therefore to make sure that savings are recycled rather than lost in a rapid bid to 'use up the money before the end of March'.

One approach to reducing costs is constantly to develop new services, increasing the size of the trust and allowing one to take advantage of economies of scale. This involves one in aggressively bidding for new services – the 'we stop at the sea' type trust. This can be expensive on senior management's time and energy. There are no grants to allay the costs of such developments, unless one trust is asked to bail out another by the region. One must make a careful assessment of the likely benefits of winning the contract and the costs in term of the morale of losing it. No matter how unlikely, losing a contract seems to knock the stuffing out of the trust senior managers for a few months.

A further way to reduce costs is to alter the type of service one is giving, to replace an old service with a new approach, as long as the effectiveness has been shown by research to be equal. One needs to know whether it is effective at answering the need within reasonable cost. If it is a little more effective, one needs to make a judgment about whether it is worth it. Is the purchaser interested or able to afford more money for a higher-quality service? Is it really a better service, or did the researchers have unrealistic expectations of their pet project? This is a very common problem; I speak as an ex-full-time researcher.

Another way of reducing costs is to move the real costs of a service from one budget to another. It may be possible to make more effective use of the patient's family, for example giving them training to help with physiotherapy. One may be able to use the resources of another trust by developing a community-or home-based service. Such services may be cheaper, as home care does not entail hotel costs. It may be possible to get the voluntary sector to cover some costs more cheaply. In my experience, the small size and high overheads of voluntary groups make them uncompetitive, although they can sometimes provide higher quality because of the nature of the work, for example in drug abuse services.

There are a number of ways of reducing costs:

- Substitution of inpatient for outpatient, or outpatient for community-based or home care.
- Reduce or increase staffing. There may be more or fewer staff than are needed, and correcting this may, overall, reduce costs.
- Reduce quality. Quality assurance aims to set a certain level of quality. If the quality is higher than necessary, it may be possible to reduce it.
- Reduce unnecessary interventions. A classic example is in the use of investigations in hospital. Unnecessary investigations are costly in themselves, but can be dangerous as some, statistically, will be abnormal, leading to unnecessary treatment. The use of protocols for admission, discharge and investigations may reduce costs.
- Cutting one's own costs (capital, energy, hotel costs, drugs) without reducing quality.

MONITORING CONTRACTS

As the year passes, the trust will keep an eye, monthly, on the way in which its contracted activity fits in with its actual activity. Table 8.2 shows a truncated spreadsheet for a medical inpatient contract with a trust and its projected difference from the contracted volumes. The data are for January, with 2 months still to run for the year's contract. All the contract currencies are finished patient episodes.

The table shows the level of activity agreed at the beginning of the year and the cumulative total up to the tenth month of the contract. The actual activity is 10% over in general medicine and 6% under in care of the elderly, and the projected end of year figures suggest a similar picture. The trust obviously

Table 8.2 Activity agreement between trust and health authority

The contract		Cumulative to current month			Projected 12 months	
Specialty	Contract level	Target	Actual activity	Variance (%)	Activity	Variance (%)
General medicine	4645	3881	4258	+10	5110	+10
Care of elderly	2075	1729	1629	-6	1955	-6
Neurology	500	417	340	-18	408	-18
Haematology	219	183	175	-4	210	-4
Cardiology	220	184	268	+46	161	+46
GP beds	315	263	214	-19	257	-19

needs to look carefully at its admission criteria for the general medical intake before the health authority will accept that this overprovision is a genuine increase in demand from patients. Similarly, general practitioner beds are heavily underused. The smaller subspecialties, such as neurology and cardiology, are often more difficult to stabilize.

'GRACEFUL DECLINE' OF HEALTH SERVICES: THE LEARNING DISABILITY SERVICE

A number of services within the health service are in graceful decline, so are therefore difficult services to manage. I have suggested that the district general hospital is an example, although this is a controversial view [131]. A service that people generally agree to be in this position is the learning disabilities service. The reason for this is a change in public, or at least professional, attitudes, resulting in a change in policy. I have outlined some of these problems in Chapter 2.

The process of 'normalization', as described by Wolfsenberger [132], crystallized a growing feeling in the health service that people with learning disabilities were partially, at least, disabled by their presence in medical inpatient care. He said that normalization was the process of using 'means which are as culturally normative as possible, to establish and/or maintain personal behaviours and characteristics which are as culturally normative as possible'. I think this means something like 'do as you would be done by'.

Wolfsenberger's work fitted with the feeling of the times about discrimination, as this was the period of the civil rights campaigns in the USA. People had a global ideal that there were inalienable rights that should be protected. Other pressures involved a bit of fighting back by the less well-paid professions, especially social work and nurses, against the dominance of the medical profession in this specialty.

The health service has therefore been gradually closing its large learning disability institutions. A central development has been the idea of multidisciplinary working, which usually involves social workers as the dominant group, with nurses and psychologists, working in community-based teams. There are usually a number of untrained people in the teams, trained by the professionals in the basic tasks of helping to care for the clients. The teams lay great stress upon multidisciplinary assessment of the needs of individual people with learning disabilities. One member of the team is then appointed as a key worker. This individual is a point of contact for the client, if the client or the family need help or advice. This approach is far removed from the hierarchical health service approach, in which the doctors assess the patient and tell the other staff what to do. In the traditional model, the central contact is between patient and doctor, but this relationship can become very one sided when the doctor is a renowned specialist. Patients may feel overawed and unable to question doctors.

The finance for the multidisciplinary teams has mostly been made available centrally. The government agreed to this on the understanding that the money released by closing the large learning disabilities hospitals would be paid back later. This whole process has taken much longer than was originally anticipated. In my health authority, for example, the closure of a large learning disabilities hospital has been planned, in detail, for 12 years. The same story has been common in two other nearby hospitals. There are now 'definite' plans that all three will close within the next 2 years.

IMPROVING THE SERVICE BY AUDITING: PRESSURE SORES

Some standards of care appear to be self-evident. An example of this is in the treatment of pressure sores.

Evidence suggests that an acute failure of the peripheral circulation causes pressure sores [133] a phase of acute illness most often initiating the problem [134]. It has been discovered that, in 7 out of 10 patients who get sores, this occurs within the first 2 weeks of admission to hospital. Some acute hospitals have a pressure sore prevalence more than three times that of others [135].

People have found that pressure sores cause a four-fold increase in deaths. When it is the main diagnosis, between one-quarter and one-third of those patients will die without being discharged. The cost of treating these sores in the UK has been estimated as being between £180m and £321m [136]. A full-thickness sore in the lower back extends the hospital stay by over 25 weeks at a cost of £26 000. The problem takes up a very large proportion of nursing time and hence resources in the health service [137]. It is unlikely that any other problem with such serious consequences and which is potentially treatable is so neglected by researchers or managers.

Effectiveness of treatment [138]

Patients in many different parts of a hospital have pressure sores, not just on the acute wards and not always in patients who are lying down. People have recorded prevalence rates between 5% and 8% in large studies of hospital and community patients. About 7 out of 10 occur in patients aged over 70 years.

Patients with fractured neck of femur appear to be especially at risk. About two-thirds of these patients develop pressure sores, especially on the heels.

Management

A range of treatment, including airwave and polystyrene bead systems, is available. None of the treatments have, at present, good evidence for their effectiveness. A description of the use of chlorinated solutions sums up the extraordinary lack of evidence in this area: 'Despite widespread use for over 70 years on all types of dirty wounds, it is not clear if these solutions actually work. . . . It is important to appreciate that chlorinated solutions kill healthy cells. If ulcer improvement occurs it may be despite their use rather than because of it.'

Pressure ulcers

Only about 1 in 10 of the papers on this subject are of a reasonable standard [139]. Despite the lack of good studies of effectiveness, there are some hints that the right approach might work. A Swiss report suggests that a combination of soft bedding support, regular turning and intensive educational programmes could reduce the incidence of pressure sores to near zero.

Researchers have written five good studies on devices that reduce pressure [140]. These devices spread the pressure between the patient and the bed and avoid high pressures in any one position. Only air-loss beds and mattresses produced pressures significantly below the critical level thought to reduce blood flow to an area. Several devices were intermediate between foam and air-loss beds. This suggests that some devices intended for pressure sore prevention are not likely to be effective. Unfortunately, trials have not been performed on most of them.

A review of alternating pressure supports [141] examined five good trials of the benefits of different types of alternating pressure mattresses and made four main points:

- Large-cell alternating pressure mattresses are more effective than small-cell mattresses in preventing pressure sores.
- Mattresses must be sufficiently robust not to break down in use.
- Clinical trials are often poor and therefore need to be checked carefully.
- Control regimes must be fully described.

A randomized controlled trial compared pressure decreasing mattresses with a special surface covering comprising small cubes of the mattress under bony protuberances of the patient that can be removed to reduce pressure locally. The researchers compared this approach with a standard hospital mattress [142]. The study was small, carried out in patients with femoral neck fractures. It showed benefits in pressure sore reduction from using this one product.

Criteria and standards for auditing

I set up a number of criteria and standards for adequate pressure sore prevention and management in the health authority.

1. Patients should have a pressure sore risk assessment performed and recorded in the notes. Standard = 100%.
2. Patients assessed as being at risk by a standard assessment score should receive preventative care. Standard = 100%.
3. Patients with pressure sores involving a skin break should be receiving recognized therapy. In this case, preventive measures should also be present. Standard = 100%.

The data for the study were obtained in a survey of all the patients in hospitals and day hospitals used as providers by the health authority. Just over 1700 patients were present on the wards on the census day. Patients with scores of 10 or more on a Waterlow assessment [143] were considered at risk.

The definition of preventive care, mentioned in criteria 2 and 3 above, was carefully drawn up to include all relevant interventions. Preventive measures should be maintained (criterion 3) where an existing bed sore is present in order to prevent further sores and to ease the pressure on the existing sore.

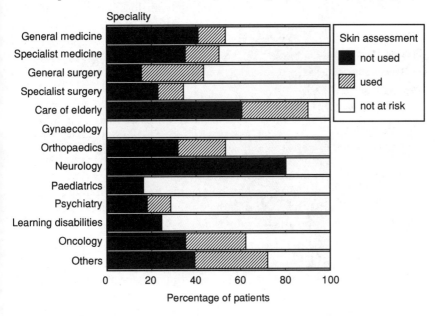

Figure 9.1 Skin assessment tool recorded for patients at risk by speciality.

Treatment for existing bed sores was carefully defined. Eight per cent of the patients had one or more pressure sores. Sores were more common in the older age groups than the younger, and there was no difference in the proportions of men and women affected.

The first audit criterion was that all patients at risk should have a pressure sore risk assessment performed on admission and recorded in the notes. The measure of 'at risk' for this study depended upon an assessment of the Waterlow score by the audit team. Figure 9.1 shows data for the patients in each specialty where the staff had used a skin assessment tool. It also shows the proportion where they had not used an assessment, despite the patients being at risk. The proportion of people at risk varied greatly from specialty to specialty: there were none in gynaecology and 90% in the care of the elderly specialty. There was also a wide range in the proportion of patients assessed for risk. This varied from none on neurology, paediatrics and learning disabilities, to almost two-thirds in general surgery. Patients in the care of the elderly, the specialty most often accepted as being particularly likely to get pressure sores, had a measure in only one-third of the patients at risk.

The next audit standard was that all patients assessed as being at risk by a standard assessment score should be receiving preventive care. The most common form of preventive care was regular turning of the patients in bed. The nurses carried this out for about one-third of the patients at risk. One-fifth received other preventive measures with regular turning; one-tenth had only the other preventive measures. One-quarter of those at risk received no

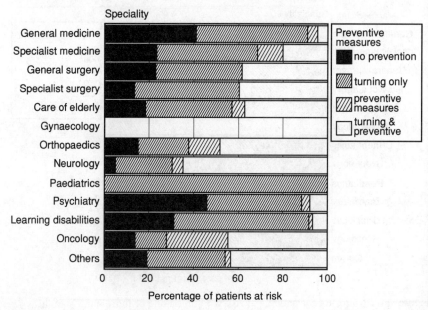

Figure 9.2 Preventive measures for patients at risk by specialty.

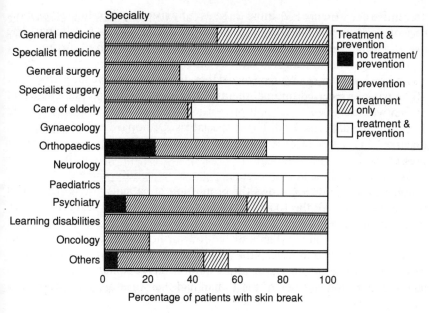

Figure 9.3 Treatment and preventive measures for patients with pressure sores by specialty.

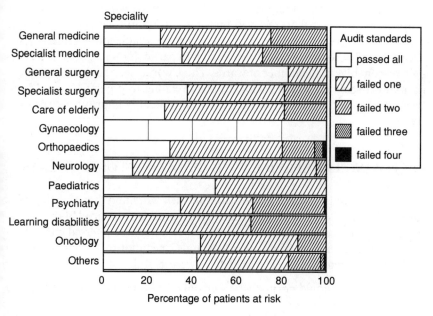

Figure 9.4 Proportion of patients at risk who failed one or more audit standards by specialty.

preventive care. Figure 9.2 shows these data by specialty. The highest proportion of patients not receiving preventive treatment was in psychiatry. The
lowest was in paediatrics, where all the patients at risk received therapy.

The last audit measure was that all patients with pressure sores involving
a skin break should receive recognized therapy and preventive measures. Half
of the patients received optimal therapy; treatment for the pressure sore and
preventive care. A further small proportion received treatment only. Figure
9.3 shows the data for the different specialties. Orthopaedics and psychiatry,
together with a mix of others, had patients who were receiving no care for
pressure sores.

I then assessed the audit measures together to identify where the foremost
problems lay. Figure 9.4 shows the proportion of patients at risk who failed
on the standards. Of the 10 patients who failed on all three of the standards,
four were in orthopaedics, two in psychiatry, one in care of the elderly and
three in other specialties. Three of the four orthopaedics cases were on the
same ward. The two in psychiatry were in wards for the elderly mentally ill.
Two of the three in other specialties were in day hospitals, the other in a
community hospital. None of the 10 had had their pressure sores when they
were admitted.

Improving the service

The study showed that there was a great variation between specialties in the
proportion of people who received prevention for and treatment of pressure
sores. This suggests that there needs to be a considerable improvement in the
approach taken to pressure sores generally. In particular, there are black spots
on a reasonably small number of wards. These wards are not necessarily those
normally associated with a major problem relating to pressure sores. Monitoring and corrective action will therefore considerably improve patient well-
being.

IMPROVING THE SERVICE WITH GUIDELINES: OUTPATIENTS

Eight consultant physicians agreed to allow their work and that of their junior
staff to be monitored with guidelines for outpatient practice [144]. The researchers surveyed a consecutive group of new attendees referred either by a
general practitioner or from other hospitals or clinics to the eight general
medical outpatient clinics. The guidelines were as follows:

- New patients should normally be seen only once and discharged to the care
  of the referring doctor.
- A follow-up appointment of new outpatient referrals is be given in the
  following circumstances:

    Diagnostic uncertainty requiring further assessment

    Monitoring of complex diseases

    Serious disease requiring further investigation and treatment by a specialist.

- A further appointment is not to be made simply to give the patient the results of tests. These results and any advice on treatment or opinion based on these results can be sent to the referring doctor, who can then take any action considered necessary.
- Diagnostic tests should only be used if the results will alter a decision; routine full blood count, ESR, urea and electrolytes, liver function tests, chest X-rays and ECGs are not justified.
- Referring doctors should normally be sent information, including the results of tests, within 10 days of the outpatient appointment or inpatient discharge. This is important when the hospital doctors do not plan to see the patients again at follow-up. If appropriate, the patient should be told that information will be sent to their general practitioner. They should be advised to contact their general practitioner in approximately 2 weeks.

The researchers printed the guidelines on a plastic card and gave this to the consultants working in four of the clinics. The consultants distributed them to their junior medical staff. At 3-monthly intervals, the staff also received a letter from the study organizer thanking them for their cooperation and stressing the importance of the guidelines. They enclosed summaries of published articles calling for a more appropriate use of hospital outpatient facilities. In other clinics, medical staff agreed to take part. The researchers did not involve them in the development or circulation of the guidelines so that these clinics acted as a control group.

Nine hundred and sixty consecutive new outpatient attenders were enrolled during the 9 months of the study. Just over one-third of patients were discharged after their first attendance. This ranged from between one-fifth and two-thirds depending on the specialty of the clinic. There were great variations in the time taken for a consultation by different consultants. Eighty different diagnostic procedures were requested during the study. The median number per patient was 2, but one-quarter of the patients had none. There were also large differences between the clinics in their use of routine tests.

Different clinics were seeing different types of patients. To take this into account, a group of patients whose main and single diagnosis was disease of the circulatory system were studied in more detail. The authors found that these patients had a wider variation in their treatment than was seen for all the patients taken together. The doctors given guidelines were significantly more likely to discharge their patients and had a slightly lower number of routine diagnostic tests compared with the doctors not given guidelines. This simple approach to using guidelines decreased the amount of unnecessary reattendance of outpatients and slightly reduced the incidence of routine diagnostic tests.

SELLING THE SERVICE

Marketing and relations with the public

There is a reluctance among clinical staff to think of the NHS in terms of marketing. There are two main reasons for this. Firstly, there is a feeling of unease caused by the association between marketing and its more obvious and dubious manifestations. Examples are adverts on television for shampoo, in which laboratories are full of glamorous women giving advice. Public relations are often typified by the 'Absolutely Fabulous' TV programme and, more seriously, the marketing of milk powder and cigarettes in developing countries. Secondly, there is political concern that marketing is closely bound up with industry and therefore the right wing in politics and privatization of the health service. However, I believe that an increase in marketing activity would be of great service to the health service.

Definition of marketing

There have been a number of definitions of marketing, but the one which most easily fits into marketing in health services comes from Drucker [145]:

> Marketing . . . is the whole business seen from the point of view of its final result, that is, from the customer's point of view.

All activities, and not simply the buying and selling going on in the organization, are therefore important to marketing. It is broader in its scope than its direct customers. It includes potential customers, potential patients. Even those who are unlikely ever to use the service need to be aware of its activities. Those people should also feel that the services are useful and of good quality.

People have recognized since its formation that the reputation of the health service is important and needs to be jealously guarded. However, in the past, patients have had little recourse if they have been taken suddenly ill near a hospital with a bad reputation. It is the job of a good marketing director to be aware of any tarnished reputation that the trust may have and try to alter it.

There is a public perception that altering the bad reputation of a business is usually attempted by putting forward a series of counter claims. The adverts on television for Sellafield, neé Windscale, for example, seem not to have altered its reputation. If anything, the adverts have increased people's suspicion that there is something to cover up. However, in a good firm, or NHS trust, the marketing director or equivalent will be a powerful figure in the organization. As such, he or she will be able to point out and help to alter those aspects of the service that are responsible for maintaining the bad reputation. Putting marketing at the centre of the business means that the business must be responsive to external pressures. Marketing directors must also be able to persuade the board to change the organization from within.

The lack of such an approach in the past may have been the cause of the renowned inability of the service to respond to patient preferences. Examples abound:

- The impossibility of providing wards with single-, two- or at most four-bedded cubicles, which patients prefer
- The appalling problems patients have in not knowing what has been, is being and is about to be done to them because of a lack of communication
- In many instances, patients simply not knowing about the existence of services vital to their well-being, incontinence laundry services, for example [146]. This makes these services easy to dispense with despite their popularity with those who do receive them.

How is marketing performed?

I have already made the point that a marketing director should be on the board of any organization that wishes to please its customers. He or she will be the most powerful person apart from the chief executive. The marketing director needs to have the information network of the organization, both formal and informal, in control; the grapevine should stop at his or her door. The marketing director will be closely involved in market research on the quality of the service provided by the trust.

A trust will therefore have to ensure that the marketing director has accurate information about what is happening. The director will also have to guarantee to customers that the trust will be able to deliver what is promised at the right time, at the right price and with a guaranteed after-sales service, the latter including a request for information from all customers about how the service could be improved. My impression is that trusts are still not taking general practitioner fundholders seriously enough when trying to agree quality of service with them. Fundholders that choose a different trust are often regarded by the spurned trust with enmity rather than a will to get back their custom. This is, of course, not a business-like approach.

Market research

Market research obviously includes the necessity of finding out, from customers, what suggestions they might have for improving the service. It is equally essential to obtain the views of the staff. Market research, however, is much broader than just filling in questionnaires.

The director will have to have information on the existing market:

- Whether demand for particular parts of the service is growing or shrinking
- Seasonal influences
- Whether it is prone to fashions
- Whether it is likely to change as a result of to new technological changes
- Which parts are being competed for.

This sort of information is as essential for an NHS trust as for any other provider of services. A small element of competition has always been available from private treatment and alternative therapies, but this is likely to be greater in future. It is well known that patients never complain about their doctors unless they are suing them for every penny; the relationship appears to have that in common with a love affair. There is therefore a great deal of literature on the problems of getting real data from patients. Despite this, a torrent of satisfaction surveys continue to flow in the NHS. Puzzled articles follow each one about why there appear to be huge discrepancies between what is known and what patients say in the surveys. My own anecdote is from an elderly lady with the most appalling health problems, including leg ulcers and dramatic incontinence, living in the Rhondda: 'My doctor's a lovely man. Haven't seen him for years. Since my husband died.'

WHAT WORKS: EVIDENCE-BASED MEDICINE

Purchasers and providers have been extremely lucky in the last 5 years. A considerable number of groups have started collecting the often confusing and always very technical data about what treatments work to help people who are ill. Much of this activity is going on in the UK. The most useful tools that have been produced are a set of systematic reviews. Iain Chalmers and his co-workers at the Cochrane Centre in Oxford were the initial driving force for these developments. Dr Chalmers was originally doing a wide range of research work into the best methods of care of mothers and babies. As a result, much of the work that the Cochrane Centre has initially published is centred on that specialty.

The point of systematic reviews is that the experts collect together research work on the topic of interest and attempt to give a summary of what all the data mean. The problem of collation is enormous. Over two million articles are published each year in the biomedical journals. If these articles were stacked up, they would rise to 500m in height. There is therefore a need to do a number of things:

- Separate those articles that are of good quality according to fixed criteria.
- Accumulate all the articles on the topic.
- Review the findings, if possible using a meta-analysis to combine comparable studies if there is no one study powerful enough to give an unequivocal opinion.
- Sum the findings from well set-up trials, preferably cumulatively. This has a slightly different function: it suggests whether trials carried out under different conditions are likely, overall, to show that the therapy is useful.
- Judge the overall power of the data and decide what they mean for patient care.

- Suggest adverse or other important effects that appear to be coming out of the research in question.
- Use the review to set up guidelines and legislation if they seem appropriate.
- Suggest areas for future research.

One approach that is central to the use of systematic reviews is the cumulative gathering of data over time. This is an alternative to looking at all the studies together at a set point and trying to make an average assessment of whether the method works. An example of the value of the cumulative approach is shown by comparing Figures 9.5 and 9.6. The figures show trials of intravenous streptokinase for reducing the damage to the heart after an acute myocardial infarction [147]. The cumulative systematic review shows the trials in chronological order. It shows that intravenous streptokinase, using the cumulative data, could have been seen to be life-saving almost 20 years before it had been approved by the US Food and Drug Administration.

Collecting together different research projects in this way is sometimes criticized. People argue that every project has some differences and that one is collecting together several studies that were restricted in size and therefore possibly restricted in quality. The argument can, however, be opposed. If the findings are consistent for trials using different population groups and in different circumstances, it suggests that the treatment being evaluated is robust and will cover a number of situations. The reviews can assess whether there is

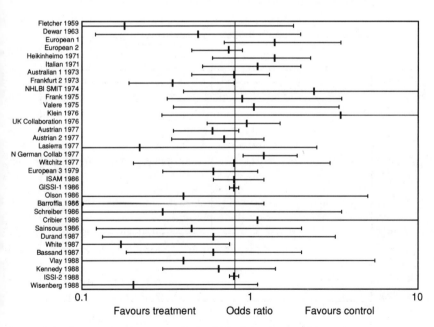

Figure 9.5 Conventional meta-analysis of 33 trials of streptokinase for acute myocardial infarction.

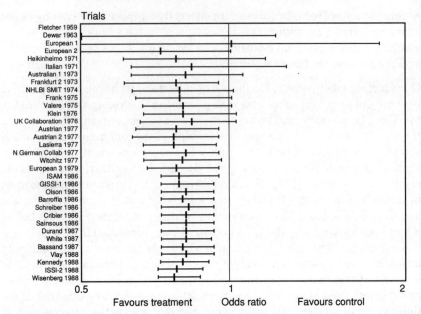

Figure 9.6 Cumulative meta-analysis off 33 trials of streptokinase for acute myocardial infarction.

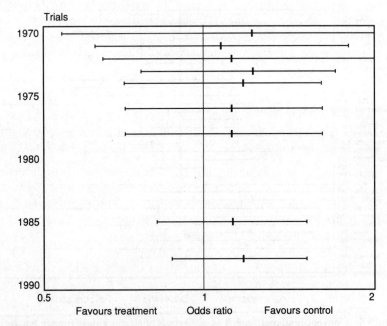

Figure 9.7 Cumulative meta-analysis of effectiveness of lignocaine.

a consistency between the studies. Perhaps the most valuable part of systematic reviews is that they apply explicit scientific principles to all the studies and suggest which are not to be trusted.

The systematic approach also aims to collect all the available evidence that exists within the area being studied. Traditional reviews have tended to be biased by the availability of some studies compared with others. The reviewers are usually biased towards work in their language and those journals that are most available locally [148]. These traditional reviews often lag a long way behind the data that are available [149], and textbooks will often lag even further behind reviews.

Figure 9.7 shows the cumulative meta-analysis of randomized controlled trials of the use of lignocaine for preventing heart rhythm disturbances after myocardial infarction and the recommendations of the clinical experts. Lignocaine showed no evidence of improvement in mortality for acute myocardial infarction from the beginning. Despite this, its use continued to be recommended for at least 20 years.

THE EVIDENCE-BASED PROCESS FOR THE INDIVIDUAL

The evidence-based health care movement has stimulated both purchasers and providers to use evidence-based data. A large number of groups including, as I have mentioned, the Cochrane Centre, the NHS Centre for Reviews and Dissemination in York and the Nuffield Centre in Leeds [150] provide information on effectiveness-based health-care. Work is also being carried out in Bristol on the need for some interventions in health care. Using evidence logically has taken off in the UK in the past 2 or 3 years.

Using evidence-based medicine in practice

When trying to decide whether a course of action that the trust is hoping to set up is in line with the evidence:

- Formulate a clear question looking at it from the perspective of the patient's problem and from your role in the provision of health care.
- Search the literature for relevant information. This is quicker if there is already a review or guideline. Large numbers of guidelines are produced in the USA, and these might be a good place to start.
- Evaluate the evidence for its validity and usefulness.
- Implement useful findings by asking about them in the clinical practice of the trust or as part of a business case.

The evidence for a particular form of therapy or other service will vary greatly, from one service to another. The strength of the evidence can be set in a hierarchy as follows:

1. Strong evidence from at least one systematic review of multiple, well-de-
    signed, randomized controlled trials. Examples of good-quality reviews
    are those using methods outlined by the Cochrane Collaboration. One
    can appraise the quality of reviews using checklists based on McMaster
    principles [151].
2. Strong evidence from at least one properly designed randomized control-
    led trial of appropriate size. One could expect evidence included here to
    meet criteria laid down in checklists based on McMaster principles.
    Evidence in this category is usually about therapy.
3. Evidence from well-designed trials without randomization, single-group
    pre-post, cohort, time series or matched case-controlled studies. Evidence
    in this category often concerns prognosis or cause of disease. McMaster
    checklists are again available (see above).
4. Evidence from well-designed, non-experimental studies from more than
    one centre or research group. Evidence in this category often concerns the
    prevalence or cause of disease.
5. Opinions of respected authorities, based on clinical evidence, descriptive
    studies or reports of expert committees.

SYNTHESIZED INFORMATION

One can find a great deal of information on-line using computers. Most good
medical school libraries will have all of these systems, and most trust libraries
should have at least Medline, the nursing database, and any specialty database
that may be relevant to the service. Many of these can be contacted on the Internet.

DARE: Database of Abstracts of Reviews of Effectiveness

*   Produced by NHS Centre for Reviews and Dissemination
*   Contains NHSCRD, INAHTA (International Network of Agencies for
    Health Technology Assessment) and other organizations and reviews iden-
    tified from the published literature
*   Some of these are quality assured (NHSCRD guidelines)
*   Some meet Cochrane criteria for classification as 'systematic'; others have
    not been screened so need critical appraisal by the user
*   Status is good; it is a well-respected database
*   Fairly cheap
*   Available in most postgraduate libraries
*   Contains only high-grade evidence
*   Comprises a relatively small number of records because systematic review
    methodology is fairly new, so not many are available
*   Is a new 'type' of literature and database, so searching is still quite crude,
    although improving.

CDSR: Cochrane Database of Systematic Reviews

- Produced by the Cochrane Collaboration
- Contains only systematic reviews carried out to very high standards by the Cochrane Review
- Groups using high-quality, randomized controlled trials only
- Highest-grade evidence only
- Fairly cheap
- Comes on a floppy or CD combined with DARE
- Is available in most postgraduate libraries. Contains a good bibliography of evidence-based methods, although there are as yet very few completed reviews.

CCPC: Cochrane Collaboration Pregnancy and Childbirth

As for CDSR, but includes good randomized controlled trials in the field.

Traditional databases

Medline

- Produced by the National Library of Medicine (the print equivalent in medicine is the *Index Medicus*)
- Extremely large database
- Covers up to the present
- Over 12 million records
- Gives references and abstracts to journal articles only from about 4000 health-related journals
- Extensive but not exhaustive coverage of primary medical, nursing and veterinary literature
- Quality of the original articles is not addressed, so they are not that easy to pick.

Interfaces allowing access

- CD ROM is one electronic medium used to store MEDLINE.

EMBASE

- Similar but not identical to MEDLINE
- European based (the printed equivalent is the *Excerpta Medica*)
- The overlap with MEDLINE is about 60–70%
- Not as widely used but necessary if exhaustive searching is necessary
- Available through JANET (the Joint Academic Network between all UK Universities and higher education establishments)

- Uses structured index terms similar to, but not the same as, those of MEDLINE.

ASSIA (Applied Social Science Index and Abstracts)

- Social sciences; not restricted to health care
- Covers well the sociological aspects of health care, for example health promotion, socioeconomic status as relating to health, community care, ageing and patients' rights.

ERIC (Education Resources Information Center)

- Database of educational materials
- 1966 to the present
- References from educational journals and research reports
- Not restricted to health care
- Includes curriculum development, communication, evaluation and adult and child education.

Other databases have data on specific disease areas and types of information. A few of the many examples are:

- CINAHL (Cumulated Index to Nursing and Allied Health Literature)
- CANCERLIT (cancer journals, books and reports)
- AIDSLINE (HIV and AIDS information)
- PSYCHLIT (psychiatry and psychology literature)
- AMED (complementary medicine).

Internet

- Provides access to reports, guidelines, discussion lists, home pages, etc.
- Quality of material is very variable (e.g. the AHCPR Guidelines are good)
- Access to information is haphazard, although attempts are being made to organize it (e.g. OMNI: Organizing Medical Networked Information). Discussing lists of interest might be evidence-based-health, public-health and primary-health-care.

Printed evidence-based sources

Bandolier

- Printed news sheet reporting on published reviews, and promotion of evidence-based practice and methods
- Produced by Oxford and Anglia Regional Health Authority

- Quick and easy access to evidence (i.e. someone else is trawling the litera-ture), so it is useful as a means of updating
- Not particularly easy to find information on specific topics of interest.

Evidence Based Purchasing

This is similar to Bandolier, and is produced by the South and West R&D Directorate.

Effective Health Care

Bulletins describing the outcomes of systematic reviews funded by the Depart-ment of Health. It includes, for example, topics on screening for osteoporosis, treatment of glue ear and implementing clinical practice guidelines.

ACP Journal Club

This is a supplement to the *Annals of Internal Medicine*, providing commen-taries and synthesis of research evidence.

Evidence Based Medicine

This is a new journal similar to the *ACP Journal Club*.

AN INFORMATION RETRIEVAL SEARCH STRATEGY

- First write an outline of information needed in your own words.
- Choose the best place to look for this information (i.e. which database or other source?).
- Idea (concept) 1. This may be a medical subject heading (MeSH) or phrase. Identify possible alternative terms.
- Idea 2. Investigate possible alternatives.
- Decide whether you want items that include both of the concepts only (AND) or whether you want both (OR).
- Find any existing information, references, authors to help you with your search:

Too many results?

Limit investigation to English only, year, review, etc., and to the level of emphasis given to the topic (e.g. a major heading). Use more precise terms to define the concepts, (and link to other topics using 'AND'.

Too few results?

Search alternative sources, and more years. Use alternative terms to broaden the search by using 'OR'. Use fewer 'AND' links.

In what form do you require your results?

This may be with or without abstracts, including author affiliation, as printout or floppy disc, etc. Keep the strategy if you wish to update the information over time.

WHO IS THE CUSTOMER?

The NHS is free at the point of delivery, apart from some charges for medicines and other services in primary care. For this reason, it is sometimes difficult for people providing the service to know who the customers are, for whom the service is being given. At one level, there is no doubt. When a doctor, nurse or therapist is dealing with a patient, the patient is the customer. But for whom is the service set up? For whose convenience? Who has the major say when changes in the way the service is provided are requested?

The money for the running of the health service comes from taxes, so ultimately tax payers own the health service. The money is passed on by the Department of Health, which sets out the policy details for the running of the health service. The Secretary of State, chief of the Department of Health, therefore has a claim to be in charge of the health service. The Secretary of State is also an elected representative, so his or her claim is that much stronger. The Secretary of State is not, of course, elected by the whole country to be in charge of the health service. The internal market, with its purchasers and providers, has added another player to the group of people who might be said to be in charge. The regional outposts of the Department of Health or the health authorities also have a claim to be in charge. General practitioners, whether fundholding or not, are being given the power, if they want it, of commissioning services from the provider trusts. They too have a claim to be the people in charge of the health service. Last, as part of the internal market, patients have been given the freedom to choose whichever general practitioner they please. They can use this right to pressure their general practitioner if they need to choose a specialist service. To some extent, the patients, as well as helping to pay, have the power to alter health services.

Who are the shareholders: the public, the purchasers?

The health service in the UK has kept its costs down compared with other countries by paying its staff badly and stifling demand. It is possible that it is also quite efficient. People reason that as demand is infinite, a service free at the point of contact could become infinitely expensive. This is not likely to be true in practice. A recent example, mentioned above, was for private nursing homes, where the service became, for a time, essentially free on demand. Demand rose but not as rapidly as might be expected [152].

In the UK, access to all health services is only possible through general practitioners. They have few expensive facilities, see many people in a short space of time and are therefore cheap to provide. Over the past decade or so, they have made themselves less available, by appointment systems and grouping together further from their patients, thus limiting their access. This has tended to drive more people to the more expensive option of going to accident and emergency departments in hospital. Countries where secondary services are available directly tend to have extremely expensive services, with a great demand for specialist secondary and superspecialist tertiary care.

If general practitioner fundholders become the norm, marketing directors in the trusts will obviously focus attention on their requirements. Services provided will therefore have to become more responsive to individual needs, both of patients and of their general practitioners. There has been some concern that general practitioner fundholding will mean that providers will concentrate on general practitioners as purchasers rather than their patients. Even this is a step forward from the previous orientation of the health service. In the past, the hospital-based providers decided what they felt was good for patients and provided that. General practitioners are unlikely to ignore completely their patients' views on their treatment as they will keep seeing them if they are not better. This is to ignore the scurrilous comment by Don Herold that 'doctors think a lot of patients are cured who have simply quit in disgust'.

There are many other groups who, as potential service purchasers, will need to be on the marketing director's visiting list. It is likely that social services will, with their management duties under the NHS and Community Care Act, wish to purchase a number of community health services. In particular, they may want to buy therapy services for disabled people at home or in day centres in order to help people to maintain their mobility. This is likely to be a more cost-effective option than expanding transport facilities for disabled people. The needs of these purchasers are likely to be very different from those of general practitioners, and a good marketing director will need to be aware of these subtleties.

PATIENT CHOICE

Patient choice is always difficult to provide within a system that has a set budget, as choice implies spare capacity.

Patient's Charter

The Patient's Charter does not lay down rights to service; it sets up standards of national performance. This encourages local purchasers, health authorities and general practitioner fundholders, to augment these with their own higher standards for the delivery of care. The Charter has so far concentrated on the time patients spend waiting for treatment in hospital outpatient or accident and emergency departments, or in the general practitioner's surgery. In April 1994 the Secretary of State announced plans to extend the range of areas covered by the Charter. This included a national target for the time patients have to wait for their first outpatient appointment. He also included a target for patients needing coronary artery bypass grafts to be admitted from a waiting list within 12 months. Other proposals to give patients more choice of food, timed appointments for community nurse visits and better complaints procedures were set up.

From January 1995

In January 1995 the expanded Charter was launched. Its contents were as follows [153]. The expanded Charter said that, among a number of other things:

- Patients have a right to know if they are going to be placed in mixed sex wards.
- National standards are needed to address security and cleanliness as well as single-sex washing and toilet facilities for patients in hospital.
- Children should normally be admitted to children's wards under the care of a paediatric consultant, rather than to adult wards.

From 1st April 1995

- An 18 month guarantee for waiting time for all inpatient treatment.
- A 26 week standard for first outpatient appointments, including a target of 90% for all trust outpatients to be seen within 13 weeks.
- A 12 month standard for coronary artery bypass grafting and some associated procedures.
- A 3–4 hour standard for emergency admission to hospital through accident and emergency departments to be strengthened to 2 hours from April 1996.

- A standard of 2 hour time bands for home visits by community nurses, and other standards addressing how quickly those visits should be made.
- A standard addressing hospital catering services.
- A series of standards for ambulance arrival.

From 1st April 1996

- A coronary bypass or similar treatment for blocked coronary arteries within a year of being diagnosed as needing one, including the waiting time for the first appointment.
- No waiting more than 4 hours in an accident and emergency department.
- Patients, when admitted, to receive written information about hospital facilities.
- Patients with serious mental illness will work with a carer of their choice and agree and keep a copy of their care plan.
- If a patient complains, he or she should receive a written acknowledgement within 2 working days and a full reply within 4 weeks.

The government have published league tables of hospital performance. Until now, the greatest variation in the measures between hospitals was with patients who had cancelled operations not being admitted within a month of the second cancellation. From none to over half of the patients fell into this category, depending on the region [154]. The government published some data from primary care, including the proportion of medical records transferred urgently or routinely, the allocation to a general practitioner and the percentage of practices who had charters. The idea of these charters is to allow people to make choices, but so far little information about clinical quality has been included.

The government have been resistant to publishing clinical information, especially about death rates. The reason is that there are differences between patients admitted by different hospitals. In some places, the age, sex and severity of the disease will be different for patients with the same condition. Some of the data are not complete. For example, deaths from an episode of illness may occur after discharge from hospital, especially if people are discharged earlier in some areas than others. It may be that, for some diseases, death is not a reasonable way of measuring the quality of the service received in hospital. It may, for example, just be the culmination of a series of different treatments, people being admitted to hospital for the last part of their illness. I mentioned in Chapter 3 that the Scots have overcome some of these problems and have published outcome data [155].

HEALTH BOARDS

There are a number of approaches for letting the public have a say in the health service that they require. Nye Bevan in 1948 was resistant to allowing locally elected politicians to run the local health authorities, as he thought that health services were too important to be subject to local party political squabbles. He therefore set up a parallel system in which the councillors were represented but the Secretary of State, a central government minister, had the final word.

I have mentioned that, until the internal market was set up in 1991, these people were chosen locally from the councillors, the great and the good. In other words, there were a number of local councillors of different political persuasion, often a number of highly placed doctors, and a number of trade unionists. I have a suspicion that Nye Bevan had quite a strong regard for doctors and wanted them to have a considerable say in 'their' service.

Since 1991 the four Secretaries of State in the UK have chosen the board members, the chairmen and the non-executive directors of trusts and health authorities. They are now from different backgrounds compared with those on the previously existing boards. Most have been chosen for their knowledge of running a company; many are directors of large firms, have businesses of their own or have financial experience with one of the big accounting groups. Given their background, their expertise is about ensuring that the finances of the board, whether trust or health authority, are in order.

The non-executive directors could not pretend to represent a cross-section of the general public. They are there to ensure that the organization is business-like. There is no doubt that the political complexion of the non-executive directors favours the right rather than the left wing of the political spectrum in the UK, which could not have been lost upon the Secretaries of State when they set up the system. Nevertheless, the ethos of paternalism does seem to have altered somewhat. The purchasing and providing system, particularly among providers, can be very competitive. Board deliberations, in my experience, revolve around how best to provide an acceptable service to customers, i.e. patients, within the money available. The expertise of people with a financial background is therefore important. These, sadly, tend to have only a right-wing perspective.

The general public's view

Given these pressures, I am concerned about the problem of the general public having a say in the way that health services develop. On the one hand, it is obviously important to keep pressure on organizations as costly as the health authorities and trusts to remain efficient. On the other, there needs to be an expertise on the boards concerning the effectiveness of the most expensive part of the organizations, the delivery of medical care. There is plenty of talk in boards about efficiency but little about effectiveness. In the UK at present, the most effective way to make changes to the health service is to depose the government of the day and therefore the Secretaries of State in a general election; this is hardly a flexible way to bring about change. One can only hope that the purchasers of health services will take more seriously the need to be aware of what the general public wants. They may then be willing to modify their plans, to some extent, towards those desires. There is a lot to do in health authorities these days with very few people to do it. It is easy to forget the delicate and complex task of asking the people out there what they want.

One of the difficulties of doing this is that the medical issues are often complex and technical and need to be translated into understandable choices, without paternalism or employing propaganda. This needs skill in communication and openness from the purchasers, which has in the past not been an obvious part of their make-up. Most health authorities have in some way or other attempted to get the views of the public or their patients about their plans. However, the central questions are often not asked. These might include the values the local public hold and whether they prefer equity of access to high-powered, centralized facilities. They may have strong views on whether some treatment services should be disadvantaged for the future development of preventive services.

A simple and obvious example will give a flavour of the problems in which the public should be involved. Screening women for cervical cancer will save a few lives and give a very large number of women reassurance that they do not have the disease. Cervical cancer is rare and the screening money would be better spent, for the number of lives saved, elsewhere. Do the public regard widespread reassurance as more important than saving some extra lives or reducing disability by spending the money on something effective at reducing disability, for example hip operations? Health authorities will make these decisions, sometimes unknowingly, but still make them without any recourse to the views of the population. Many health authority purchasers themselves have no stated set of values that would guide them into choosing one option or the other for cervical cancer. Most authorities try to get away with doing a bit of everything to keep the public and politicians quiet, while pretending to do everything.

I have not mentioned the community health councils which, during this time, are supposed to have represented the general public's view to the health authorities. They have not, in my experience, had any effect upon policy or planning within the health service, but have been more successful at acting as advocates for individual patients who have fallen foul of the system.

The Bath experience

Researchers in Bath Health Authority surveyed 1500 people in their area [156]. Just under half of the questionnaires were returned. The researchers asked people how important they believed a selection of 10 services were. Two services – family planning and help for people who want to stop smoking – were said to be very important by one-third of the people who answered. Table 10.1 shows the importance attached to different aspects of the quality of the services in the order of importance.

Table 10.1 Aspects of the health service thought to be important

Aspects of service	Percentage who thought it important
Clear information	76
Modern equipment	68
Value for money	58
Seeing the same doctor if you return to a clinic	58
Friendly staff	33
Tasty and nutritious food	26
Signposts around the hospitals	26
Comfortable waiting areas	10

People were asked who should make decisions about the health authority. There was support for suggestions that the health authority should give people more information about what it does and about the services provided for them. The services chosen by people did not particularly reflect what professionals would regard as good value for money. Haemodialysis, for example, costs £14 000 for one quality-adjusted life, whereas advice to help people stop smoking costs £167 for the same benefit [157]. People gave a low priority to helping smokers. It is not clear whether this reflects a lack of sympathy with smokers or poor information about the relative benefits.

People did not give a particularly high priority to some aspects of quality highlighted in the NHS reforms, such as comfortable waiting areas. They considered clear information about their illness and treatment to be much more relevant. People also felt that they should have more say in decision making for the health service, although the study did not look into the best means of how to achieve this.

EFFECTIVE THERAPY OF WHICH PATIENTS ARE WARY: MINIMAL ASSISTANCE ANTENATAL CARE

There has been a growing worry that much of antenatal care has become an unthinking ritual with few returns and great inconvenience for pregnant women [158]. We have inherited the scheduling of clinic visits from the 1920s, when the risks from pregnancy were quite different. Many people believe that, today, women make too many antenatal visits to see too many different professionals in too many settings. Until recently, all women were seen at set intervals, increasing in frequency as the date of delivery became closer.

Several people have suggested improvements, with less antenatal care. Experts have suggested that each visit should have an explicit clinical purpose, and it is believed that there should be different contributions by general practitioners, midwives and obstetricians. At present, obstetricians disagree on whether they should, or should not, be involved in the antenatal care of all healthy women with normal pregnancies [159, 160].

There is little quantitative evidence to help in these debates. A few random-ized trials have assessed the effects of combined antenatal care and childbirth. The trials have involved using midwives and domiciliary care for women who have no complications. Researchers have carried out four randomized trials of different patterns of antenatal care. The first two were small [161, 162], but two much larger trials have also been published [163]. A Scottish trial com-pared routine antenatal care delivered by general practitioners and midwives with conventional care involving specialist obstetricians [164]. A trial in London [165] compared the traditional British antenatal schedule of routine visits with a markedly reduced number.

Antenatal care aims to provide many different sorts of benefit, including clinical improvements, education and psychological and social support. Poor clinical outcomes, and death or disability affecting the mother or baby, are very rare. Because of this, even the larger trials mentioned are not large enough to draw conclusions about whether the types of antenatal care have an effect upon serious life-threatening outcomes. The Scottish trial found fewer women with complications in the group cared for by general practitioners and mid-wives. It is important to establish whether this is due to failure to detect the abnormalities or because the care was better.

The new trials do provide important information about the views of pregnant women. In the London trial, women in the group receiving fewer visits were less satisfied than were the group getting more. They were more likely to worry about their baby both before and after the birth. They were also more likely to have negative views about their baby, and more likely to be dissatisfied by the number of antenatal visits they received. This finding fits with earlier data from Aberdeen, which started the reassessment of antenatal care in the UK [166].

It may be that pregnant women have learned, from their friends and family, what they are likely to receive when they are having a baby and expect the same degree of attention. Whatever the case, it is essential that the arrange-ments are responsive to the needs and expectations of pregnant women. It would be unfortunate if women saw an attempt to improve the quality of care as disregard for them and their babies. Some parts of the approach, including care that involves consultant obstetricians only when problems arise, appear to be acceptable. However, the London trial should save the maternity services from making the mistake of implementing unpopular, infrequent timings for antenatal visits without a lot more thought.

EXAMPLES OF PATIENT SATISFACTION SURVEYS

The British social attitudes survey has since 1983 been asking people what they think of the health service. The researchers gather information through interviews carried out by Social and Community Planning Research in a nationwide representative sample of people. It is known that the views people have of the service have an important effect upon the way in which they behave, particularly in going to their doctor and following their treatment.

Many people have found that there are difficulties with looking at people's satisfaction with services. The health service is such a large organization that different people, when responding to a questionnaire, may be thinking about different parts of the organization. If one compares the results of the national surveys in 1983, 1989 and 1993, one finds that there was a reduction in overall level of satisfaction with the health service between 1983 and 1989. There was subsequently, in 1993, a slight rise, but not reaching the level of satisfaction in 1983.

Different areas of the country showed the same pattern of a drop and then a rise. London remained the most dissatisfied with the NHS throughout. Different social classes were reasonably similar in 1983 and 1989. In 1993 professional groups remained dissatisfied, whereas the other groups improved. Women reported slightly higher levels of satisfaction in all age groups than did men. About half of the young men were dissatisfied with the health service in 1989, compared with only 1 in 10 of the oldest group of females.

In 1983 patients were asked specifically about their satisfaction with their general practitioner. The extent of the satisfaction was greater than with the rest of the NHS. The pattern again showed that people in London and young men were the most dissatisfied. The main difference between the satisfaction with general practitioners and the NHS as a whole was that there was little change over the years in satisfaction with the general practitioners. Again, more women than men were satisfied with their general practitioner.

The researchers asked a further series of questions about being in hospital. The main difference in the pattern was that there was a gradual increase in satisfaction over the 3 years of reporting of the study. There was a difference between those who had recent experience of being an inpatient or having a member of family or friend admitted, compared with those who did not have such experience. Those with recent experience reported higher levels of satisfaction than did those who had not been admitted or been in contact with someone who had been admitted. Those who had been admitted also showed a slight improvement in the level of satisfaction between 1989 and 1993. This is good news for the hospital service and possibly suggests that becoming a trusts has required hospitals to improve their services.

The researchers asked people what improvements to the services they would suggest. The main problem that patients had with general practitioners was the appointment system. Four out of 10 people recommended some change. As far as hospital services were concerned, most people were satisfied with the quality of medical treatment, especially nursing care, but waiting times for non-emergency operations caused considerable concern. There was also some concern about the physical layout of hospitals.

There was a marked change over the years in answer to a question about whether the government should increase taxes so that spending on health, education and social benefits could be improved. Between 1983 and 1993 double the percentage of people, from one-third to two-thirds, thought that increased taxes should be spent. Interestingly, during this period, people voted for the political party that promised to cut taxes.

INEFFECTIVE BUT ESTABLISHED SERVICES: COUNSELLORS IN GENERAL PRACTICE FOR MENTAL DISORDERS

Definition of counselling

Counselling is the skilled and principled use of relationships to help the client develop self-knowledge, emotional acceptance and growth, and personal resources [167].

Uses of counselling

Counselling has been used for patients with anxiety, depression and problems with relationships. People have suggested it for alcohol misuse, postnatal depression and addiction to tranquillizers in the mental health field. It has been used for people suffering from trauma.

Effectiveness

Many attempts to evaluate its effectiveness have shown little or no benefit [168–172]. When researchers have claimed benefits, these have been small compared with the resources employed. Caution is needed in the face of this evidence [173]. Despite the lack of evidence of its efficacy, many general practitioners believe in the value of counselling and of counsellors in general practice. Between 10% and 30% of consulting patients have mainly emotional problems, so the scope for increasing general practitioners' counselling skills or referring to an in-house counsellor is substantial.

Reason for the expansion of counselling

The main reason for general practitioners' enthusiasm for counselling may be a desire to reduce contact with a very demanding group of patients [174]. If this is so, increasing the counselling skills of general practitioners may be preferable to widening the primary health care team. Counselling requires a move away from the model of distance, diagnosis and reassurance, towards a model that recognizes and promotes a person's autonomy. Many general practitioners may find this difficult.

Since 1990 the general practice contract has allowed reimbursement for the costs of employing counsellors. The staffing budget is cash limited, and some practices may have to accept less than 70% reimbursement if their application is successful. Fundholding practices have more control over staffing, and many consider counsellors, along with physiotherapists and chiropodists, to be their highest priority. Many practices have applied to run health promotion clinics for managing stress, which are disguised counselling sessions.

The future

The stage therefore seems set for an explosion of counselling. Whether effective or not, counselling can, in the wrong hands, be damaging. Practices would be wise, therefore, not to appoint unqualified people just because they seem to have good listening skills. However well intentioned an amateur counsellor might be, there are profound professional, ethical and clinical issues. Sibbald and colleagues have shown that fewer than half of all present counsellors have received specialist training in counselling [175].

Counsellors should be accredited by the British Association for Counselling or be chartered psychotherapists recognized by the British Psychological Society [176]. They must keep accurate records, but the requirements of confidentiality may require keeping some disclosures from the patients' doctors. They should have debriefing sessions with their own counsellor at least monthly and should have a commitment to audit and reaccreditation. Some practices may not wish this degree of rigour, especially with the relative scarcity of trained counsellors. Every health authority should enter into discussions with its general practitioners to establish guidelines, if they must, for the employment of counsellors. It is important that the current demand for counsellors does not lead to a lowering of standards [177].

PURCHASING SERVICES IN THE VOLUNTARY SECTOR: EXAMPLE OF A CONTRACT

Voluntary organizations can bid for money from the health service for providing services expected to have a positive effect upon the health of the patients, as long as it is in line with the health authority's strategy and fits in with the annual purchasing plan.

Contract between (Purchasers) and (Provider)

Services Covered:	As outlined in section 3 of the contract
Contract Duration:	1st April 199X to 31st March 199X, subject to annual review at times mutually agreed between both parties
Contract Value:	£75 000
Party 1:	Purchasers: **Health Authority**
Party 2:	Provider

For and on behalf of the Purchaser:

Signature: ....

Designation: ....

Date: ....

For and on behalf of the Provider:

Signature: ....

Designation: ....

Date: ....

Introduction

Following a review and evaluation of the service you provided under contract to the Health Authority during 199X, the following is an agreement to fund the named project. The project is funded under the terms of section 23 of the National Health Service Act 1977 according to the criteria outlined in the following contract.

Name of Project to be Funded

- Drop-in centre: Service in xxxx
- Shop: Service in xxxx

Estimated costs:

Recurring	Non-recurring	Total amount for 1995/96
Shop: £12 000	£000	£12 000
Drop-in centre: £63 000	£000	£63 000

Services to be provided within the above sum

Services to be provided are those outlined in the business case. Particular note will be taken of the following.

Drop-in centre

To provide the aspects of the service outlined in the business case submission of November 199X as:

- To provide support information, counselling, crisis assistance, advocacy and befriending for people with mental health problems outside the hours normally operated by community services
- To provide weekend meals for those with serious mental health problems who require them
- To support users with paid staff and with volunteers who will be trained and supervised to a high standard
- To provide specialist drop-in sessions for specific groups of people suffering mental ill-health

Cafe

- To continue to facilitate through paid workers the cafe in xxxx, which is staffed by service users
- To continue to provide the sandwich making and delivery services to offices in XXXX town centre
- All the above criteria will be considered in discussions in the 6 monthly review meeting.

Monitoring information

Information required by the Health Authority should be returned on a half-yearly basis (that is in the fifth and the twelfth months). A review meeting will be arranged for the sixth month to monitor progress and suitability of the contract to date. Information should be returned to xxxx.

Information required by the health authority on a half-yearly basis includes:

- The numbers attending weekend and evening sessions
- Feedback from a user group established to draw up and audit quality standards for the service
- Records to monitor the training and use of volunteers
- An annual users' 'satisfaction survey' report.

Information required by the Purchaser on an annual basis includes:

- a comprehensive annual report on services throughout the year
- a detailed statement of accounts for the year.

Service criteria

The decision to fund this scheme has been made according to the business case submitted on xxxx.

Method of payment

Payment will be made on a quarterly basis.

General contract conditions

All aspects of the General Contract Conditions (attached) will apply.

Notice of withdrawal of contract

The period of notice required by either side will be 6 months.

Named contact in each organization

    Provider: Purchaser:

GENERAL CONDITIONS FOR CONTRACTS WITH NON-STATUTORY PROVIDERS OF HEALTH CARE

Introduction

This section of the contract documentation is common to all contracts held between non-statutory providers of mental health care and xxxx Health Authority.

Objectives and duration

The objective of the contract is to secure, for the residents of the Health Authority, the provision of a range of health care for defined client groups and specialities. This is at a defined level of quality, with appropriate levels of skill and care being exercised, for an agreed price, for one year from 1 April 199X. The Health Authority requires that they are informed of any significant intended changes in existing or future capacity, including that arising from other purchaser intentions.

The provision of this contract is for the financial year 199X/9Y.

This agreement is underpinned by the commitment of both parties to the objectives of the Secretary of State's focus on:

- Ever-improving health
- Real choice for patients
- Stewardship.

Both parties also agree to work together to seek to achieve the highest quality of health care and to incorporate priorities for maintaining and developing services that take account of:

- Local needs
- How clinical effectiveness can be enhanced
- How the speed of access to appropriate health care can be improved

- How the quality of the environment within which patients are treated and cared for can be improved
- How the standard and level of communication with patients and relatives can be improved.

Quality

Standards incorporated in the above sections and adopted by the Authority have been based on previous years' experience, professional guidance, the Patient's Charter, Caring for the Future and health strategies. Providers are expected to address each of the standards and work towards achievement by reporting on the performance against using the relevant agreed indicators within the stated time scales.

To monitor the performance against the quality specification and to gauge conformance, reports will be required at fixed intervals. The form of the reports will be agreed with Providers. Along with Provider reports, the Authority will receive information for monitoring purposes from its patient satisfaction surveys, visits and information from other departments within the health authority. The information gathered will be shared with the Providers and the outcomes and action plans agreed.

Variations of contract terms

There may be exceptional circumstances during the year that are beyond the reasonable control of either party which prevent the discharge of the contract in whole or in part. When this becomes apparent, both parties must discuss any proposed variations and agree a timetable leading to the resumption of normal contracting arrangements. This is important so that any charge of non-performance by either party can be avoided. The Provider shall not be liable for failure to perform the agreement directly or indirectly caused by *force majeure*. This term includes Acts of God, Acts of Parliament, Fire, War, Embargoes, Strikes and any other recurrence [whether or not similar in nature to those specified] beyond the control of the Provider.

Information monitoring

The Provider is required to maintain systems that will produce accurate information to allow its services to be monitored. The Provider will give the Purchaser the following information as agreed. It is recognized that services provided by the non-statutory agencies address issues of quality of life. Attempts will be made accordingly to remember this in requests for monitoring information. During the contract period, monitoring visits will be undertaken. Such visits will give regard to the operation of the provider with the continued care of patients.

Performance review

For the purposes of monitoring the agreement, the Purchaser will hold performance review meetings with the Provider. The agenda for these meetings will be formed from the Provider's quarterly reports with the key agenda items being:

- quality
- targets and guarantees
- a review of client or patient satisfaction.

Confidentiality

The Purchaser and non-statutory Provider in this case agree always to maintain a high standard of confidentiality. They will respect the need for such confidentiality as part of the contract between them. In addition, both will uphold the normal and accepted rules of confidentiality concerning information regarding patients or clients.

LINKING GUIDELINES AND ASSESSMENT OF QUALITY

Guidelines and reviews are designed to help clinicians and others assess their care. However, there is no standard method for developing these. Guidelines are set up to help clinicians to keep a good standard of service. They do this by getting the providers in a specialty to agree a certain minimum of care that all patients should receive. Reviews may be set up after the guidelines are in place, to give information about whether the guidelines are being followed. The reviews can be used to monitor performance and can be used to guide the more stringent process used in clinical audit [178].

Example of guidelines

The guidelines of the British Hypertension Society say that 'great emphasis should be placed on encouraging patients to stop smoking as the coexistence of smoking as an additional risk factor in hypertensive patients confers a much increased risk of subsequent cardiovascular events' [179]. The guidelines can instruct clinicians to review whether the guideline has been followed as:

The records show that at least annually:
- There has been an assessment of smoking habit
- Appropriate advice has been given to smokers.

The review criteria make clear what information is required to assess compliance, how the information is obtained and the time over which smoking habit needs to be assessed.

Table 10.2 Definitions of guidelines, criteria and protocols for clinical practice

Clinical practice guidelines	Systematically developed statements to assist decisions for practitioner and patient about appropriate health care for specific clinical circumstances
Review criteria	Systematically developed statements that can be used to assess the appropriateness of specific health care decisions, service and outcomes
Protocol	A comprehensive set of criteria for a single clinical condition or aspects of an organization
Standard	The percentage of events that should comply with the criterion

Recently, researchers have suggested the development of systematic guidelines based on evidence, which may offer an approach to incorporating the findings of research into routine clinical practice [180,181]. Guidelines can encourage improvements in performance when properly implemented [182,183]. The NHS Management Executive has recognized the part that guidelines could play in improving clinical effectiveness, and I would suggest that general guidelines should be incorporated in contracts [184]. However, using guidelines does not guarantee success [185–187], and the way in which clinicians work depends on more than guidelines. There needs to be a campaign to encourage their acceptance. Table 10.2 shows a series of commonly used phrases in this area and their definitions.

Useful sets of requirements for review criteria have been developed [188,189]. Evidence from research should be evaluated properly to differentiate criteria for which there is strong supporting evidence from those for which evidence is less clear or completely lacking [190]. One should provide data as a review of the research literature, and how research reports were evaluated. This is aimed at increasing the confidence of clinicians in the practical value of the criteria and their impact on the outcome of care.

Several classification systems for prioritizing review criteria have been suggested [191]. To meet the needs of clinical audit for a system that is easy to understand, some researchers have devised a classification of 'must do', 'should do' and 'could do' criteria [192]. The 'must do' criteria are those for which there is solid evidence from research of substantial impact on outcome. 'Should do' criteria are those for which there is good evidence, but the impact is less substantial or the evidence is less strong. 'Could do' criteria are those elements of care for which evidence of impact is inconclusive. If it cannot be shown that an element of care is either beneficial or harmful in clinical or economic terms, there is little to be gained by undertaking an audit to ensure that that element of care is provided. Such criteria should not therefore be routinely included in assessments of the quality of care.

Feeling an ownership for the guidelines is often seen as an important part of whether the criteria or guidelines are used [193]. People say that ownership depends on whether people who use the criteria helped to developed them. In a recent review of methods for the implementation of guidelines, however, the evidence did not show that ownership was critically important. Local development need not be the only way to ensure that clinicians accept and use the criteria. Ownership is helped by allowing clinicians the freedom to choose whether performance is judged against 'must do' criteria or 'must do' plus 'should do', and to select the most appropriate standards for their circumstances.

Overcoming problems | 11

SERVICES DIFFICULT TO PURCHASE

Chronic diseases

Long-term diseases, especially those that require coordinated work with other services, such as social services, housing and education, have special problems. Mental illness services, learning disability services and services for disabled elderly people are classic examples, but some health problems classically thought of as belonging to acute medicine can also be associated with problems. I worked with a group many years ago who showed that a major improvement in the mental and physical state of men with myocardial infarction occurred when they went back to work [194]. In these men with a classic acute illness, social factors were an overwhelming part of their getting back to health.

Forensic psychiatry

Purchasing forensic psychiatry services is problematical because the number of cases is small and the highly specialist facilities required are available on a national or regional, rather than a local basis.

Introduction

Forensic psychiatry is a sub-specialty of psychiatry established within the NHS in 1972 with a specialist section within the Royal College of Psychiatrists. It is concerned with patients who overlap between psychiatry and the law. Much of the confusion in the press about mentally ill people being involved in violence, and tabloid attacks on 'care in the community', concern this group of patients. They are in fact no more commonly cared for in the community now than they have been for the past 20 years, largely due to a lack of provision, as we shall see. Many move from gaol to secure health service accommodation and back with depressing frequency.

These patients, because of their interaction with the law, often have to be confined. There are therefore four main categories of need within forensic psychiatry. These are patients requiring:

- High secure units or special hospitals
- Medium secure units (regional secure)
- Low secure units
- Specialist teams in the community.

Not all mentally ill patients who offend or are violent are treated by specialist forensic psychiatry teams. Most of those at levels of security lower than medium security are cared for by general psychiatric services. It is important to see the service as an integrated whole for patients, rather than treating each category of care separately. Liaison and cooperation between professionals responsible for the different services is vitally important. It is also extremely difficult as several of the levels of security are managed by different organizations and are likely to be considerable distances from each other.

Effectiveness of services

Special hospitals
In 1994 more than half of the 1700 patients in special hospitals suffered from schizophrenia, 25% from psychopathic disorder and 9% from learning disability. Sixteen per cent were women. One in seven was not an offender [195,196]. Twice as many men as women in these places were convicted for homicide. Property offences were more common among women: 40% had been convicted for arson or criminal damage. For men, homicide or violence were more common with mental illness; sexual offences and arson were more commonly found with psychopathic disorder and mental impairment. Some follow-up studies of patients discharged or transferred from special hospitals are summarized in Table 11.1 [197]

Table 11.1 Outcomes of discharges and transfers from special hospitals

Main author and length of follow-up	Reoffending rate	Special hospital	Prison	NHS hospital	Community
Acres[198](93) 2 years	67% MI 18% MH	17%	13%	2%	50%
Dell[199](105) 2 years	7%	6% MI 6% MH		38% MI 19% MH	
Black[200](128) 5 years	10%	20%		20%	50%

Figures in round brackets are numbers of patients in study.
MI, mental illness; MH mental handicap.

Acres followed up patients discharged to the community from special hospitals. Most offences were acquisitive; there was one murder, one rape, two sexual assaults and 13 violent offences. Supervision reduced the chance of re-offending. Dell studied patients transferred from special hospitals to NHS care; only eight caused major difficulties following transfer. Black followed up men discharged from Broadmoor, of whom half had originally committed homicide. There were no homicides in the first 5 years after release, but there were two later.

Bowden [201] reviewed the progress of patients leaving special hospitals. One in five returned to special hospitals, 1 in 2 were subsequently convicted, usually of trivial acquisitive offences, and 1 in 10 were involved in serious or homicidal acts of violence. Four-fifths of serious reoffenders among patients discharged from Park Lane special hospital to the community were diagnosed as having personality disorder, as were nine-tenths of all reoffenders [202]. Sexual offences, prior imprisonment and absolute discharge were associated with higher rates of reconviction. Previous sexual index offences and a sexual element to the initial offence tended to lead to higher rates of reconviction for serious offences. The number of previous convictions and the probability of reconviction were directly related [203].

Medium, low and specialist community services
There is no evidence for the effectiveness of these services. Government policy gives guidance on the methods to be employed [204]. It seems sensible that all patients should be at the lowest level of security consistent with a reasonable degree of safety for themselves and society at large. Policies on the provision of care for forensic psychiatry patients are as much to do with protecting the public as with the care of the individual.

Existing demand for services

An assessment of the need for services for forensic patients in North and South Wales [205] gave a point prevalence for such patients of 164 for the North and 342 for the South. These included patients with brain injury, personality disorder, psychosis, other mental illness and learning disabilities. For mental illness alone, the prevalence was 148 in the North and 254 in the South. The survey response rate in the North was higher.

The availability of the four levels of provision available or planned in Wales are shown in Table 11.2. An additional survey of forensic psychiatric referrals was undertaken in North Wales, identifying an additional 30 people who required services.

Special hospitals
Special hospitals are not at present a health authority provision or responsibility but will become so with the development of the High Security Purchasing

Table 11.2 Places available for forensic psychiatry in Wales

Type of Provision	Names	Number of places for Welsh patients
Special Hospitals (high secure)*	Ashworth	50
	Broadmoor	12
	Rampton	7
Regional (medium) secure and equivalent	Caswell clinic	33
	Ty Llywellyn, Llanfairfechan (not yet built)	25 + 10 (learning disabled— not yet approved)
	Llanarth Court (private)	62
Low secure	Ward W3 Whitchurch	10 + 7 rehab
Specialist community services	North Wales	Forensic team
	South Wales	Forensic trained CPNs

*No limit on places—demand specific

Table 11.3 Number of clients in special hospitals

Health authority	Welsh surveys: North 1993 South 1995. (Figures in brackets give numbers not identified by surveys)		Most recent data-All Wales point prevalence (estimates)
	Past	1993/1995	
Dyfed and Powys	3	1(7)	6
Morgannwg	4	4(5)	8
Bro Tâf	8	9(16)	24
North Wales	10	16(2)	16
Gwent	6	6(10)	15
Total	31	36(40)	69

Table 11.4 Number of clients estimated to be in medium secure facilities (mental illness, learning disability and brain injury)

Health authority	Medium secure: North 1993, South 1995		Private facilities: mostly medium secure
	Past	1993/1995	1993/1995
Dyfed and Powys	4	6	4
Morgannwg	1	3	7
Bro Tâf	7	9	15
North Wales	2	3	12
Gwent	7	5	7
Total	21	26	4

Table 11.5 Number of cases in low secure accommodation (mental illness, learning disability and brain injury)

Health authority (estimated)	Low secure: physically or high staffing – North 1993, South 1995	
	Past	1993/1995
Dyfed and Powys	2	3
Morgannwg	5	9
Bro Tâf	3	2
North Wales	21	26
Gwent	2	12
Total	33	52

Board that has replaced the Special Hospitals Service Authority [206]. This was established in shadow form in September 1995.

Table 11.3 shows the demand for special hospital care and how it has increased over time. This has been largely due to a lack of medium secure and low secure facilities.

Medium secure facilities
Table 11.4 shows the data from the needs assessment exercises for existing and previous demand for medium secure facilities.

Low or local secure facilities
The needs assessment work divided these facilities into those which are physically secure and those which have high staffing. There is only one facility in Wales. Patients who are highly disturbed in other counties may be admitted to intensive care facilities for a short time, or may be sent to the unnecessarily restrictive medium secure facilities.

The needs assessment data on the low secure units are shown in Table 11.5. The data have been adversely affected by a low response rate in the assessment of needs from the Bro Tâf area, a point prevalence then would have shown about 10 cases.

There has been a dramatic rise in the demand for this type of facility.

Specialist community services
The level of demand for specialist community services is unknown, and the number of people involved in such services is, at the moment, small. It involves people who have been followed up by forensic psychiatry teams, following an inpatient stay in secure units or following referral for assessment from the courts.

Non-specialist community services
It must be remembered that about three-quarters of the patients who could be classified as forensic cases are being managed by the general adult services.

Table 11.6 Clients in prison in Welsh survey (North 1993, South 1995)

Health authority	Past	Present
Dyfed & Powys	6	6
Morgannwg	12	7
South Glamorgan	26	6
Gwent	19	8
North Wales	23	12
Total	86	39

These figures are necessarily less easy to verify for separate authorities. The needs assessment survey included 181 people who were living independently or with their family.

Future needs: pressures upon demand

Prison
The Reid report [207] suggested that there is a need to review prisoners in gaol for mental illness. The authorities assessed the needs of prisoners for mental illness services. It is assumed that most of these will require a medium secure unit care, although some may require special hospitals. The Reid report suggests that there may be 800 prisoners falling into this category in the UK. This would result in the release of an extra 30–40 patients into Welsh medium secure provision, with perhaps 10%, i.e. 3–4, of them requiring special hospital support.

In the South Wales survey, 25% of the 27 presently sentenced prisoners who required NHS care were considered suitable for transfer to this level of security (Table 11.6). If the numbers for the whole of Wales follow this pattern, this suggests a present demand for special hospitals from the prison service of 5–10 patients. The demand in the past year from the prison service for less secure services has been increasing markedly.

A study [208] has found that 4% of sentenced prisoners required transfer to NHS care. In 1994 it was estimated that 78 additional Welsh prisoners might have been better served by transfer to NHS care. Using the rates obtained in the surveys, this would mean 20 special hospital places, 10 medium secure places and 39 low secure places. These figures have been included in the estimated future demand for services.

Misplacement
An external independent audit of the placement of one health authority's patients in secure environments [209] showed that about one-third of the patients in medium secure accommodation could be managed in a less secure environment. A small number required longer-term, medium secure care, and some should have been released. The reports showed that the initial assessment, risk assessment and monitoring procedures were poor in all the facilities

used by this group of patients except one. Admission to that unit was difficult to achieve.

Future demand

Special hospitals
Sixty-nine Welsh patients are estimated to be in special hospitals, but, by the estimate of the hospitals themselves, 29 do not require this degree of security [210]. Of the other 40, the needs assessment studies suggested that many would be able to be managed in alternative arrangements in future, but there will be some pressure from the gaols to take more cases. The Special Hospitals Service Authority, before it became the High Security Purchasing Board, estimated that 30–50% of its patients could be in medium secure accommodation. This was a lower estimate than in the Welsh studies, possibly because the latter allowed the estimates of future need to be up to 2 years hence.

The Welsh needs assessments suggested that the future need for special hospital places was 33. This figure assumes that the rates obtained from people identified in the surveys could be applied to those not identified. If rates from other studies are used on the unidentified population, 39 places may be required. If the highest rates from all the studies are applied to unidentified patients, up to 60 places may be required. A target of 45 special hospital places for the Welsh population would seem reasonable in the medium term. Authority estimates are obtained by proportion of present use (Table 11.9). This approach will tend to overestimate the need in rural, and underestimate the need in urban, authorities.

Medium secure and low secure beds
Table 11.7 shows the needs assessment data for the future demand on medium secure and low secure hospital places. Demand will alter in this way:

- If the surveys of professional opinion are right
- If the facilities can be built or adapted and staffed.

Table 11.7 Future estimates of need for medium and low secure hospitals

Health authority	Medium secure: all sources	Low secure
Dyfed and Powys	2 (12)	17
Morgannwg	12 (13)	31
Bro Tâf	25 (18)	29
North Wales	29 (16)	47
Gwent	13 (14)	15
Total	87[a] (73)[b]	139[a]

[a] Authority figures based on needs data.
[b] Authority figures based on population data. (Figures based on All Wales Advisory Group in brackets.)

Table 11.8 Need for other provision

Health Authority	Local non-secure provision	Independent living	Other
Dyfed and Powys	4	19	14
Morgannwg	9	32	14
Bro Tâf	14	51	14
North Wales	12	69	23
Gwent	18	46	17
Total	57	217	82

Community-based care

There is a demand for other services, including local non-secure provision, independent living, supported living schemes, specialist rehabilitation for head injury and many others. Table 11.8 shows the predicted needs for these people based on the surveys. These are likely to be minimum requirements in the long term.

There is also a demand for a service that provides an assessment of offenders, advice about the management of behaviourally disturbed patients and outpatient and outpatient treatment. This is estimated to come to about 200 new referrals a year per million population. In Wales this would be about 586 per annum (see Table 11.9).

One health authority has a mental health assessment and diversion scheme at the local magistrate's court, supported by the health authority, the probation service and the police. One specialized community psychiatric nurse works in the community with a specialized social worker in the health authority. There is a problem of isolation of these people.

Future developments

A large number of trusts in Wales have shown an interest in developing, at one level or another, a forensic psychiatry service, mainly low security and community services. This should help to reduce the number of patients kept in high security when they do not require it, as well as improve the care at lower levels of security. Many of the problems posed by placing patients who require secure care revolve around the need for a good initial and follow-up assessment service for patients. This helps to establish the priorities and helps the health authorities to decide how many places are needed at each level of security.

Work needs to be done on the needs of patients with psychopathic and personality disorder, in particular, the confusion that arises in the legal profession when different consultant psychiatrists regard and treat these patients differently [211].

Table 11.9 Future estimated annual number of cases for high, medium, low secure hospitals and community places

Health authority	High secure (see text)	Medium secure (see Table 11.7)	Low secure (see Table 11.7)	Community places (see text)
Dyfed and Powys	4	8 (12)	17	95
Morgannwg	5	12 (13)	31	101
Bro Tâf	16	25 (18)	29	146
North Wales	10	29 (16)	47	132
Gwent	10	13 (14)	15	112
Total	45 (33–60)	87 (73)[b]	139[a]	586[b]

[a]Authority figures calculated by needs assessment.
[b]Authority figures calculated by population sizes.

Conclusions

Individual health authorities will be dealing with quite small numbers of very expensive patients. It is obviously sensible for the purchasers to keep in close touch with each other when commissioning these services. There seems little doubt that there are insufficient places for the lower levels of security needed by a proportion of these patients, especially high-staffed, low security and specialist community services. The pressures on higher levels of security depend critically on whether these develop. They will also depend upon the demand for high secure places from the criminal justice system and other psychiatric services.

The development of medium secure places will depend critically upon low secure and community-based places. The present and planned medium secure beds should be sufficient. These changes will need considerable retraining of manpower. The need for such specialist medical nursing and social work care may well prove to be the main block to expansion of the less restrictive services.

Table 11.9 shows an estimate of the need for different types of service in the future.

AN EXAMPLE FROM ACUTE SERVICES: CANCER SERVICES

Commissioning and providing cancer services is not easy. Hypocrites, 2500 years ago, pointed out that patients with internal cancers who were treated survived for a shorter time than those who were left alone. A number of people, including some doctors, feel that the same holds true even today for some of the common adult cancers. The need for services is considerable. At any one time, about a million people in the UK have cancer, and although some types of cancers are increasing and some decreasing in number, overall the numbers do not appear to be changing.

In the UK, there has been resistance to the development of cancer treatment as a separate specialty, possibly exacerbated by the existence of different Royal Colleges for surgeons, physicians and radiologists. This makes it difficult to develop a common training for the specialists [212]. A report [213] has recently proposed a countrywide network of services linking cancer units. It suggests specialist cancer centres in larger hospitals, mainly the medical schools, with lesser centres in some but, controversially not all, district general hospitals.

The report underlined the large number of different groups involved in treating patients with cancer. It suggested more non-surgical cancer specialists and that cancer surgeons need to treat a certain minimum number of cases in a year to be effective. This means that, in some hospitals, surgeons will have to stop doing cancer surgery. The report encourages purchasers to follow this route by making contracts specific for different tumour sites and allowing only people with considerable experience in the field to care for a particular cancer. The letter accompanying the report suggested that the recommendations be funded from within available resources. This has caused some controversy, especially among those directly involved in the field [214].

OPPORTUNITIES AND PROBLEMS OF NEW SERVICES

Problems of new technology: percutaneous endoscopic gastrostomy

Percutaneous endoscopic gastrostomy (PEG) is a fairly typical example of a new advance in treatment that is first introduced by a number of enthusiasts. The general medical community became interested through descriptions in journals and at conferences. It rapidly became the norm for a high proportion of patients unable to eat, resulting in a heavier workload for a wide range of other people in other services.

There needs, with all such developments, to be a moment of truth when the hard questions are asked:

- Is it preferable to the existing method (see, for example, Maxwell's criteria in Chapter 3 to decide what is meant by 'preferable')
- What are the criteria for contraindications to its use?
- How many will be needed? Will this increase or decrease over time?
- What effect does it have on the rest of the service, either as workload or costs?
- Who pays?

Background to the use of PEG feeding

Gauderer and associates were the first to report placing a feeding tube using PEG and local anaesthesia [215]. Enthusiastic reports of modifications of and improvements in the technique by those authors have followed. Hospital specialists have widely embraced the treatment. It seems to be safe, cost-effective and well tolerated by patients [216,217]. Despite this, there are some complications. Careful comparison of PEG and surgical gastrostomy with proper patient selection and comparison of the benefits has been difficult as the simpler procedure, PEG, appears to be self-evidently superior. As a result, no researchers have felt that they could set up a trial. Comparison with the use of a nasogastric tube has emphasized the limited time during which the tube can be tolerated.

This problem is very common. The enthusiasts who develop a new technique are not interested in comparing it with the older approach. Within a short time, the new one becomes established and no-one feels able ethically to perform the trial. Archie Cochrane suggested that 'the first case should be randomised'; in other words every new technique, from its inception should be scientifically compared with the old one. The problem is that the safety of new treatments improves rapidly as people become more skilled. Most new treatments would be rejected in their early stages if it were not for the enthusiasts.

Selecting patients

The most common reason for PEG is a neurological disorder that impairs the patient's swallowing, for example a stroke, so that food can inadvertently pass into the windpipe. Patients who are unconscious might also inhale. Another common reason for needing a PEG is cancer of the head or neck, causing a blockage to normal feeding. The procedure, like conventional surgical gastrostomy, is generally not advised in any patient with a severely limited life expectancy or who will not, because of confusion, leave the tube in place.

Tube placement complications

I have said that complications may occur after putting in a PEG tube. The overall rate of complications is reported to be 13% for minor complications and 3% for major complications [218]. This can be reduced by carefully choosing which patients receive the PEG and special care of the wound after feeding begins.

The death rate for the procedure itself is about 1%. The death rate within 30 days of the PEG being put in is about 16%, but the great majority of deaths are due to the underlying disease rather than the PEG. It is obvious, in retrospect, that these cases were badly chosen. People have found a similar rate of complications in PEG and the standard operative gastrostomy. However, PEG avoids the risks of general anaesthetic and can be performed at the bedside. It is therefore less expensive. A PEG tube can also be removed easily, and the remaining wound usually closes in 7–10 days. This is important because up to 14% of patients regain their ability to eat, making the gastrostomy tube unnecessary.

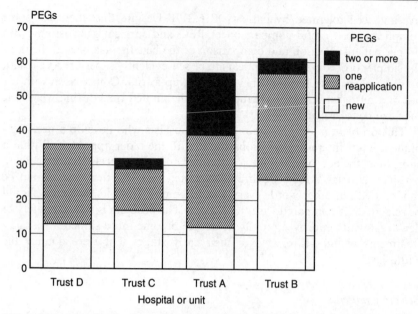

Figure 11.1   New applications and number of reapplications in past six months.

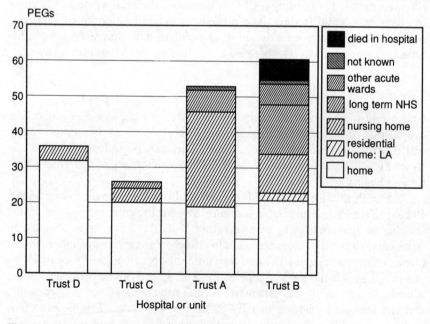

Figure 11.2   Trust or unit of those with PEGs by destination.

Use of PEG and gastrostomy

I carried out a retrospective 6 month survey of PEG in the health authority, the aim of which was to provide data about the use of the procedure and its indications, and as a background for developing an authority policy on the use of PEG. Figure 11.1 shows the number of PEGs, both initial and replacements, inserted by local provider trusts.

Clinicians give the great majority of PEGs to patients with a stroke. There was a wide range of reasons for other patients, some neurological, some due to carcinoma of the head or neck. A significant number, 20, was given to children with cystic fibrosis. Figure 11.2 shows the destination of those who received PEGs during the period by trust or unit. A large proportion of those leaving trust A go into nursing homes, whereas a higher proportion of those leaving trust B go into long-term NHS beds.

Figure 11.3 shows details of those who have new PEGs and those who have had replacements once, twice or more times in the 6 months of the survey. Multiple replacements are more common for patients discharged to nursing homes, suggesting that more attention needs to be paid to the care of such patients.

Policy problems

There have been comments by the provider trusts that PEGs are a considerable additional expense to the service, especially the community nursing service,

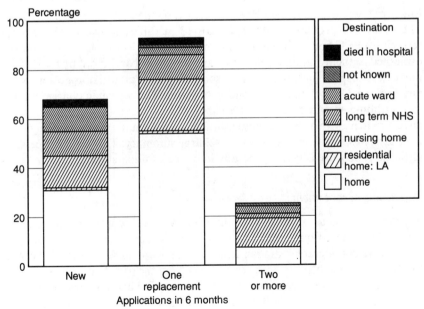

Figure 11.3   New applications against old in 6 months by destination.

both at home and in private nursing homes. There is some discussion about whether specialist nurses from the trusts should assist the nursing and residential homes to manage the PEGs. There have also been comments made that PEGs are being inserted 'too freely'. There are suggestions that they are being inserted inappropriately in elderly people with strokes and severe dementia. Many of these patients are not likely to survive for long, so the effect of the PEG is only to cause unnecessary distress.

Guidelines

Clinical contraindications to the insertion of a PEG mentioned above are mainly about the technical possibility of insertion. PEGs are not unique as a method of providing feeding for any group of patients. They are a more convenient method for some groups, so some thought must therefore be given to which patients require a PEG. Suggested indications are:

- PEGs are intended as medium- to long-term feeding methods. They should not be inserted for people who are likely to die within the next 4 weeks.
- They should not be given for people likely to regain the ability to take food by mouth within a month.
- The tube requires a certain amount of cooperation from patients. Those who are disturbed and likely to harm themselves by removing it should not be offered a PEG.

Many patients will have their PEGs managed by themselves or their relatives. The cases will probably need to be costed at different levels. All patients receiving a PEG and returned home should have the details of its management explained to them and their relatives. This should be carried out by the district nurse or a hospital liaison nurse very soon after their arrival home, along with any explanation they may have had in hospital. The person in charge of their case at home should give the latter explanations. General practitioners who have a patient with a PEG at home should receive details of the guidelines for the use of PEGs with each patient's discharge summary. This will be necessary until the procedure is better generally known and understood.

Purchasing arrangements

An important knock on effect of using PEGs was that people discharged home with them required quite intensive care from the community nursing service, which was a considerable extra burden on the service at home. The costs of caring for the PEG were therefore transferred away from the trust that inserted it.

This was even more complicated for patients discharged to private nursing homes, where there was a demarcation problem. If the procedure was regarded as routine, the nurses in the nursing home would be required to care for the

PEG. If it was seen as a specialist procedure, the NHS was required to assist the nursing home staff. This needed to be resolved. I suggested:

- The provider inserting the PEG should be responsible for monitoring it, and knock-on payments, for example nurse visits, should be covered by the trust inserting the PEG. This arrangement should last until there was some stability in the numbers being used.
- The purchasers should purchase the whole service from the inserting trust. Inserting trusts would subcontract maintenance care. Monitoring numbers would be the responsibility of the provider inserting the PEGs.
- Once the numbers had stabilized, for example after 2 years, the purchasers would transfer the money required to maintain the PEGs to the provider who was carrying out that maintenance.
- Complications requiring operative or inpatient intervention would be paid for by the inserting provider in all cases, probably as part of the original contract.
- The care of PEGs should initially be seen as a specialist nursing procedure, until nurses in the nursing homes were trained in how to care for them, when it would become routine.

Conclusions

In the right conditions, PEGs are a useful adjunct to the care of patients with feeding disorders. They are not unique, and a number of health authorities do not purchase them at all. They are less resource consuming and safer than an operative gastrostomy and can often replace the need for one. Nasogastric feeding is more cumbersome and uncomfortable for patients over the medium term but is probably less dangerous over the short term (less than a week). Having said this, the approach relies on common sense. There have been no formal trials, so there is no strict evidence that PEGs should be used. The procedure has a mortality and morbidity and should therefore be restricted to cases who will have appreciable excess benefit.

Operational policies must try to address the complex ethical issues of, for example, inserting PEGs into elderly people with a degree of dementia, with or without other disease. Authors have discussed this a little more freely in the literature [219]. There also needs to be more guidance on the care of PEGs at home, for example indications for training patients or their family to feed themselves. Nursing homes appear to require some assistance with the management of patients with PEGs, as they seem to have some difficulty in maintaining such patients.

The health authority will routinely collect information on the cost of PEGs to the providers and the health authority, and continue to look for evidence of effectiveness.

Opportunities using less costly approaches: hospital-at-home

One way of improving the cost-effectiveness of services is to give a similar service in a different setting, one candidate for which is the hospital-at-home service. If good community services already exist, hospitals-at-home may be an offshoot of those services. Most of the trusts based in the community see advantages in diverting some of the patients presently treated in hospital to receive their diagnostic work up and therapy in the community. I have mentioned that the trend for curative work has been moving away from superspecialists and surgeons towards the physicians and general practitioners. A move towards hospital-at-home schemes is part of this trend.

The Americans have developed some remarkable community-based hospital back-up services. Marks [220] has described the South Hills Health System Home and Health Agency, which is the largest home help agency in the USA [221]. This was established in Pittsburgh in 1963. It serves nine hospitals, treating an average of 3000 patients each day and employing over 300 staff: nurses, therapists and health care aides. Its services cover psychiatry, paediatrics, physiotherapy, occupational therapy, speech therapy, social work and home care. Health education and nutritional advice are available to support the services. It can provide care at home at virtually any level, including intravenous antibiotic therapy and nutritional care, and includes the use of life support machines.

The services are planned on a geographical basis. The team helps to develop discharge plans for patients in hospital and coordinates services making sure that equipment is available and that staff produce and amend care plans. A member of the team attends discharge planning rounds on each nursing unit within the hospitals in the system and visits the patient at home within 48 hours of being discharged. The system is expensive, except in comparison with the cost of inpatient beds, so that while it is reducing length of stay, it is cost-effective. There is a temptation for such services to be less aware of the importance of discharging patients from their care than hospitals, in which case the overall costs can rapidly increase. Most UK health authorities would have some, but not all, of the services of the South Hills agency. Such a close integration with hospital care is still a dream for most areas.

A succession of other experiments have been set up, especially in Canada [222] in which acute curative care is offered entirely outside the hospital. The best known, if rather smaller, UK scheme has been running in Peterborough for some years. It treats patients at home who would otherwise be admitted to hospital. It aims either to prevent admission or to reduce length of stay by taking patients after an early discharge. The scheme now admits up to 400 patients per year, mainly suffering from stroke, cancer, hip fractures and elective hip and knee replacements. In addition, children on traction with congenital dislocation of the hip or fractured femur are nursed at home [223]. The main users of the service are elderly people with terminal disease or who require quite intensive rehabilitation.

Setting up a hospital-at-home scheme

In the UK, new hospital-at-home schemes are likely to be set up by community-based health trusts or those with a combined hospital and community service. They will see them as a patient-friendly, cost-effective way of caring for acutely ill patients compared with inpatient care. Researchers have shown that patients prefer hospital-at-home to going into an institution, but there is a dearth of information about comparative costs in the UK.

There appears to be little doubt that developing a hospital-at-home is more cost-effective than expanding or building a new general hospital [224]. What is not clear is whether hospital-at-home is cheaper than using pre-existing district general hospital premises. Because of the great variability of costs in the hospital sector, it is desirable to set up cost-effectiveness projects in each place, before opening a new hospital at home scheme. One needs to take into account a number of points.

Patients

Patients may feel vulnerable if they are treated at home. Some prefer the thought of being in a hospital ward with a large number of facilities available for them if the worst should happen. Hospital at home, while likely to provide better creature comforts and a familiar environment for patients, nevertheless puts a certain amount of onus upon them to be involved in their own cure. This is likely to be a bonus for the speed of recovery, but some patients prefer to leave it to the doctors and nurses, preferring a formal approach that does not require self-analysis or much effort beyond forbearance. It is likely that such people will not fare particularly well in hospital either, as an acute general ward is not always a therapeutic environment.

The need for good and intensive training of patients to help them in their process of recovery is self-evident when they are being treated at home. No-one is forgotten in the side ward or in the corner at the end, as happens on wards. The active involvement of patients is also a required part of community and home care. Patients do not have a great deal of knowledge about the processes involved and what is to be expected. For this reason, some hospital-at-home groups have an audiovisual programme and instruction manual to be used by patients, families and professionals. This direct involvement of patients must, in most cases, be beneficial.

Problems of assessing cost-effectiveness

The best means of assessing the cost-effectiveness of hospital-at-home services is by using a randomized controlled trial. It is important in this sort of study to look at the cost of running the service and the costs to all of those people concerned: patients, their families and carers, and the community at large.

This can be tricky because one has to make decisions about how one should measure the cost of, for example, pressure on family members as a result of being disturbed in the night. Researchers have suggested [225] that a proper analysis would involve measures of mortality, morbidity, disability, discontent and discomfort, together with their economic social and psychological effects on patients and their family. The difficulty with such a range of measures is how to judge one against the other if some are improved but others are not. One can most sensibly list them and ask the patient which means most to him or her.

Hedrick and co-workers have put together a good review of the effects of home care [226]. They state that the early studies were poor and that the majority of these were assessed by the people running the scheme, who were biased. Hedrick looked at 12 home care programmes that had a reasonable research design. There were considerable problems with bringing these together, but the authors tentatively suggested that home care programmes do not affect death rates nor increase the use of nursing homes, although they may have increased the use of outpatient services. Costs seem to be less in some cases than in others, but the cost of home care is never greater than that in hospital. Most of the studies assessed refer to acute care for elderly people rather than acute treatment in younger adults.

Assessing total costs

The costs of treatment for acute care are highest in the period immediately after the onset of the acute episode of disease. Home care schemes that take patients early on are therefore likely to be more costly than those aimed at reducing hospital length of stay, or which take only patients who require rehabilitation. They also have the greatest opportunity for saving money. Adler [227] itemized the benefits of home care services for patients, their families and society at large, making the point that all of these are important when assessing the impact of the treatment. A study of families with very seriously ill children kept at home on respirators [228] found that 4 in 10 of the families incurred considerable costs, which often caused serious financial problems. In these cases, an important means of producing savings for the health service was using family instead of professional nursing.

The potential for saving is greatest, as I have said, for early acute treatment. Care at home gives relatives a number of benefits that are difficult to quantify in financial terms, such as a better understanding of the disease process, with less overprotection of the patient. It also helps to transfer the skill of managing patients with diseases to the patients themselves and their families. It seems likely that these experiments, from small beginnings, will develop and become more adventurous. People have suggested that virtually all medical care, apart from the most highly intensive, could be carried out in the home [229].

Opportunities for new services: nurse practitioners

Nurse practitioners have for some time been doing some of the work previously identified as traditionally concerning doctors. A shortage of junior hospital doctors has accelerated this process. Other pressures to find alternatives to junior doctors have been the legal moves to reduce junior doctors' hours [230] and the Calman report's recommendations for shortened specialist training [231].

In response to these pressures the United Kingdom Central Council for Nursing, Midwifery and Health Visiting published new regulations in 1992 which meant that nurses were allowed to undertake a number of activities outside basic nursing [232]. Researchers have now set up a pilot project to look at the extent to which nurses have been taking over junior hospital doctors' work [233]. The aim of this project was to describe how nurses had taken over jobs thought of as belonging to the medical profession and the extent to which this would require new forms of training.

This work is at an early stage. The project looked at only three posts, two of which were partially subsidiary, to the work of the preregistration house officer, particularly the routine clinical work. Nurses did not undertake emergency admissions or diagnoses nor ask for investigations and treatment. Neither did they do tasks such as prescribing, which are legally confined to qualified medical practitioners. Another study described the work of a nurse who took virtually all the clinical work of a senior house officer apart from those tasks confined legally to medical practitioners. In these studies, nurses coped well with the type of work involved.

Problems of new services: costs of screening for breast cancer

Screening for breast cancer is a difficult subject. It is being carried out at present in the UK as a national policy as a result of evidence of effectiveness, but there have been some detractors suggesting that screening is not effective. The point of this example, however, is not to reach a conclusion about breast cancer screening *per se* but to suggest a method of comparative costing. Figure 11.4 shows the general outline of a study carried out by the Health Insurance Plan in the USA. Sixty-two thousand women were involved in the study; half were screened, while the rest were not. Thirty seven women less died in the study group compared with the control group.

Patients who are true positives, i.e. they appear on the screening test to have the disease and subsequently prove to have it, are screened, tested in hospital and treated. False positives – those who are positive for screening but are subsequently cleared – are screened and tested when they are found to be clear. It may be easier to diagnose false positives, so their testing may be cheaper than that of true positives. It is important to move fast from a positive screen to hospital testing for both of these groups of women to allay their anxiety.

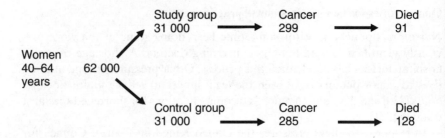

Figure 11.4 HIP cancer screening study.

People who are found to be false negatives are screened, mistakenly cleared, but later develop symptoms, are retested in hospital and are then treated. The second hospital test and treatment costs are therefore costs in a later period. There is a tendency for these women to be seen later in the stage of their disease and to be more severely affected when they report symptoms, as they have wrongly been given a clean bill of health. Overall they are costly, although some of the cost is spread out. True negatives, those who are negative on testing and do not have the disease, are screened and have no further tests.

Women with conventional treatment present to the doctor with symptoms, are tested in hospital and treated. Their costs will arise later than for true positives, and the detection stage will probably be later. Worried well people present for testing but at a later stage than those who are screened.

Figure 11.5 shows the screened group in more detail, in particular the number with different numbers of screens. If the proportions are added up, it can be seen that only 65% of the study population were screened.

Initial screen	2 screens	3 screens	All 4 screens
7%	7%	12%	39%
of 31 000	of 31 000 x 2	of 31 000 x 3	of 31 000 x 4
=2170	=4340	=11 160	=48 360

Total number of screens = 66 030

Figure 11.5 Details of the screened group.

Table 11.10 Rates of referral in the original study

Referrals	1st screen/1000 people	2nd screen/1000 people
Reviewed	88	97
Cysts aspirated	8	5.5
Referred to surgeon	20	6.4
Biopsy		
Benign	9.7	2.8
Cancer	5.5	0.9

Table 11.10 shows the rate of referrals at the first and second screening. I will be using the data for the first screening only, but considerable variations can be noticed between the first and second screens. These have been ignored in this costing process, although they are obviously important.

Translating the research findings to the local health authority

A health authority with a population of 400 000 has 42 646 females between the ages of 45 and 64. There were 99 deaths from breast cancer in the year. Approximately 86 of these were in the over 50s, and this is the group likely to benefit from screening. They would enjoy a reduction in mortality of one-third because of screening. Thus the health authority may save 28 lives in a year. The referrals as a result of the research screening process are as follows:

- 42 646 women aged 45–64 in the health authority
- It is estimated that 30.4% will be screened per annum
- Therefore 12 964 screens *per annum* in the health authority.

Costs

Table 11.11 shows the typical costs of the treatment undergone in breast cancer screening (1989 prices).

Information about the costs of the screening and follow-up processes can usually be obtained from the finance department of the trust involved. Note

Table 11.11 Costs of treatment associated with screening for breast screening

Procedure	Costs
Screening	
Mammogram	£8
Clinical examination and overheads	£14
Total	£22
Treatment	
Aspirate cyst	£50
Outpatient attendance	£25
Biopsy	£50

Table 11.12 Costs of the whole screening and treatment service for the health authority

Process	Cost
12 964 screens per annum @ £22 per screen	£285 208
Review of 88/100 = 1140 @ £10 per review	£11 400
Cysts aspirated 8/1000 = 104 @ £50 per cyst	£5 200
Referral surgeon 20/1000 = 259 @ £25 per referral	£6 475

Table 11.13 Comparing costs of screening and not screening

Service provided	Costs for screened patients	Costs for not screened patients
Screening	£285 208	
Review	£11 400	
Cysts aspirated	£5 200	£5 200
Referral surgeon	£6 475	£6 475
Biopsies	£9 900	£9 900
Mastectomies	£63 900	£63 900
Total	£382 083	£85 475

the relative unimportance of such costs as equipment costs for each screen. At these prices, a mastectomy costs about £900.

Table 11.12 shows the 12 964 screens a year for the health authority and their costs totalled. Notice the high cost of the screening compared with the other costs. Any inaccuracies will be relatively unimportant when compared with the multiplied inaccuracies of the screening process. The cost of mastectomies is large, but relatively few are performed, so that any inaccuracies in the costing of the operation will not be greatly exaggerated. However, inaccuracies in the numbers performed will be a problem. These inpatient data are normally accurate in routine returns.

Table 11.13 shows a comparison between the costs of screening in a year compared with the same population not screened. The unscreened population will be referred later, so not all the costs will occur in the same year. The service costs £296 600 for the saving of 28 lives, which is a cost of £10 593 a life. This is good value. There is a prolongation of life of 7 years based on Shapiro. There is no information about the negative psychological aspects of screening or the quality of life of these women.

The general method therefore is to look at a good randomized trial to look at effectiveness, and then, using costing information, much of which you will have in your head, to work out the cost-effectiveness.

Conclusion: difficult cases 12

USING EXISTING KNOWLEDGE

Pressures promoting new expensive medicines

One of the main problems in managing the health service is that we know more than we think we know. Researchers have described a good example of this with a group of antidepressants, the selective serotonin reuptake inhibitors (SSRIs). These were described in March 1993 as being expensive and of uncertain additional value over existing antidepressants. This evidence was produced in an issue of *Effective Health Care* and in the *British Medical Journal* as a meta-analysis [234], and later in an issue of the *Drugs and Therapeutics Bulletin*. In January 1994 the *Effective Health Care Bulletin* was issued to all general practitioners, with a covering letter from the Chief Medical Officer recommending the contents it contained.

Figure 12.1 shows the increased use in prescribing SSRIs. Despite the evidence, Figure 12.2 shows that the cost of prescribing the SSRIs rose. The figure shows a sharp dip in the cost immediately after publication of the bulletin, but this was due to a reduction in price of one of the antidepressants. The evidence presented showed the company that their product was expensive for little additional benefit. The company reduced the cost of the drug but this was unlikely to be entirely, if at all, due to public pressure. It had, in fact, reached the upper boundary of its prescribing limits and had to reduce profits from the NHS. It may be, of course, that they chose this particular drug because of the pressure.

Figure 12.3 shows the market share of different types of antidepressants after the *Effective Health Care Bulletin* and meta-analysis in the *British Medical Journal* was produced. I have presented this for costs and volumes. The older tricyclics have about 60% of the total volume of treatment and 20% of the overall cost. The SSRI's comprise about 20% of the volume with 60% of the total costs. In the meantime, the industry was progressively marketing their new products and the rate of SSRI prescribing continued to increase

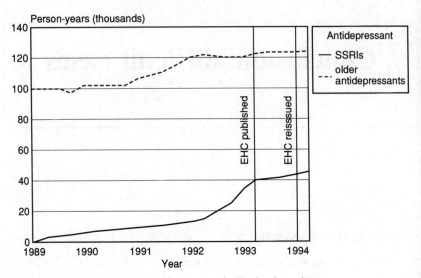

Figure 12.1   GP-prescribed antidepressants in England – volume.

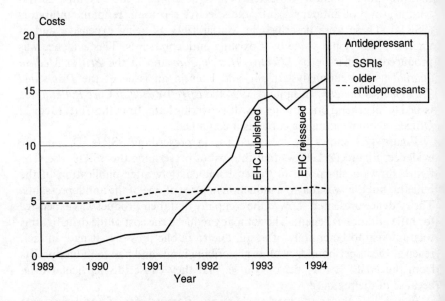

Figure 12.2   GP-prescribed antidepressants in England – cost.

dramatically. We need some change in policy to moderate the extreme influence of the pharmaceuticals industry in promoting practice that does not represent a good use of NHS resources.

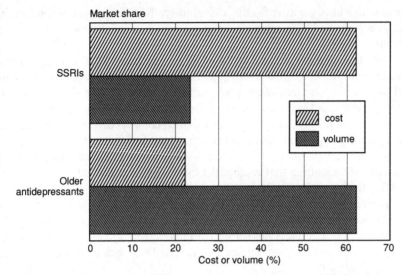

Figure 12.3 Market share for different antidepressants by cost and volume.

Services that are necessary to provide by law but appear to be ineffective: case management in mental illness

A central part of the NHS and Community Care Act 1990 was a requirement that care for people managed in the community would be provided using the care management approach, which workers in the USA have used for some time for mentally ill patients. It was part of the development of community-based psychiatric and social care to replace the large mental hospitals. The idea was that a designated person, the care manager, took responsibility for the client in the community. The care manager assessed the client's needs and used a care plan to outline the services needed. The care manager also monitored the services [235].

The literature on care management makes it clear that the term can mean two things, and the confusion between them does not appear to be entirely luck. In the first definition, care managers offer a service to about 30 patients whom they see infrequently; some may carry a small case load. The second approach is more interventionist. This approach has a team of health professionals, usually including a psychiatrist. The care managers have about 10 patients and treat them directly. Team members work with patients as and when their particular skills are required. The team concentrates on avoiding hospital admission and developing patients' living skills. They make strenuous efforts to keep in contact with patients [236].

There are to date 13 randomized controlled trials of the second type of care management in the literature, 12 of which have found the approach to be beneficial. There are at least nine randomized controlled trials of the former approach and two well-designed, non-randomized controlled studies, all but one of which have negative findings. Curiously, the whole thrust of community care policy in the UK is towards the implementation of the former type. It is, of course, cheaper.

Care management arrived in the UK in the late 1980s, leading to two parallel but closely related developments: social services 'care management' and the health services 'care programme' approach. Social services care management was the first to take off, after the publication of the Griffiths report on community care [237]. This report recommended that care management provided by social services should be at the heart of community care for severely mentally ill people. Griffiths saw care management as a way of giving efficient care, meaning that each patient got what was needed and no more.

After the Griffiths report, people set up a number of different approaches for different patient groups, especially mentally ill people. In some areas, social workers were withdrawn from clinical duties to act as purchasers of care [238]. In other areas, social services set up care management teams to provide care in parallel with existing mental health services. There was no evidence of their efficacy [239,240].

Meanwhile, the care management idea was also imposed on the health service. The approach was originally reserved for the most severely ill patients, for whom the mental health services were required to appoint key workers. The patients received an assessment of need, a written care plan and regular reviews organized by the key worker. It is possible to see how, with proper funding and guidance, this approach might have evolved into an effective service. In fact, the approach, through a combination of lack of funding, paperwork and its extension to all psychiatric patients has had little effect. No-one has properly evaluated it, but a partial evaluation in a recent randomized controlled trial showed a doubling of hospital admission rates rather than a reduction [241].

This type of care management has little justification but has displayed an astounding ability to flourish in the age of evidence-based medicine. There is a simple explanation for care management's immunity to scientific analysis: in the UK it is no longer just an intervention but government policy.

CONSENSUS APPROACHES: COMMISSIONING CHILD HEALTH SERVICES

This section describes an approach to refocusing children's services in a health authority. Its aim is to provide a combined child health service, providing preventive, primary, secondary and tertiary care. This required four provider trusts and several other agencies to work in harmony to bring it about.

For the new child health services there needs to be a unified medical career structure which:

- Provides care centred on the child within the family rather than within an institution such as the hospital
- Provides continuity of care between hospital and community and encourages communication
- Provides support services wherever they are sited to work closely with the primary care team
- Identifies the health needs of children at social disadvantage
- Recognizes responsibilities beyond contacts initiated by the child and family
- Provides continuity between prevention and treatment, with health promotion as part of each element of the service
- Avoids duplication of, for example, medical records.

Commissioning plan

The philosophies and principles for this plan have been set out in many recent publications.

These are:

- *Health and Social Gain for Children*
- *Local Strategy for Health; Maternal and Child Health*
- *UN Convention on the Rights of Children*
- *Children's Rights – UK Agenda for Children*
- *Children's Rights – Together Towards a Better Future*
- *Children First*
- *Seen but not Heard.*

Outline of current services for children

Services within the health authority at present do not follow the principles set out above. In 1992 the authority recognized this deficiency and proposed a single children's unit. At present, services for children are still structured and purchased in sectors (primary, secondary and tertiary) and are fragmented across the authority area. They are also contained in four provider units (acute and community). Services are purchased from each provider unit and pay little attention to continuity of care. The plan attempts to deal with these shortcomings. Whilst mainly dealing with the health services for children, it attempts to clarify the links with other agencies.

Aim of the service

The aim of the service is to add to the potential of children by identifying their needs and providing effective and efficient health care in the most appropriate setting. It also aims to meet those needs within the resources available.

Outline of plan

This model requires a strong primary and community care base and a single children's unit that will be the focus of child-centred secondary (community and acute) and specialist care. This will act as the coordinating and resource centre for care within the community and liaison with other agencies.

The plan comprises four changes to the current services:

- A combined child health service with a local focus on multidisciplinary teams working with other agencies
- Outpatients, day care and other non-hospital services for children in the health authority to be provided as near to children's homes as possible
- A single children's inpatient unit, in the same hospital as the accident and emergency department, with a regional neonatal intensive care unit and a paediatric intensive care unit
- The children's unit to act as the centre of the combined child health service encompassing all services (community and hospital) for children, working closely with general practitioners and other agencies.

Care will be focused on primary, community, day and outpatient care in appropriate settings. Thus outpatient or ambulatory centres could exist in neighbourhoods and, where appropriate, in a general practice. Support within the community will have to be developed. This will include community paediatricians, paediatric community nurses, outreach nurses, liaison with other agencies and communication between all elements of the services. Collaboration with other agencies is particularly important for, for example, children with chronic conditions and children with special physical, behavioural and psychological needs. Some of the services provided to children, for example child protection, fostering and adoption, are most effectively organized and managed at a health authority level.

Achieving the aim

Each step is described as function, structure, process and outcome or key measures of success. Under the heading of outcome or key measure of success, some examples are given, and details will be worked through later.

Step 1: Consolidation of the primary care base, including relationships with other services

Function: To ensure effective, appropriate and efficient provision of care.

Structure:
- Adequately staffed and trained primary health care teams
- Clear lines of communication
- Commissioning advisory group for children's services (wide representative membership).

Process: • Purchasers to support primary health care teams through the contracting process (for example, maximizing secondment, and basing services in the practice setting wherever possible).

Step 2: Integration of community child health and secondary hospital children's services

Function: To provide continuity of care with the maximum access to services for families.

Structure: • Collaboration
             • Common career structure
             • Single managed service, joint working, single case notes
             • Local focus
             • Supporting primary care
Process: • Agree roles and responsibilities
             • Maintenance of strong professional clinical links
             • Whole service specification: specifications defining details of service, standards required (including joint protocols and audit) and joins between the services.
             • Contracts.

Outcome or key measures of success:
             • General: more effective and efficient child-centred service
             • Improved continuity of care
             • Specific: intact, district-wide child protection service.

Step 3: Further development of ambulatory (including outpatient) service

Function: To avoid unnecessary hospital admission wherever possible and to provide child-centred care as close to home as possible.

Structure: • Peripheral outpatient clinics with appropriate support
             • Assessment units
             • Good community support services
Process: • Develop peripheral general clinics for children (beginning in areas with greatest need)
             • Develop referral guidelines with general practitioners for common causes of referral
             • Develop assessment units and review admission policies
             • Further develop community children's nursing (general and specialist outreach as appropriate)
             • Achieved through specifications and contracts.

Outcome or key measures of success:
             • Reduction in the number of inappropriate hospital admissions

- Reduction in the number of readmissions
- Reduction in the numbers of visit to hospital-based outpatient departments
- Increased child, parent and primary health care team satisfaction.

Step 4: Develop nursing support for children within the community (both general and specialist outreach nursing)

Function: To support children at home, minimize hospital admissions where appropriate (particularly for children with chronic conditions, including learning disability) and to enable the earliest possible discharge.

Structure:
- Establish community nursing support for children
- General paediatric community nursing teams liaising and collaborating closely with the primary health care team as well as secondary care teams and other agencies (a role for district nurses or health visitors)
- Specialist outreach nurses
- School nursing service.

Process:
- Pilot a model of general paediatric community nursing service
- Strengthen and develop specialist outreach nursing
- Ensure community support for those with learning disability
- Specification and contracts.

Outcome or key measures of success:
- Decrease in the number of hospital admissions for chronic conditions
- Increased satisfaction of child, parents and primary health care team
- Improved liaison between the primary health care team, other agencies and the hospital.

Step 5: Clarify joint roles and responsibilities with other agencies as well as points of contact

Function: To provide continuity of care from assessment to treatment and care as effectively, appropriately and efficiently as possible.

Structure:
- Through an effective joint planning mechanism (ideally a joint commissioning mechanism)
- Multiagency assessment and protocols.

Process:
- Joint advisory group (comprising key representatives from major agencies) to inform policy makers in education, social services and health.

Outcome or key measures of success:

- Individual care plans
- More effective protection of children at risk
- More appropriate and rapid placement of children in need
- One strategy for children's services.

Step 6: Move gradually towards a single children's unit

- Move children's inpatient services to a preferred site
- Move the accident and emergency department to a preferred site.

Function: To make a child centred-service maximizing the available resources.

Structure:
- Providers A and B to combine
- Transfer children's inpatient services provision from provider A to the preferred site
- Transfer the remaining inpatient care from all sites to the preferred site
- Further develop day case facilities for children
- Transfer accident and emergency services to the preferred site (provider B).

Process:
- Make progress with the strategic plan
- Implement recommendations of audit report
- Specifications and contracts.

Outcome or key measures of success:

- No inpatient children's services located at provider A
- Resources identified and reallocated
- Adequately staffed (including training) children's wards
- Better clinical outcomes (morbidity and mortality) for children
- All inpatient care on one dedicated site, achieving the aim of lessened morbidity and mortality for children
- Decrease in unnecessary hospital admissions, with more care being appropriately provided within the community
- No children nursed on adult wards, adult intensive care, adult day case units or any adult facility
- Teenagers cared for in adolescent facilities
- Good paediatric cover for the accident and emergency department, with advanced resuscitation facilities on site
- Enhanced under-and postgraduate education.

Contracting models

Considerable thought will have to be given to the method of contracting for such a service:

- A contract with a single provider who would also manage and provide the service
- A single provider (lead provider) to manage the service but subcontract out
- Several contracts let with different provider units

If the authority chooses the third model, an eye must be kept on liaison between the trusts. This will also need close monitoring of the specification and contract.

Time scale

First year:

- Obtain agreement on plan
- Progress interim arrangement in respect of Cardiff Royal Infirmary
- Children's inpatient services
- Progress steps 1–4.

Second year:

- Progress steps 1–4
- Detailed services specifications should be developed during the year in readiness for the next year's contracting round
- Finalize the timetable for step 5
- Develop detailed plans, guidelines and specifications for step 6.

Third year:

- Consolidate steps 1–4 and introduce step 3 county-wide.

Fourth year:

- Contract for combined child health service, with a local focus and a single acute inpatient unit.

MANAGED MARKETS: FUTURE TRENDS

The past 10 years have seen the instigation of planned markets in health care in many developed countries. The UK, Sweden and Finland rely on much of their health care being publicly funded. They have all introduced considerable changes to the ways that their health care systems work, which have all separated the funders or purchasers of health care from those who treat patients directly. The three countries are using slightly different methods to identify the purchasers and providers in their respective systems. All three agree about the advantages of tax-based, government-owned finance for the services.

Other countries, especially the USA and the Netherlands, have used competition at the financing end of the market by using large numbers of private insurers. In the USA, these are mainly for profit, in the Netherlands not for profit. These countries believe that competition between the providers is not enough to raise standards, despite the increased costs that multiple insurers seem to allow, compared with countries with a centralized source of finances. The centralized system, if government owned, appears to be better able to resist pressures from the providers to spend more.

Similarities and differences in the internal markets

There is, as I have said, almost a consensus among the main developed nations that some separation of the purchasers from those who provide the service is advantageous. However, there is some disagreement about who should be the purchasers. In the UK and Finland, purchasers are at the equivalent of the county level or slightly larger, with populations of between 400 000 and 700 000. In Sweden, the population unit is smaller, although the purchasers are still public bodies. In Finland, the purchasers are at a municipal level. In the USA and the Netherlands, the purchasers are private, nationally based companies. In the UK, some of the purchasers are general practitioners, although there is a close oversight of these from the health authorities, whereas in the USA the purchaser is quite often a private individual, this being one of the few developed countries where this is still common.

The purchasers come from a variety of backgrounds. In Sweden, they are planners with elected politicians on their boards; in the UK, nationally appointed trustees, mainly with a business background, or general practitioner fundholders. In the Netherlands and the USA, they are commercial businessmen, whereas in Sweden patients lead the new market arrangements. In Finland and Sweden, these groups are purchasing all hospital services, in the UK elective and diagnostic hospital services, and in the Netherlands and the USA primary and hospital services. Community care may be added as in the UK and the Netherlands.

There are different views on the nature of the contract between the purchasers and providers. People have suggested that some of the costs of setting up the contract could be reduced by using nationally designed model contracts. However, the gains made in saving transaction costs might prevent new innovative ideas coming forward and not allow for local differences in the structure of different populations. This has been an important freedom for the trusts in the UK. Many of the best ideas have developed in response to a general call for innovative ideas rather than a standard method of developing services. There is also an obvious balance to be achieved between developing complex tightly controlled contracts, which will be efficient but expensive to set up and monitor, and loose contracts, which will be cheap to set up but within which the costs of the service may go out of control. The UK appears to have moved from the latter to the former over the past 5 years or so.

I remember the health authority that I worked in in the mid 1970s deciding to go 10% over its annual budget and face the consequences with the government department concerned (which happened to be the Scottish Home and Health Department). There was a feeling that we were being bold but moral by setting the budget high. There was no question of trying to make the service more efficient by cutting back on, for example management costs, as there is these days. The authority was given a severe talking to, but the money was forthcoming. No-one lost their job. The general feeling was that if the clinicians said that they needed something to provide a good service it should be provided, not necessarily this year but probably next. We were very naive.

Patient choice and internal markets

Many countries have also had to face difficulties with allowing patients some choice in a planned market. In the UK and Sweden, patients have, theoretically, an unrestricted choice of general practitioner. In other countries, patients have their choices restricted to general practitioners working for a particular municipality (Finland) or private insurer (USA). In the Netherlands and the USA, patients may have to go to general practitioners with contracts from a particular private insurer. The Netherlands and the USA consider the choice of purchaser, i.e. the insurer, to be a more important freedom than the choice of provider. It is believed that, by choosing a strong advocate and the advocates competing with each other, patients will have more power over the quality and cost of the provider.

Where public agencies purchase on behalf of patients, these are elected directly in Sweden and Finland, or in the UK are appointed by the elected government. In the Swedish internal market, patients can choose providers outside their district. In the USA, patients with insurance can choose someone other than the private insurer's contracted providers if they pay more than the average. In the UK and Finland, patients are generally expected to get most of their care within a set group of providers, chosen by the purchasing authority, which in the UK, may be a fundholding general practitioner. There is the possibility for occasional extracontractual referrals. In the USA, patients using the health maintenance organizations are restricted to a group of providers. A few local governments in Sweden have limited experiments using vouchers for some home care and transport services.

Future organization

The structures set up for the internal market – the purchasing and providing groups – may force structural change on the health services using them. To simplify the contracting process, both general practitioner fundholders and health authorities are collaborating or merging. General practitioner fundholders are already grouping together to hire managers to handle the details of contracting. This process could result in a handful of new semi-private corporations that could control most primary care services in the UK.

In Chapter 6, I mentioned the similarity between this approach and some of the health maintenance organizations in the USA. The hospitals may begin to take on salaried general practitioners as part of their work. Community trusts, which are increasingly managing the primary care team for general practitioners, might favour this approach, and indeed one community trust has already started this process [242]. At present, they find themselves squeezed between the hospitals and the primary care services. Alternatively large groups of total fundholders might be tempted to try to control their local hospital service. The result, in either case, would be a large, multifaceted health complex with integrated primary and secondary care. The UK has, since 1948, put a barrier between primary and secondary care that either of these models would overturn.

Who will run the health service?

The service purchasers and providers are controlled by one of four factors:

- The democratic process
- Market mechanisms
- Formal regulation
- Professional ethics.

People believe democratic processes to be a strong way of making the services accountable. The difficulty is that we need to keep the population well informed to make decisions about as technical and complex an organization as a health service. This needs to be the first process. Allowing politicians to speak on behalf of the population results in considerable and regular interference in the running of health services by politicians. It is difficult to see how, in countries where many of the services are publicly funded, the health services can be isolated from the political process, as health services are expensive and therefore inevitably an important political issue.

In most internal markets, patients can complain and be sent to another provider, resulting in the first provider having a smaller market share. This approach is rather cumbersome for an individual patient who has concerns, but a provider consistently giving a bad service will notice the loss of revenue. General practitioner fundholders who are not happy with their community services, in particular, are turning to other providers. The occasional one can be laughed off at a board meeting, but a series will cause fundamental questions to be asked. Purchasers may require providers to reach some general benchmark of standards rather than asking for directly competitive prices and quality of services; the health authorities might be able to stir up a competitive spirit between their providers by using such an approach. My experience with trusts so far has been that they continually need reassurance.

In a number of areas, this competitive approach has been undermined by dividing the large commissioning populations of, say, three quarters of a million into local groups and commissioning from that population group. Typically, such population sizes of about 200 000 fit nicely with a single district general hospital. The pressure for such commissioning tactics has come from the government, which requires purchasing to be general practitioner led. This would be impossible without dividing the patch into smaller groups, but it does reduce the ability of purchasers to compare directly, and pressure providers to improve quality or reduce costs.

Traditionally, formal regulation has been built into the publicly financed health system in the UK. For internal markets to work best, the market needs to measure and compare what the trusts provide – their outputs. Regulations are better at controlling input, especially finances and how they are earmarked. Regulation does not seem to work very well to improve quality of care. Nursing homes for elderly people are some of the most regulated services world wide, yet they continually cause some of the most common scandals. Regulatory sanctions also require expensive documentation and proof, much of which will be surrogate measures for quality but not relevant to more direct measures. They are typified by managers complaining that they need more data and that the data they have do not appear to be relevant to what they want to know.

Ethical accountability to patients has traditionally been based on professional responsibility, self-regulation and trust. The system has depended upon training and the sanction of losing professional prestige and esteem if one strays. There has been a noticeable impact in the UK with the emergence of self-governing trusts and fundholding general practitioners on physicians' professional autonomy. The shift from self-control for physicians towards a mix of managerial and professional oversight undermines the strength of the professions. It may help to control maverick consultants from arm's length, but it is impossible and counterproductive to try to control all the consultants.

The future for managed competition: beautiful animal or myth?

The mix of state regulation and market incentives found in different models suggests that we are still at the experimental stage with managed markets. There is no doubt that further changes will radically alter the present state of affairs. What does appear certain is that earlier, more ambitious attempts to move publicly operated health systems closer to the pure market model have now drawn back. The notion of creating fully competitive markets among health care providers is being replaced by less disruptive notions such as comparative pricing and comparing outcomes. My feeling is that this has been more because the government fears losing control if it allows the markets more leeway, rather than because the more competitive approach has failed.

The original intention of including large numbers of private as well as public suppliers in the health care markets has not worked. Private providers require high profits; public institutions have lower transaction and other operating costs and have therefore kept the private providers out of the market.

There are pressures on the contracting process to go in opposite directions at present. On the one hand, there is a school of thought that believes that the future is likely to see the development of trust-based contracts covering a wide range of services. This scenario suggests that there will be increased cooperation between providers engendered by these wide-ranging contracts. There is pressure for them to develop as a result of the need to coordinate efforts between primary and secondary care and between hospital and community services. An example of such an approach is in children's services, as described in this chapter above. Another pressure will be for superspecialist groups, such as oncologists or transplant specialists, to be able to care for patients at an affordable price. This will mean reducing the highly technical end of care to a minimum, with close cooperation between the acute and less acute sectors.

Evidence that high tech seems to be better than medium tech in the treatment of cancer surgery, for example, means that the superspecialists will be under pressure to do more. Coordinating their services with rehabilitation and other facilities will be the only way that they can survive, as finances fail to keep up with the developments.

Another possibility is that contracting will become more and more detailed. The move towards contracting according to diagnosis-related groups has been mentioned. This will allow close comparisons between providers, including comparisons of patient outcomes, and therefore closer competition. This is likely to result in trusts amalgamating and becoming more entrepreneurial. There are likely to be rapid changes in the way in which care is provided, for example by moving more acute service into primary and community care, and using less highly trained individuals where possible.

The second model should allow patients to have more say in the type of care they get and who provides it because the comparative outcome data will, almost certainly, be made publicly available for different diagnostic groupings. It will be fascinating to see whether the general public will be swayed by such data or whether their present preference to go to the nearby hospital will alter. There needs to be a cadre of people able and ready to translate these outcome data for the public. It could be public health consultants or an independent group such as a *Which?* for health, but there is so far little sign of such a group developing at national level. Community health councils may develop alliances with one group or the other and make their presence felt.

It must be said that, at this time, the drive during the first years of the 1990s towards planned markets internationally appears to have moderated, leaving a larger proportion of the previously existing health system than might have been expected. In Sweden, for example, Social Democrats received majorities in all 26 countries in the 1994 election, based on their stated intention to preserve service levels in the publicly operated health system.

There is also a quiet move towards rehabilitating professionals, especially doctors. In the 1950s and 1960s medical practitioners were seen as selfless individuals who received high esteem as well as high rewards from society. By the 1980s physicians were caught up in the criticism of all professionals. This was engendered, among others, by right-wing economists and their political followers. Most notable of these was Margaret Thatcher, who appeared to view all professionals as self-interested, especially concerning their incomes. In some countries, perhaps less so the UK, doctors lost some public respect. The role of planned market mechanisms in the UK has been to remove authority from physicians towards managers. At this stage, a new respect for physicians within knowledge-based hospitals and primary care centres is needed. Here their work will remain crucial.

The ability of patients to select their provider is being seen, in some countries, as an increasingly important safeguard. This, especially if local health authority board members are elected, may give patients more leverage over the health service. If planned markets persist in letting experts decide both the purchaser and provider for patients, there will be no real choice for them. In democratic societies where people can choose the conditions in which they live, it is likely that they will also want to choose and influence their health care.

The ultimate test of the planned market era of health reform will be relatively straightforward: it will be the extent to which these reforms are better able to provide good quality, effective, accessible health care reasonably equitably to the whole population. Planned markets will not be judged on the cleverness of their economics, but on their ability to provide patients with the care they need. My main concern is that, even if they do, we will not measure it, and even if we measure it we will still try to fix it, even if it ain't broke.

References

1. Butler, J. (1994) Origins and early development, in *Evaluating the NHS Reform* (eds R. Robinson and J. Le Grand), Kings Fund Institute, London.
2. Fowler, N. (1991) *Ministers Decide: A Personal Memoir of the Thatcher Years*, Chapman, London.
3. DHSS (1983) *NHS Management Inquiry* (the Griffiths Report), DHSS, London.
4. DHSS (1983) *Competitive Tendering in the Provision of Domestic Catering and Laundry Services*, HC(83) 18, London.
5. Houseman, S., Hunter, D. and Pollitt, C. (1990) *The Dynamics of British Health Policy*, Unwin Hyman, London.
6. Hoffenberg, R., Todd P.I. and Pinker, G. (1987) Crisis in the national health service. *British Medical Journal*, **295**, 1505–6.
7. Enthoven, A.C. (1985) *Reflections on the Management of the National Health Service*, Occasional Paper No. 5, Nuffield Provincial Hospitals Trust, London.
8. Binstock, R.H. and Post, S.G. (eds) (1991) *Too Old for Health Care. Controversies in Medicine, Law, Economics and Ethics*, Johns Hopkins University Press, Baltimore.
9. Culyer, A. and Brazier, J. (1988) *Alternatives for Organising the Provision of Health Services in the UK*, IHSM, London.
10. Department of Health (1989) *Self Governing Hospitals*, Working Paper No 1, HMSO, London.
11. Aaron, H. and Schwartz, W. (1984) *The Painful Prescription*, Brookings Institute, Washington DC.
12. Abel-Smith, B. (1964) *The Hospitals, 1800–1948*, Heinemann, London.
13. Doll, R. (1989) Demographic and epidemiologic trends today. *Arzneimittel Forschung*, **39**, 943–7.
14. Editorial (1990) *The Economist Annual Review*, December.
15. Katz, S., Branch, L.G., Branson, M.H., Papsidero, J.A., Beck, J.C. and Greer, D.S. (1983) Active life expectancy. *New England Journal of Medicine*, **309**, 218–23.
16. Manton, K.G. (1991) The dynamics of population aging: demography and policy analysis. *Millbank Quarterly*, **69**, 309–39.
17. Bebbington, A.C. (1988) The expectation of life without disability in England and Wales. *Social Science and Medicine*, **27**, 321–6.

18. Petersen, M.E. and Dickey, R. (1995) Surgical sex reassignment: a comparative survey of international centers. *Archives of Sexual Behaviour*, **24**, 135–56.
19. Snaith, P., Tarsh, M.J. and Reid, R. (1993) Sex reassignment surgery. A study of 141 Dutch transsexuals. *British Journal of Psychiatry*, **162**, 681–5.
20. American College of Physicians (1995) *Clinical Practice Guidelines*, American College of Physicians, Philadelphia, PA.
21. Court, C. (1996) NHS Handbook criticises evidence based medicine. *British Medical Journal*, **312**, 1439–40.
22. *Proverbs* 29 v. 18.
23. Wall, A. (1993) *Values and the NHS: a Briefing Paper*, Institute of Health Service Managers, London.
24. Seedhouse, D. (1988) *Ethics: The Heart of Health Care*, John Wiley, London.
25. Klein, R. (1991) On the Oregon trail. *British Medical Journal*, **302** 1–2.
26. West, M. and Anderson, N. (1993) Fire fighting. *Health Service Journal*, **103**, 20–4.
27. Department of Health (1994) *The Operation of the NHS Internal Market: Local Freedoms, National Responsibilities*, HSG(94)55.
28. National Audit Office (1995) *Contracting for Health Care in England*, Report by the Controller and Auditor General, HC 261, HMSO, London.
29. McKeown, T. (1979) *The Role of Medicine. Dream, Mirage or Nemesis*, Blackwell, London.
30. Barrett, S. and Fudge, C. (eds) (1981) *Policy and Action*, Methuen, London.
31. Friend, J., Power, J.M. and Jewlett, C.J.L. (1974) *Public Planning: The Intercorporate Dimension*, Tavistock, London.
32. Lawrence, W.G. (ed.) (1982) *Exploring Individual and Organisational Boundaries*, John Wiley, Chichester.
33. Davidson, S.M. (1983) Planning and coordination of social services in multi-organisational contexts. *Social Services Review*, **50** (1) quoted by Tibbitt, J. in Williamson, A. and Room, G. (1983) *Health and Welfare State in Britain*, Heinemann, London.
34. Challis, L., Fuller, S., Henwood, M., Klein, R., Plowden, W., Webb, A., Whittingham, P. and Wistow, G. (1988) *Joint Approaches to Social Policy*, CUP, Cambridge.
35. Victor, C.R. and Vetter, N.J. (1988) Preparing the elderly for discharge from hospital: a neglected aspect of patient care? *Age and Ageing*, **17**, 155–63.
36. Newton, J.N., Henderson, J. and Goldacre, M.J. (1995) Waiting list dynamics and the impact of earmarked funding. *British Medical Journal*, **311**, 783–5.
37. Audit Commission (1995) *For Your Information*, HMSO, London.
38. Audit Commission (1995) *Setting the Records Straight*, HMSO, London.
39. Davenport, R., Dennis M.S. and Warlow, C.P. (1996) Effect of correcting data for case mix: an example from stroke medicine. *British Medical Journal*, **312**, 1503–5.
40. McCormick, A., Fleming, D. and Charlton, J. (1993) *Morbidity Statistics from General Practice. Fourth National Study 1991–1992*, HMSO, London.
41. Bunker, J.P., Frazier, H.S. and Mosteller, F. (1994) Improving health: measuring effects of medical care. *Millbank Quarterly*, **72**, 225–8.
42. Charlton, J.R.H. and Velez, R. (1986) Some international comparisons of mortality amenable to medical intervention. *British Medical Journal*, **292**, 295–300.

43. Clinical Outcomes Working Group (1995) *Clinical Outcomes Indicators*, Scottish Office, Edinburgh.

44. Farmer, J. and Chesson, R. (1996) The informers. *Health Service Journal*, **106**, 28–9.

45. Appleby, J., Walsh, E. and Cayham, C. (1995) *Acting on the Evidence NAHAT Research Paper No. 17*, NAHAT, Birmingham.

46. Goldberg, D. (1991) Filters to care – a model, in *Indicators for Mental Health in the Population*, (eds R. Jenkins and S. Griffiths), HMSO, London.

47. Meltzer, H., Gill, B., Pettigrew, M. and Hinds, K. (1995) *The Prevalence of Psychiatric Morbidity among Adults Living in Private Households*, OPCS Surveys of Psychiatric Morbidity in Great Britain, Report 1, HMSO, London.

48. Holland, W.W., D'Souza, M.D. and Swan, A.V. (1978) Is mass screening justified? *Transactions of the Society*, **56**, 22–5.

49. Reading, R., Colver, A., Openshaw, S. and Jarvis, S. (1994) Do interventions that improve immunisation uptake also reduce social inequalities in uptake? *British Medical Journal*, **308**, 1142–4.

50. Edwards, N. and Werneke, U. (1994) In the fast lane. *Health Services Journal*, 8th December, 30–2.

51. Department of Health (1991) *Health of the Nation*, HMSO, London.

52. Maxwell, R. (1984) Quality assessment in health. *British Medical Journal*, **288**, 1470–2.

53. Martin, J., Meltzer, H. and Elliot, D. (1988) *The Prevalence of Disability among Adults*, OPCS Surveys of Disability in Great Britain, Report 1, HMSO, London.

54. Paraphrased from Tropman, J.E. (1987) Organisational excellence and the nursing home: a new perspective on quality of life. *Danish Medical Bulletin*, Special Supplement Series No. 5, 2–6.

55. Laing, W. (1991) *Empowering the Elderly: Direct Consumer Funding of Care Services*, IEA Health & Welfare Unit, London.

56. Salvage, A.V., Jones, D.A. and Vetter, N.J. (1988) Awareness of and satisfaction with community services in a random sample of over 75s. *Health Trends*, **20**, 88–92.

57. Donaldson, L.J. and Jagger, G. (1983) Survival and functional capacity: three year follow-up of an elderly population in hospitals and homes. *Journal of Epidemiology and Community Health*, **37**, 176–9.

58. Gibbins, F.J., Lee, M., Davison, P.R. *et al.* (1982) Augmented home nursing as an alternative to hospital care for chronic elderly invalids. *British Medical Journal*, **284**, 30–3.

59. Challis, D., Darton, R., Johnson, L., Stone, M. and Traske, K. (1991) An evaluation of an alternative to long-stay hospital care for frail elderly patients. 1. The model of care. *Age and Ageing*, **20**, 236–44.

60. Department of Health (1994) *NHS Responsibilities for Meeting Long Term Health Care Needs*, HSG(94), Department of Health, Leeds.

61. Atkinson, D.A., Bond, J. and Gregson, B.A. (1986) The dependency characteristics of older people in long-term institutional care, in *Dependency and Interdependency in Old Age* (eds C. Phillipson, M. Bernard and P. Strang), Croom Helm, London.

62. Salvage, A.V., Vetter, N.J., and Jones, D.A. (1988) Attitudes to hospital care among a community sample of people aged 75 and older. *Age and Ageing*, **17**, 270–4.

63. Donaldson, C. and Bond, J. (1991) Cost of continuing care facilities in the evaluation of experimental National Health Service nursing homes. *Age and Ageing*, **20**, 160–8.

64. Kesby, S.G. (1991) *Continuing Care for Elderly People in South East Thames Region*, Interim discussion paper, South East Thames Regional Health Authority, London. (This document confirms that it is virtually impossible to make theoretical decisions about the number of long-term beds needed in a district.)

65. South Glamorgan Health Authority (1994) *Future Purchasing of Long Term Health Care for Elderly People in South Glamorgan*, South Glamorgan Health Authority, Cardiff.

66. Hughes, D. (1990) Same story, different words. *Health Service Journal*, 22nd March, 432–4.

67. Welsh Office VFM (1994) *Waiting List Good Practice Guide*, WO, Cardiff.

68. Welsh Office (1996) *Guidance on the Protection and Use of Patient Information*, DGM(96)43, WO, Cardiff.

69. National Health Service Executive (1996) *NHS Information Management and Technology Security Manual*, HSG(96)15, NHSE, Leeds.

70. National Health Service Executive (1996) *The Protection and Use of Patient Information*, HSG(96)18, NHSE, Leeds.

71. Harris, A. (1993) Developing a research and development strategy for primary care. *British Medical Journal*, **306**, 189–92.

72. Anglia and Oxford Regional Health Authority (1994) *Getting Research into Practice and Purchasing (GRiPP) Four Counties Approach.* NHS Executive, Oxford.

73. Simpson, M., Buckman, R., Stewart, M. *et al.* (1991) Doctor–patient communication: the Toronto consensus statement. *British Medical Journal*, **303**, 1385–7.

74. Hobbs, R. (1995). Rising emergency admissions. *British Medical Journal*, **310**, 207–8.

75. Department of Health (1994) *An Accountability Framework for General Practitioner Fundholding*, EL (94) 92, Department of Health, London.

76. Anon. (1996) Fundholders urged to give up savings. *Health Services Journal*, **106**, 5.

77. Stuart-Brown, S., Surender, R., Bradlow, J., Coulter, A. and Doll, H. (1955) The effect of fundholding in general practice on prescribing habits three years after introduction of the scheme. *British Medical Journal,* **311, 543–7.**

78. Bradlow, J. and Coulter, A. (1993) The effect of fundholding and indicative prescribing schemes on general practitioners prescribing costs. *British Medical Journal*, **307**, 186–9.

79. Coulter, A. (1993) General practice fundholding. Time for a cool appraisal. *British Journal of General Practice*, **45, 119–20.**

80. Orton, P. (1994) Shared care. *Lancet*, **344**, 1413–5.

81. Gilliam, S.J., Ball, M., Prasad, M. and Varidis, G. (1995) Is outreach care cost-efficient? A case study in ophthalmology. *Family Practitioner*, **12, 262.**

82. Monkley-Poole, S. (1995) The attitudes of British fundholding general practitioners to community psychiatric nursing services. *Journal of Advanced Nursing*, **21**, 238–47.

83. Whynes, D.K. and Reed, G. (1994) Fundholders' referral patterns and perceptions of service quality in hospital provision of elective general surgery. *British Journal of General Practice*, **44**, 557–60.

84. Coulter, A. and Bradlow, J. (1993) Effects of NHS reforms on general practitioners' referral patterns. *British Medical Journal*, **306**, 433–7.

85. Howie, J.G., Heaney, D.J. and Maxwell, M. (1995) Care of patients with selected health problems in fundholding practices in Scotland in 1990 and 1992: needs process and outcome. *British Journal of General Practice*, **45**, 121–6.

86. Howie, J.G., Heaney, D.J. and Maxwell, M. (1994) Evaluating care of patients reporting pain in fundholding practices. *British Medical Journal*, **309, 705–10**.

87. Dixon, J., Dinwoodie, M., Hodson, D. *et al.* (1994) Distribution of NHS funds between fundholding and non-fundholding practices. *British Medical Journal*, **309**, 30–4.

88. Audit Commission (1996) *Fundholding: The Main Report*, Audit Commission, London.

89. Singer, R. (1994) Needs assessment: beyond the fundholding perspective, in *Royal College of General Practitioners Commissioning of Care. A Digest of the Proceedings of a One Day Conference*, Royal College of General Practitioners, London.

90. Hart, J. (1988) *A New Kind of Doctor*, Merlin Press, London.

91. Charlton, B.G., Calvert, N., White, M. (1994) Health promotion priorities for general practice; constructing and using 'indicative prevalences'. *British Medical Journal*, **308**, 1019–22.

92. Shanks, J., Kherej, S. and Fish, S. (1995) A better way of assessing health needs in primary care. *British Medical Journal*, **310**, 480–1.

93. Murray, S.A. and Graham, L.J.C. (1995) Practice based needs assessment: use of four methods in a small neigbourhood. *British Medical Journal*, **310**, 1443–8.

94. Hopton, J. and Dlugolecka, M. (1995) Patients' perceptions of need for primary health care services: useful for priority setting? *British Medical Journal*, **310**, 1237–40.

95. Starfield, B. (1994) Is primary care essential? *Lancet*, **344**, 1129–33.

96. Cragg, D.K., Campbell, S.M. and Roland, M.O. (1994) Out of hours primary care centres: characteristics of those attending and declining to attend. *British Medical Journal*, **309**, 1627–9.

97. Glennerster, H. and Matsaganis, M. (1993) The UK health reform – the fundholding experiment. *Health Policy*, **23**, 179–91.

98. Dickson, J. (1994) Can there be fair funding for fundholding practices? *British Medical Journal*, **308**, 772–5.

99. Department of Health (1993) *General Practitioner Fundholder Budget Setting Guidance 1993/4*, Department of Health, London.

100. Sheldon, T.A., Smith, P., Borowitz, M., Martin, S. and Carr Hill, R. (1994) Attempt at deriving a formula for setting general practitioner fundholding budgets. *British Medical Journal*, **309**, 1059–64.

101. Hill, R.A. Carr, Hardman, G., Martin, S., Peacock, S., Sheldon, T.A. and Smith, P. (1994) A formula for distributing NHS revenue based on small area use, Centre for Health Economics Occasional Paper, University of York, York.

102. Glennerster, H., Matsaganis, M. and Owens, P. (1992) *A Foothold for Fundholding*, King's Fund Institute, London.

103. Glennerster, H., Matsaganis, M., Owens, P. and Hancock, S. (1994) *Implementing General Practitioner Fundholding*, Open University Press, Buckingham.

104. Glennerster, H. and Cohen, A. (1994) *Embedding Primary Care in Purchasing*, London School of Economics, London.

105. Butler, P. (1996) Andover fist. *Health Service Journal*, 11th July, 10.

106. Coulter, A. and Bradlow, J. (1993) Effect of NHS reforms on general practitioners' referral patterns. *British Medical Journal* **306**, 433–7.

107. Surender, R., Bradlow, J., Coulter, A., Doll, H. and Stewart-Brown, S. (1995) Trends in referral patterns in fundholding and non-fundholding practices in the Oxford region, 1990–4. *British Medical Journal*, **311**, 1205–8.

108. Allen, I. (1996) Career preferences of doctors. *British Medical Journal*, **313**, 2.

109. Fayol, H. (1916) *Planning General and Industrial Administration*, London.

110. Victor, C.R. and Vetter, N.J. (1985) The early readmission of the elderly to hospital. *Age and Ageing*, **14**, 37–42.

111. Boyce, W.J. and Vessey, M.P. (1985) Rising incidence of fracture of the proximal femur. *Lancet*, **1**, 150–1.

112. Spector, T.D., Cooper, C. and Fenton Lewis, A. (1990) Trends in admission for hip fractures in England and Wales, 1968–85. *British Medical Journal*, **300**, 173–4.

113. Wickham, C., Cooper, C., Margetts, B.M. and Barker, D.J.P. (1989) Muscle strength, activity, housing and the risk of falls in elderly people, *Age and Ageing*, **18**, 47–51.

114. Brocklehurst, J.C., Exton-Smith, A.N., Lampert Barber, S.M., Hunt, L. and Palmer, M. (1976) *Fracture of Femoral Neck: A Two Centre Survey*, Report No. 1, DHSS, London.

115. Prudham, D. and Grimley Evans, J. (1981) Factors associated with falls in the elderly: a community study. *Age and Ageing*, **10**, 141–6.

116. Effective Health Care (1996) Preventing falls and subsequent injury in older people. *Effective Health Care*, **2**(4), 1–15, Nuffield Institute for Health, Churchill Livingstone, London.

117. Vetter, N.J., Lewis, P.A. and Ford, D. (1992) Can health visitors prevent fractures in elderly people? *British Medical Journal*, **304**; 888–90.

118. Wickham, C., Cooper, C., Margetts, B.M. and Barker, D.J.P. (1989) Muscle strength, activity, housing and the risk of falls in elderly people. *Age and Ageing*, **18**, 47–51.

119. Cook, P.J., Exton-Smith, A.N., Brocklehurst, J.C. and Lampert Barber, S.M. (1982) Fractured femurs, falls and bone disorders. *Journal of the Royal College of Physicians of London*, **16**, 45–9.

120. Holbrook, T. L., Barrett-Connor, E. and Wingard, D. L. (1988) Dietary calcium and risk of hip fracture: 14 year prospective population study. *Lancet*, **2**, 1046–9.

121. Blake, A.J., Morgan, K. and Dallosso, H. *et al.* (1988) Falls by elderly people at home: prevalence and associated factors. *Age and Ageing*, **17**, 365–72.

122. Vetter, N.J., Lewis, P.A. and Ford, D. (1992) Can health visitors prevent fractures in elderly people? *British Medical Journal*, **304**, 888–90.

123. Law, M.R., Wald, N.J. and Meade, T.W. (1991) Strategies for prevention of osteoporosis and hip fractures. *British Medical Journal*, **303**, 453–9.

124. Ions, G.K. and Stevens, J. (1987) Prediction of survival in patients with femoral neck fractures. *Journal of Bone and Joint Surgery*, **69B**, 384–7.

125. Wood, D. (1990) Predicting Outcome for Patients with Fractured Neck of Femur. Dissertation, University of London.

126. Gilchrist, W.J., Newman, R.J., Hamblen, D.L. and Williams, B.O. (1988) Prospective randomised study of an orthopaedic geriatric inpatient service, *British Medical Journal* **297**, 116–8.

127. Sikorski, J.M., Davis, N.J. and Senior, J. (1985) The rapid transit system for patients with fractures of the proximal femur. *British Medical Journal*, **290**, 439–43.

128. Pryor, G.A. and Williams, D.R.R. (1989) Rehabilitation after hip fractures. Home and hospital management compared. *Journal of Bone and Joint Surgery*, **71B**, 471–3.

129. Vetter, N.J. (1992) How to assess the value of the geriatric day hospital: a problem in operational research. *European Journal of Gerontology*, **1**, 194–205.

130. Cameron, I.D. and Quine, S. (1994) External hip protectors: likely non compliance among high risk elderly people living in the community. *Archives of Gerontology and Geriatrics*, **19**, 273–81.

131. Vetter, N.J. (1995) *The Hospital: From Centre of Excellence to Community Support*, Chapman & Hall, London.

132. Wolfsenberger, W. (1972) *The Principle of Normalisation in Human Services*, National Institute on Mental Retardation, Toronto.

133. Editorial (1990) Preventing pressure sores. *Lancet*, **335**, 1311–12.

134. Norton, D., McLaren, R. and Exton-Smith, A.N. (1975) *An Investigation of Geriatric Nursing Problems in Hospital*, Churchill Livingstone, Edinburgh.

135. Allman, R. (1989) Epidemiology of pressure sores in different populations. *Decubitus*, **2**, 30–3.

136. Department of Health (1993) *Pressure Sores: A Key Quality Indicator*, Department of Health, London.

137. Hibbs, P. (1988) *Pressure Area Care for the City and Hackney Health Authority*, City and Hackney Health Authority, London.

138. Young, J.B. and Dobrzanski, S. (1992) Pressure sores: epidemiological and current management concepts. *Drugs and Aging*, **2**, 42–57.

139. Krainski, M. (1992) Pressure ulcers and the elderly: a review of the literature, 1980–1990. *Ostomy/Wound Management*, **38**, 22–37.

140. Hedrick-Thompson, J.K. (1992) A review of pressure reduction device studies. *Journal of Vascular Nursing*, **X**, 3–5.

141. Bliss, M.R. and Thomas, J.M. (1993) Clinical trials with budgetary implications: establishing randomised controlled trials of pressure relieving equipment. *Professional Nurse*, **8**, 292–6.

142. Hofman, A., Geelkerken, R.H., Wille, J., Hamming, J.J., Hermans, J. and Breslau, P.J. (1994) Pressure sores and pressure decreasing mattress: controlled clinical trial: *Lancet*, **343**, 568–71.

143. Waterlow, J. (1991) A policy that protects. The Waterlow pressure sore prevention and treatment policy. *Professional Nurse*, **6**, 262–4.

144. Hall, R., Roberts, C.J., Coles, G.A. *et al.* (1988) The impact of guidelines in clinical outpatient practice. *Journal of the Royal College of Physicians of London*, **22**, 244–7.

145. Drucker, P. (1954) *The Practice of Management*, Harper and Row, London.

146. Salvage, A.V., Jones, D.A. and Vetter, N.J. (1988) Awareness and satisfaction with community services in a random sample of over 75s. *Health Trends*, **20**, 88–92.

147. Lau, J., Antman, E.M., Jimenez-Silva, J., Kupelnick, B., Mosteller, F. and Chalmers, T.C. (1992) Cumulative meta-analysis of therapeutic trials for myocardial infarction. *New England Journal of Medicine*, **327**, 248–54.

148. Mulrow, C.D. (1987) Medical review article: state of the science. *Annals of Internal Medicine*, **106**, 485–8.

149. Antman, E.M., Lau, J., Kupelnick, B., Mosteller, F. and Chalmers, T.C. A comparison of results of meta-analyses of randomised controlled trials and recommendations of clinical experts. *Journal of American Medical Association*, **268**, 240–8.

150. NHS Management Executive Information Group (1993) *Information for Effective Purchasing*, Department of Health, Leeds.

151. Sackett, D.L., Haynes, R.B. and Tugwell, P. (1990) *Clinical Epidemiology*, Little, Brown, Boston.

152. Laing, W. (1991) *Empowering the Elderly: Direct Consumer Funding of Care Services*, IEA Health and Welfare Unit, London.

153. Department of Health (1995) *Patient's Charter*, HSG(95), Department of Health, London.

154. Harrison, A. and Bruscini, S. (1995) *Health Care UK 1994/95*, King's Fund Policy Institute, London.

155. Scottish Home and Health Department (1994) *Clinical Outcome Indicators*, MEL 1994 (82), Scottish Home and Health Department, Edinburgh.

156. Richards, A., Charny, M. and Hanmer-Lloyd, S. (1992) Public opinion and purchasing. *British Medical Journal*, **304**, 680–2.

157. Williams, A. (1985) Economics of coronary bypass grafting. *British Medical Journal*, **291**, 326–9.

158. Hall, M.H., Chng, P.K. and MacGillivray, I. (1980) Is routine antenatal care worthwhile? *Lancet*, **1**, 78–80.

159. Walker, P. (1995) Should obstetricians see women with normal pregnancies? Obstetricians should be included in the integrated team. *British Medical Journal*, **310**, 36–7.

160. James, D.K. (1995) Should obstetricians see women with normal pregnancies? Obstetricians should focus on problems. *British Medical Journal*, **310**, 37–8.

161. Reid, M.E., Gutteridge, S. and McIlwaine, G.M. (1983) *A Comparison of the Delivery of Antenatal Care between a Hospital and a Peripheral Clinic*, Report to Health Services Research Committee, Scottish Home and Health Department, Edinburgh.

162. Giles, W., Collins, J., Ong, F. and MacDonald, R. (1992) Antenatal care of low risk obstetric patients by midwives. A randomised controlled trial. *Medical Journal of Australia*, **157**, 158–61.

163. Neilson, J. (1996) Antenatal care on trial. *British Medical Journal*, **312**, 524–5.

164. Tucker, J.S., Hall, M.H., Howie, P.W. *et al.* (1996) Should obstetricians see women with normal pregnancies? A multicentre randomised controlled trial of routine antenatal care by general practitioners and midwives compared with shared care led by obstetricians. *British Medical Journal*, **312**, 554–9.

165. Sikorski, J., Wilson, J., Clement, S., Das, S. and Smeeton, N. (1996) A randomised controlled trial comparing two schedules of antenatal visits: the antenatal care project. *British Medical Journal*, **312**, 546–53.

166. Hall, M., MacIntyre, S. and Porter, M. (1985) *Antenatal Care Assessed*, Aberdeen University Press, Aberdeen.

167. Rowland, N. (1992) Counselling and counselling skills, in *Counselling in General Practice*, (ed. M. Sheldon). Royal College of General Practitioners, London.

168. Ashurst, P.M. and Ward, D.P. (1985) *An Evaluation of Counselling in General Practice*, Mental Health Foundation, London.

169. Martin, E. and Martin, P. (1985) Changes in psychological diagnosis and prescription in a practice employing a counsellor. *Family Practitioner*, **2**, 241–3.

170. Robson, M.H., France, R. and Bland, M. (1984) Clinical psychologist in primary care. *British Medical Journal*, **288**, 1805–8.

171. Teasdale, J.D., Fennel, M.J.V., Hibbert, G.S. and Amies, P.L. (1984) Cognitive therapy for major depressive disorder in primary care. *British Journal of Psychiatry*, **144**, 400–6.

172. Earll, L. and Kincey, J. (1982) Clinical psychology in general practice. *Journal of the Royal College of General Practitioners*, **32**, 32–7.

173. Corney, R.H. (1990) Counselling in general practice – does it work? *Journal of the Royal Society of Medicine*, **83**, 253–7.

174. Gray, P.G. (1988) Counsellors in general practice. *Journal of the Royal College of General Practitioners*, **38**, 50–1.

175. Sibbald, B., Addington-Hall, J., Brenneman, D. and Freeling, P. (1993) Counsellors in English and Welsh general practices: their nature and distribution. *British Medical Journal*, **306**, 29–33.

176. Newman, C.V. (1990) Advice on the appointment of psychologists and counsellors within general practice. *British Journal of General Practice*, **40**, 388–9.

177. Pringle, M. and Laverty, J. (1993) A counsellor in every practice? *British Medical Journal*, **306**, 2–3.

178. Field, M. and Lohr, K.N. (eds) (1992) *Institute of Medicine Guidelines for Clinical Practice. From Development to Use*, National Academy Press, Washington DC.

179. Sever, P., Beevers, G., Bulpitt, C. *et al.* (1993) Management guidelines in essential hypertension: report of the second working party of the British Hypertension Society. *British Medical Journal*, **306**, 983–7.

180. Grimshaw, J.M. and Russell, I.T. (1993) Achieving health gain through clinical guidelines. I. Developing scientifically valid guidelines. *Quality in Health Care*, **2**, 243–8.

181. Grimshaw, J.M. and Russell, I.T. (1994) Achieving health gain through clinical guidelines. II. Ensuring guidelines change medical practice. *Quality in Health Care*, **3**, 45–52.

182. Grimshaw, J.M. and Russell, I.T. (1993) Effect of clinical guidelines on medical practice: a systematic review of rigorous evaluations. *Lancet*, **342**, 1317–22.

183. Grimshaw, J.M., Freemantle, N., Grimshaw, J. *et al.* (1995) Developing and implementing clinical practice guidelines. *Quality in Health Care*, **4**, 55–64.

184. NHS Management Executive (1993) *Improving Clinical Effectiveness*, EL(93)115, Department of Health, Leeds.

185. Lomaz, J., Anderson, G.M., Domnick-Pierre, K., Vayda, E., Enkin, M.W. and Hannah, W.J. Do practice guidelines guide practice? The effect of a consensus statement on the practice of physicians. *New England Journal of Medicine*, **321**, 1306–11.

186. Jones, R.H., Lydeard, S. and Dunleavey, J. (1993) Problems with implementing guidelines: a randomised controlled trial of consensus management of dyspepsia. *Quality in Health Care*, **2**, 217–21.

187. Neville, R.G., Clark, R.C., Hoskins, G. and Smith, B. (1993) National asthma attack audit 1991–2. *British Medical Journal*, **306**, 559–62.

188. Kessner, D.M., Kalk, C.E. and Singer, A.A. Assessing health care quality – the case for tracers. *New England Journal of Medicine*, **288**, 189–94.

189. Irvine, D. (1990) *Managing for Quality in General Practice,* Medical Audit Series 2, King's Fund Centre, London.

190. Oxman, A.D. (1994) Checklists for review articles. *British Medical Journal*, **309**, 648–51.

191. Donabedian, A. (1978) The quality of medical care. Methods for assessing and monitoring the quality of care for research and for quality assurance. *Science*, **200**, 856–63.

192. Baker, R., Khunti, K. and Lakhani, M. (1993) *Monitoring Diabetes*, Eli Lilly National clinical Audit Centre, University of Leicester.

193. North of England Study of Standards and Performance in General Practice (1992) Medical audit in general practice: effects on doctors' clinical behaviour and the health of patients with common childhood conditions. *British Medical Journal*, **304**, 1480–8.

194. Cay, E.L., Vetter, N.J., Philip, A.E. and Dugard, P. (1972) Psychological influences determining return to work after a coronary thrombosis. *Rehabilitation*, **81**, 27.

195. Chiswick, D. (1994) High security for mentally disordered people. *British Medical Journal*, **309**, 423–4.

196. Home Office (1993) *Home Office Statistical Bulletin, Statistics of Mental Disordered Offenders, England and Wales 1991*, Government Statistical Service, London.

197. Hamilton, J. R. (1985) The special hospitals, in *Secure Provision: A Review of Special Services for the Mentally Ill and Mentally Handicapped in England and Wales* (ed. L. Gostin), Tavistock, London.

198. Home Office (1975) *Report on the Committee on Mentally Abnormal Offenders*, Cmnd 6244, HMSO, London.

199. Dell, S. (1980) *The Transfer of Special Hospital Patients to NHS Hospitals*, Special Hospitals Research Report, No. 16, Special Hospitals Service Publications, NHS, London.

200. Black, D.A. (1982) A five year follow up of patients discharged from Broadmoor Hospital, in *Abnormal Offenders: Delinquency and the Criminal Justice System*, (eds J. Gunn and D. F. Farrington), John Wiley, Chichester.

201. Bowden, P. (1981) What happens to patients released from special hospitals? *British Journal of Psychiatry*, **138**, 340–5.

202. Bailey, J. and MacCulloch, M.J. (1992) Characteristics of 112 cases discharged directly to the community from a new special hospital and some comparisons of performance. *Journal of Forensic Psychiatry*, **3**, 91–112.

203. Jones, C., MacCulloch, M., Bailey, J. and Shahtahmasebi S. (1994) Personal history factors associated with reconviction in personality disordered patients discharged from a special hospital. *Journal of Forensic Psychiatry*, **5**(2), 249–61.

204. Department of Health (1994) *Guidance on the Discharge of Mentally Disordered People and their Continuing Care in the Community*, HSG (94) **27**, Department of Health, London.
205. Rogers, C. (1995) *Services for Mentally Disordered Offenders and Others with Similar Needs. A Needs Assessment for South Wales*, Clwyd Health Authority, Clwyd.
206. Welsh Office (1995) *High Security Psychiatric Services: Changes in Funding and Organisation*, Welsh Office, Cardiff.
207. Department of Health (1994) *Report of the Working Group on High Security and Related Psychiatric Provision*, (the Reed Report), Department of Health, London.
208. Gunn, J., Maden, T. and Swinton S. (1990, revised 1991) *Mentally Disordered Prisoners*, Home Office, London.
209. Williams, T. (1994) *Review of South Glamorgan Psychiatric Patients in Secure Environments*, South Wales Forensic Psychiatric Service, Bridgend.
210. Department of Health (1995) *A Progress Report on High Secure Forensic Services and Changes to their Funding and Management*, Department of Health, London.
211. Department of Health and Home Office (1994) *Report of the Department of Health and Home Office Working Group on Psychopathic Disorder*, Department of Health and Home Office, London.
212. Standing Sub-Committee of the Standing Medical Advisory Committee (1984) *Report on Cancer Services*, SMAC, London.
213. Chief Medical Officers' Expert Advisory Group on Cancers (1995) *A Policy Framework for Commissioning Cancer Services*, Department of Health and Welsh Office, London and Cardiff.
214. Whitehouse, M. (1995) A policy framework for commissioning cancer services. *British Medical Journal*, **310**, 1425–6.
215. Gauderer, M.W., Ponsky, J.L. and Izant, R.J. (1980) Gastrostomy without laparotomy: a percutaneous endoscopic technique. *Journal of Pediatric Surgery*, **15**, 872–5.
216. Drickamer, M.A. and Cooney, L.M. (1993) A geriatrician's guide to enteral feeding. *Journal of the American Geriatrics Society*, **41**, 672–9.
217. Raha, S.K. and Woodhouse, K.W. (1993) Who should have a PEG? *Age and Ageing*, **22**, 313–15.
218. Ponsky, J.L. and Gauderer, M.W. (1981) Percutaneous endoscopic gastrostomy: a non-operative technique for feeding gastrostomy. *Gastrointestinal Endoscopy*, **27**, 9–11.
219. Watson, R. (1990) Feeding patients who are demented. *Nursing Standard*, **4**, 28–30.
220. Marks, L. (1991) *Home and Hospital Care: Redrawing the Boundaries*, King's Fund Institute, London.
221. Frasca, C. and Christy, M.W. (1986) Assuring continuity of care through a hospital based home health agency. *Quality Review Bulletin*, **12**, 167–71.
222. Wynn, L., Dingle, J., Hogan, D. *et al.* (1989) *Before and After the New Brunswick Extra Mural Hospital: An Analysis of Traditional Hospital Utilisation*, Dalhousie University Medical School, Halifax, Nova Scotia.

223. Anand, J.K. and Pryor, G.A. (1989) Hospital at home. *Health Trends*, **21**:46–8.
224. Ferguson, G. (1987) The New Brunswick extra mural hospital: a Canadian hospital at home. *Journal of Public Health Policy*, **8**, 561–70.
225. King Edward's Hospital Fund for London (1973) *Accounting for Health: Report of a Working party on the Application of Economic Principles to Health Service Management*, King's Fund, London.
226. Hedrick, S.C. and Inui, T.S. (1986) The effectiveness and cost of home care: an information synthesis. *Health Services Research*, **20**, 851–80.
227. Adler, M.W., Waller, J.J., Creese, A. and Thorne, S.C. (1978) Randomised controlled trial of early discharge for inguinal hernia and varicose veins. *Journal of Epidemiology and Community Health*, **32**, 136–42.
228. Aday, L.A., Wegener, R.M., Andersen, M.J. and Aitken, M.J. (1989) Home care for ventilator assisted children. *Health Affairs*, **14**, 137–47.
229. Welsh Health Planning Forum (1992) *Health and Social Care 2010*, Welsh Office, Cardiff.
230. NHS Management Executive (1991) *Junior Doctors. The New Deal*, NHS Management Executive, London.
231. Department of Health Working Group on Specialist Medical Training (1993) (Chairman Calman), *Hospital Doctors: Training for the Future*, Department of Health, London.
232. Department of Health and Social Security (1977) *The Extending Role of the Clinical Nurse. Legal Implications and Training Requirements*, HC (77)22, DHSS, London.
233. Dowling, S., Barratt, S. and West, R. (1995) With nurse practitioners, who needs house officers? *British Medical Journal*, **311**, 309–13.
234. Song, F., Freemantle, N., Sheldon, T.A. *et al.* (1993) Selective serotonin reuptake inhibitors: meta-analysis of efficacy and acceptability. *British Medical Journal*, **306**, 683–7.
235. Shepherd, G. (1990) Case management. *Health Trends*, **22**, 59–61.
236. Bond, G.R., McGrew, J.H. and Fekete, D.M. (1995) Assertive outreach for frequent users of psychiatric hospitals: a meta-analysis. *Journal of Mental Health Administration*, **22**, 4–16.
237. Griffith, R. (1988) *Community Care: An Agenda for Action*, HMSO, London.
238. Marshall, M. (1996) Case Management: a dubious practice. *British Medical Journal*, **312**, 523–4.
239. Marshall, M., Lockwood, A. and Gath, D. (1995) How effective is social services case management for people with long-term mental disorders? A randomised controlled trial. *Lancet*, **345**, 409–12.
240. Ford, R., Repper, J., Cooke, A., Norton, P., Beadsmoore, A. and Clark, C. (1993) *Implementing Case Management*, Research and Development for Psychiatry, London.
241. Tyrer, P., Morgan, J., Van Horn, E. *et al.* (1995) A randomised controlled study of close monitoring of vulnerable psychiatric patients. *Lancet*, **345**, 756–9.
242. Butler, P. (1996) Trust may turn into purchaser in unique merger. *Health Service Journal*, 4th July: 6.

Index